THEOLOGICAL BIOLOGY

The Case for a New Modernism

Kenneth Cauthen

Toronto Studies in Theology
Volume 62

The Edwin Mellen Press
Lewiston/Queenston/Lampeter

Library of Congress Cataloging-in-Publication Data

This volume has been registered with The Library of Congress.

ISBN 0-7734-9655-6

A CIP catalog record for this book
is available from the British Library.

The Edwin Mellen Press
Box 450
Lewiston, New York
USA 14092

The Edwin Mellen Press
Box 67
Queenston, Ontario
CANADA L0S 1L0

The Edwin Mellen Press, Ltd.
Lampeter, Dyfed, Wales
UNITED KINGDOM SA48 7DY

Printed in the United States of America

To My Parents:

JOHN WILFRED and BEULAH HARRIS CAUTHEN

They gave me life.
They gave me love.

Who could ask for anything more!

LIFE

. . . I have set before you life and death, blessing and curse;
therefore choose life . . .

Deut. 30:19 (RSV)

All life is driven by a three-fold urge . . .
 "to live,
  to live well,
   and to live better."

Alfred North Whitehead

. . .to live,
 . . .to learn,
  . . . to love.

 . . . to live to learn,
  . . . to learn to love,
   . . . to love to live.

   . . . to live to learn to love,
    . . . to learn to love to live,
     . . . to love to live to learn.

Kenneth Cauthen

TABLE OF CONTENTS

PREFACE

My aim is to make the case for a new modernism in religion. If some want to call the attempt post-modern, I will not object. I do not use that variously defined term, although it is currently in fashion. Nevertheless, the relativism, pluralism, and pragmatism I espouse is related to some efforts that claim that designation. This essay is positioned within the larger tradition of American religious empiricism and in particular the left-wing of contemporary process-relational thought.

I am both a Christian theologian and a philosopher of religion. Functioning as both at the same time is made possible by the fact that I am a neo-modernist. I stand in the Christian tradition and work out my views in conversation with Scripture and the history of thought that has developed within that framework. But I insist that all religious doctrines must be tested by reason and experience. These are the criteria employed by philosophers of religion.

What follows, then, can be read both as an essay in philosophical theology and in philosophy of religion. At nearly every point I address issues of concern to both. I do not take up those specific issues that are the special province of Christian dogmatics -- the trinitarian conception of God, Christology, the doctrine of the church, ministry, and sacraments, and so on. I deal rather with those overlapping areas that interest both philosophers and theologians -- the problem of knowledge, cosmology, the concept of God, the enigma of evil, freedom, the meaning of history, the religious implications of evolutionary science, and the like.

The effort is related to the older discipline of natural theology but is not identical with it. In agreement I employ only the resources of reason and do not appeal to Scripture or Christian tradition as warrants or norms of truth. Unlike many natural theologians of the past I recognize the historical relativity of religious thought. Justification of basic claims is internal to the point of view being tested. The appeal to what all reasonable persons in all times and places must believe when thinking rightly is a futile move. Hence, I acknowledge that my outlook is conditioned by my location in the Christian community. From that perspective I look at the world seeking for the most compelling interpretation of human experience relevant to intelligent practice in quest of the highest ends of life. I do insist that it is philosophically legitimate to seek insight from the Bible as well as from Plato, Kant, or Dewey. Everybody is located somewhere, looks at the world from a particular angle, stands in some tradition of thought. This point is so widely assumed by philosophers and theologians these days that no elaboration or defense is needed here.

In the first chapter I critically evaluate several schools of contemporary theology and elaborate on the need for a new modernism. Chapter II takes up the issue of knowledge, its sources, norms, and procedures of justification. Chapter III attacks the notion of divine perfection found in classical theism, mainly because of the difficulties posed by the massive evils on earth. In

chapter IV I propose the doctrine of a finite, opportunistic God based on evidences of divine purpose in the
evolution of life and in the experience of goodness in
human existence. The final chapter spells out that notion
in a form of naturalistic panentheism.

The category of life is used as the central clue to
the world process and to God. The universe is infused
with life-producing tendencies that are actualized
wherever conditions permit. God is the All-Inclusive Life
who works opportunistically to create and maximize the
enjoyment of living creatures great and small in all
their various and splendid forms. A limited, suffering
Cosmic Purpose struggles with evil but cannot fully
overcome it. This perspective is worked out in close
connection with a scientific understanding of life as an
evolutionary phenomena. In some ways the book is an essay
in theological biology.

As a theologian I call for a new modernism that will
preserve only the highest and best of Scripture as that
is measured by the highest and best we know from any and
all sources. The Bible itself is a prime treasury of
religious wisdom. Religious beliefs are functional
formulas that must be consistent with the whole inventory of ideas by which we elucidate the whole of experience. Religion is a way of coping with the threats and
terrors of existence and of responding to experiences of
goodness and enjoyment. Religious beliefs function to
interpret the relation of selves to the ultimate realities and to facilitate the quest for fulfillment by
uniting us with the superhuman positive graces in the
very nature of things that produce and sustain life. They
cannot do that unless they are plausible. Yet being
credible to us does not guarantee that the universe is
what we think it to be. Students tell me they have
experienced healing in answer to prayer. I insist they

have experienced healing. They interpret it as an answer
to prayer. Their interpretation may be correct. Part of
my task will be to show that this way of looking at
religious belief does not erode vital faith.

Doctrines about ultimate matters of fact are
theories that their sponsors usually or often intend to
be true, where truth means correspondence with reality.
But we have no way of knowing whether our beliefs about
God are, in those terms, true or false. Methods used to
test theories about ultimate matters operate in circular
fashion. Justification of truth claims proceeds on the
basis of principles assumed by the system being assessed.
Tests of coherence within a conceptual system and of
adequacy in accounting for evidence may be met. Yet we
have no way of knowing whether the theories that result
are in accord with reality. All theories about God but
one are necessarily partly wrong if they intend to
describe ultimate facts. Since they contradict each other
right and left, not all can be closest to the truth. Propositions about God can be regarded as true only in terms
of their relative adequacy in organizing systematically
the whole range of experience yielding understanding that
functions to promote the art of living. That opens the
possibility of there being many operational religious
truths. The alternative, however, when truth is defined
as correspondence to reality, is to have no certainty at
all. The middle ground by which truth becomes warranted
consensus overcomes relativism only verbally. The usual
way to defeat relativism is for thinkers to declare
boldly that their refutations are successful in slaying
the dragon. Humility is the chief theological virtue. My
assumption, nevertheless, is that experience is of something objectively there. Reality that matters is what is
experienced. Reality for us is its total effects on
us. But interpretations may or may not be reliable as

accounts of experienced reality. Straight sticks stuck in water may be seen as crooked. Colds may be caused by a virus. The folk culture I grew up in held that colds were caused by drafts, getting wet and cold, etc. Others might believe they are punishments from God, whatever the natural mechanisms involved. Reality transcends experience and interpretation. The problem is how to determine when interpretation is adequate to experienced reality. I will insist repeatedly on the distinction between experiencing something and interpreting the experience. We nearly always mean _interpreted_ experience when we appeal to _experience_ as a test of truth, religious and otherwise. Our epistemological predicament is that reality, experience, and interpretation are connected in ways that prohibit a precise disentanglement.

Finally, a personal word may be addressed to readers. In my intellectual pilgrimage I have, in a fashion, recapitulated the theological history of the last century. I embraced in my childhood a form of revivalistic Baptist pietism that developed in America during the 19th century. In college I was introduced to liberal theology through the writings of Harry Emerson Fosdick and Shailer Mathews. Both were Baptists reared in a religious environment similar to mine. They were providing answers to the questions I was asking as I learned about science, evolution, higher criticism of the Bible, modern philosophies, and a broad range of post-Enlightenment developments in Euro-American culture.

From H. Richard Niebuhr's The Social Sources of Denominationalism and Liston Pope's Millhands and Preachers, I learned how race, class, and nationality, as well as differing interpretations of the Bible, shaped denominations. Social factors are as important as theological considerations in church life. At Yale

Divinity School I was indoctrinated into neo-orthodox ways of thinking that helped me employ the religious vocabulary of sin and grace I learned in my childhood. Reinhold Niebuhr and Emil Brunner became by primary guides. Two lectures on A. N. Whitehead and Charles Hartshorne by William Christian stimulated me to begin a largely self-guided effort to learn process philosophy. A doctoral dissertation at Vanderbilt on the liberal movement in American theology completed my formal education. This journey has led after three decades more back to Shailer Mathews. The empirical modernists and naturalistic theists hold most promise for the reformulation of theology today.

I beg critical friends and unfriendly critics not to hold back from pointing out the errors into which my pilgrimage has led. I ask only that in so doing they honor the motive that over many years has produced the left-wing position taken in this book. When I had already experienced one intellectual conversion before I was twenty years old, I committed myself to follow the truth, as I could come to know it, wherever it took me. The faith and the doubt expressed herein are the product of that sometimes agonized quest in which there were no dogmas exempt from testing, no questions that could not be asked, no traditions that could not be scrutinized, no orthodoxy beyond criticism, no reigning theology whose limits could not be probed. I have increasingly sought to determine the down to earth implications for life of every doctrine. At the same time I have demanded correspondence between belief and experience and coherence within the total system -- within the limits of my fallible reason.

A philosophical pilgrimage of more than forty years lies behind me. One of my teachers, H. Richard Niebuhr, said that for an ideological dwelling place he preferred a tent -- a home that could be moved. That fits my own history. The revivalistic evangelicalism of my youth has led through several intervening stages to the empirical, pragmatic, naturalistic version of Christian modernism that informs these pages. Each perspective gave way, not without carryovers of course, to its successor as "interprience" (my word for interpreted experience) failed to sustain the doctrines I currently espoused. An early rationalism, empiricism, and skepticism that I must have been born with developed into a relativistic pragmatism that tolerates no belief whose meaning and consequences cannot be defined and tested by reference to experience.

Everyone needs some conceptual framework by which to articulate religious questions and answers. I am not convinced that only those in vogue at the moment are worthy. They will be succeeded by exaggerated claims about what is then new. I have long ago given up on the game of "At last we've got it!" It is, however, still the favorite game in town. Many of today's students, for example, are not aware of how limited the concept of liberation is as a summary of the Gospel. They may be offended by aging professors who raise the point. Liberation theology is a powerful corrective to es- tablished outlooks and a potent constructive effort of the highest importance. Nevertheless, it has shortcomings that the next generation of students will readily recognize. Having played "At last, we've got it" and repented, I perhaps may be excused for my amusement and impatience with those who still find it a profitable game. I follow Whitehead's example. Having accepted Newtonian physics as the last word about nature and seeing it replaced by radically different ways of conceiving the world, he said, "I'll be damned if I'll ever be burned again.

I am not helped by complaints that what some hold essential is left out. Of course it is! Otherwise, I would not have any reason to try an alternative. I offer a minority report that most theological students and professors will find lacking in traditional substance. Even so, I will not easily be persuaded out of my current stubbornness. On the other hand, I will not be unappreciative of those who hold contrary views, if we can all recognize the partiality of our efforts.

One final comment can end this beginning. I have long been interested in the relation of theology to other disciplines. Much of my work has been interdisciplinary. I have been particularly concerned with the natural and social sciences. I have sought to create a synthesis between theology and other ways of knowing the world. In pursuing this task, one runs the risk of being a dilettante who knows a little about a lot of things but not much about anything. That is a hazard I am willing to live with in return for the broader vision it enables. Interdisciplinary tasks have to be taken on "by marginal scholars who are willing to be incompetent in a number of fields at once."[1] If I exceed in nothing else, I exemplify what this willingness taken to great extremes can accomplish.

Kenneth Cauthen
July 20, 1991
Rochester, New York

1. Donald Campbell, quoted by Michael Ruse in Taking Darwin Seriously, p. xiii.

Chapter I

A CALL FOR A NEW MODERNISM

It is time for theology to resume the path being followed by some branches of American liberal thought when it was rudely interrupted by the onslaught of neo-orthodoxy.[1] I refer to the modernistic liberals, many of whom were in the "Chicago school." These theologians defined themselves as modern intellectuals informed by empirical sciences and historical disciplines that had undermined the Protestant orthodoxy of their youth. They called for a radical rethinking of the Christian message. Without such a reconstruction Christianity would cease to be credible and important for life in the 20th century. The modernists assumed that all social systems and conceptual schemes are historically relative and culturally conditioned. They also stood in the Christian tradition, believing that it contains permanent truths and values that could be reclaimed. The call for a recasting of orthodoxy has, of course, been a common theme since the Enlightenment and is the defining characteristic of "modern" Christian thought.[2]

The intent of the liberal movement in theology was to make it possible to be, in the memorable words of Harry Emerson Fosdick, both "an intelligent modern and a serious Christian." The evangelical liberals claimed to recapture the heart of the ancient Gospel in modern categories. The empirical or scientific modernists of the Chicago school took a more radical stance. They gave up the notion of an identifiable Christian essence persisting throughout all its historical forms. For Shailer Mathews Christianity was whatever it had become over the long centuries of its development. A Christian is anyone who claims loyalty to Jesus. The modernists vowed to re-present as binding on contemporary belief only what is valuable to the present age as that is judged by contemporary criteria. Scientific methods of inquiry into nature and history provided for them the most reliable form of knowledge about the source of human good.[3]

The overly optimistic estimate of human possibilities associated with liberal theology (along with other factors) produced a revulsion against it. Many of its typical themes -- the immanence of God, confidence in science and human progress, emphasis on experience as the source of religious truth, a focus on the historical Jesus -- were abandoned in neo-orthodoxy. Discontinuity replaced continuity as the central informing motif. Paradox, ambiguity, and tension replaced liberal harmony and rational unity. In neo-orthodoxy attention shifted from autonomous reason and human possibilities to God's self-initiated self-disclosure in certain crucial events of salvation history. Divine revelation judged and contradicted cultural wisdom, so that a leap of faith was required to appropriate it. Jesus was no longer primarily the moral example and spiritual ideal to be emulated. Emphasis was put on the Christ-event -- the paradox of the God-man. Jesus embodied God's Word of grace to sinful humanity. The Bible had authority as the decisive witness to divine revelation, although it was interpreted by liberal methods. Augustine, Luther, and Calvin -- generally scorned by liberals -- were warmly embraced because they affirmed the transcendence of God, the depravity of humanity, and salvation by grace. These themes spoke powerfully to a civilization whose foundations had been shaken, reeling and rocking from the massive evils of the first half of the 20th century.[4]

The revival of orthodoxy was incorporated into a more humane post-Enlightenment framework that rejected many of its repulsive aspects. The inheritance of depravity and the damnation of non-elect children had no standing. Established findings of empirical science and of historical criticism were affirmed. Classical doctrines of creation, incarnation, and consummation were regarded as myths to be taken "seriously but not literally" (Reinhold Niebuhr). Hence, American neo-orthodoxy was, in these respects, a thoroughly modern theological outlook. The aim of speaking to the present age was so strong in Reinhold Niebuhr, Paul Tillich, and Rudolf Bultmann that they could also be called neo-liberal.[5]

While neo-orthodoxy served its generation well by bringing good news to a bad news generation, theology needs to take a different direction today. Difficulties in contemporary American theology also justify a call for a new modernism. Two problems will be highlighted: (1) the question of method and authority and (2) the reality and activity of God.

CONTEMPORARY THEOLOGY AND THE AUTHORITY QUESTION

A variety of outlooks since 1960 -- most prominently, black, feminist, and process theologies -- shifted attention away from the neo-orthodox theme of recovering the "message" of the Bible. The new focus was on the "situation" to which the Gospel is to be addressed and on human experience as a source of theology.[6] This is a relative distinction, since all modern theologies want to be both biblical and relevant. Another relative distinction is between those perspectives that focus on the particularities of somebody's experience (some specific groups and individuals) and those that base their thinking on the universalities of everybody's experience (all individuals and groups). Black and feminist perspectives exemplify the former, while process theologies are examples of the latter. Making experience the starting point is a stance shared with the older liberals. Some black theologians, however, spoke with a neo-orthodox accent blended with a reliance on the history and culture of black Christians.[7] The early theology of hope espoused by Jürgen Moltmann continued to base theology on the Word of God.[8] Process theologies, however, are more neo-liberal. They refer to universal human experience as a source of truth that can be harmonized with the crucial biblical theme of a God of unbounded love who is affected by and responsive to events in time and history.[9] Other revisionist theologians, assuming a self-conscious identity as secular modern persons, have sought to correlate the meanings contained in classic Christian texts with interpretations of common human experience.[10]

Revisionist methodology unites classic Christian motifs with modernity but sees the results as a defensible synthesis that transforms both ancient orthodoxy and modern secularism. Process theologies, for example, contradict notions of divine omnipotence and eliminate use of coercive power to fulfill the divine purpose. Revisionists want to be biblical like the neo-orthodox and modern like the liberals. Yet, as defined by David Tracy, it is philosophical reason that finally determines what truth claims are valid. That is a modernist theme, although the older liberals believed in the harmony of revelation and reason. Revisionists appear to be evangelically liberal or neo-orthodox in claiming to re-present from the classical texts what is central and vital to those ancient authorities.[11] Hence, Tracy-type revisionism appears to be on the boundary between a liberal/ neo-orthodox and a modernist outlook.

What, then, is to guarantee either the Christian or the secular character of the result if each transforms the other? It is the interpreter, of course, who makes this happen. By eliciting the meanings found in Christian texts and in common human experience and then doing the testing, a particular theologian can practically guarantee a valid outcome! Theologies are true to the Gospel and pertinent to the situation only as somebody judges them to be so. No revisioning will satisfy everybody. Pluralism is inescapable and can only be partially and never satisfactorily overcome. This does not negate the considerable overlapping that occurs among the many circles of interpretation whose centers may be close to each other.[12] Some thinkers appear to be moving closer to the new modernism I advocate.[13]

Tracy and others champion the need for a "public theology." Public means an appeal to what is reasonable within the framework of contemporary secular consciousness. Rules of evidence established by the various university disciplines must be followed. Theologians cannot appeal to the Bible or a particular tradition of thought as warrants for their claims. They must argue for them on the basis of public sources and norms of truth. Common human experience is the point of reference. Ruled out are statements of the form "X is true because the Bible (or the Pope or the creed, etc.) says so, period." This establishes criteria specific enough to eliminate Christian tradition or the cultural reason of other societies or epochs as intrinsically authoritative. It is sufficiently general, however, to permit a wide variety of fundamentally conflicting claims based on reason and common human experience. Accepting the "morality of scientific reason" might persuade biologists, psychologists, sociologists, and philosophers to admit theologians to the conversation. Even if Bibles are left at home when they go to the seminar, however, will theologians convince any non-believers with their rational God-talk and with their assurances that they too are university intellectuals, one of them at heart? How far does being secular and reasonable take theology in practical terms toward a universal audience? Which public does theology take into account in announcing its warrants and making its claims? To which contemporary philosopher does the theologian turn for a reasonable interpretation of common human experience -- Ayer, Russell, Heidegger, Sartre, Whitehead, Dewey, Derrida, Rorty, or Woody Allen? Can philosophy or theology add anything to the description of matters of fact not discoverable by scientific methods of inquiry? Contemporary cultural reason is divided on this crucial question. The metaphysical philosophy advocated by Tracy as his instrument of going public with theology is rejected out of hand by large segments of the secular intellectual community to which he would speak.

Tracy holds that warrants employed by public theology are available in principle to all reasonable persons, although in fact everybody reasons from within particular traditions and communities.[14] He provides no resolution of this predicament. There is, in fact, no universally satisfactory way for theology to be both "public" in appealing to contemporary rational criteria and "confessional" in witnessing to the Gospel. No consensus exists in culture regarding what is reasonable as descriptions of reality and no agreement is present in the church about what is essential to Christian witness. Tracy, like everybody else, is caught in the dilemma posed by the desire for objectivity and universality in the search for truth and the fact of particularity and relativity that divides humanity into a plurality of competing communities.

The modernist is more consistently pluralist, particularist, and relativist. Public theology is a neither a rational nor a theological necessity. Its pragmatic success rate is questionable. It is a preference and a choice for which good reasons can be given. But it is not demanded by necessary principles of rationality obvious to all reasonable persons. Christian theologians do not even agree among themselves about the sources and norms of religious truth. Whose or which theology are we to offer unbelievers? The post-liberals represented by George Lindbeck, Hans Frei, and the Yale school of theology think that the revisionist way is more likely to compromise the Gospel than to persuade worldly thinkers.[15] Can Tracy show by universal reason that Karl Barth was wrong in appealing to the Word of God as the norm of Christian truth? Will reasoning with atheists provide a higher conversion rate than quoting Scripture to them? I doubt it. Nevertheless, it is doubtful that any two world-views -- Christian and otherwise -- constitute circles totally outside each other. Hence, meaningful conversation can, if enough good will is assumed, take place among thinkers of radically diverse traditions of thought that may produce widening areas of mutual understanding. Consensus on certain points may exist or be eventually attained. On rare occasions conversion to other points of view may occur. At no point, even assuming universal agreement, is certainty about ultimate matters of fact guaranteed.

Black and feminist perspectives have been particu-
laristic, centering on the experience of blacks and of
women respectively.[16] Yet they claim to have found in the
liberation motif the authentic Christian message. Liberation theologians tend to assume the truth of the Gospel
and focus on its power to emancipate the oppressed. Black
and feminist theologians, however, confront the fact that
oppressive practices like slavery and the subordination
of women are present without condemnation in many places
in both the Old and the New Testaments. Moreover, it is
not self-evident that liberation in the Bible is always
the same thing contemporary black and feminist theologies
are talking about. Liberation theologies are frequently
obscure or ambiguous about how the liberation they speak
of relates to liberation in Scripture.

In the New Testament liberation is primarily from
sin and death, not from various forms of political and
social oppression. It is achieved fully only at the
Endtime consummation when all of nature as well as
society is perfected by a new creative act of God. When
an apocalyptic outlook reigns, liberation (and that word
alone is inadequate to describe biblical hope) occurs
only in a divinely coerced cosmic transformation.
Contemporary theologians want economic, social, and
political justice in this world. They want it fully and
now or as soon as possible, not in some sweet by and by
that keeps getting put off further into the future. The
deliverance of Israel from Egyptian slavery was a social
liberation event. Yet neither in the wilderness nor in
Canaan was liberated life all that happy, prosperous, or
free.

In any case, liberation theologians do not expect that release from oppression will be accompanied by the kind of supernatural intervention that rescued Israel from the Pharaoh. Moreover, Israel continued to be oppressed periodically and eventually nearly all the time. Nor were the magnificent predictions of the new Isaiah(s) (Is.40-66) of a New Creation fulfilled in the post-Exilic period. The apocalyptic expectations of the New Testament never came to pass. Rev. 21 is not what black and feminist theologians want most. This is not to deny that secular social justice is a prominent Old Testament theme, less so in the New Testament. Nevertheless, liberties are taken in redefining liberation in more systemic, sociological terms than the New Testament in particular will sustain.

To find the ultimate liberation event and paradigm in the resurrected Christ, as Cone does,[17] is to engage in the kind of spiritualizing and transcendentalizing that liberation theologies object to in other perspectives. The social order following the resurrection remained full of suffering and injustice and still does. To reinterpret the consummation referred to by the apostolic witness as yet to come, as fundamentalist, neo-orthodox, eschatological, and liberation theologies routinely do, may be a theological necessity. The result hardly qualifies as a re-presentation of what the Bible says. To reinterpret the time-frame of the promised consummation in the radical way required is a modernist move. The usual claim is that this is a minor point incidental to the essence. If such a drastic recasting of biblical assumptions is undertaken to accommodate the historical facts and the modern consciousness, what is the crucial sense in which the product can be said to be biblical? At what point does reconstruction become destruction? And must not the truth-claims of the new eschatology be judged by reason, since the Bible's own definition of what liberation and consummation mean has already been rejected?   That the New Testament message must be restated within a modern framework is, of course, a familiar claim in post-Enlightenment theology. However, the reinterpretation needed is more fundamental than many contemporary thinkers who would be both Christian and modern acknowledge. Methodological integrity is threatened unless the hermeneutical procedures explicitly adopted allow or require a reconstruction as thorough-going as that actually performed.

James Cone asserts that the two measuring rods of black theology are Christ and black liberation. He unites these, of course, by rejecting interpretations of Christ contrary to black liberation.[18] Cone strongly affirms the particularity, subjectivity, and relativity of all theology. He chastises white theologians for claiming objectivity. Yet in the end he affirms that the liberating theme defines the objective Gospel and is not merely a specific concrete norm for a given situation. The poor and oppressed are empistemologically privileged. The non-oppressed cannot challenge such a claim. So once again, despite all the affirmations of the relativity of all human efforts, it is maintained that a particular interpretation has grasped the objective truth of faith. Of course, specific forms of liberation theology are acknowledged by him to be limited, partial, and in need of revision. That the many stories of the afflicted must be reformed in light of the one Story, he readily allows. In the end, however, Cone does not go beyond the familiar neo-orthodox framework that assumes a Christological canon within the canon, an abstractable vital core that can take various conceptual forms. For all his

flirting with radical particularity and relativity,[19] he
-- like nearly everybody else -- in the end purports to
know the normative content of Scripture. All non-liber-
ating views are heretical. Either they miss the point or
are distorted by the social location and interests of
their adherents and thus are wrong. Calvin, Luther,
Harnack, and Rauschenbusch all played "At last, we've got
it." Cone plays it too. A pluralist, relativist, and
pragmatist asks: Is liberation theology as he understands
it one plausible modern reading, or has he discovered the
universal Gospel residing in an internally self-defined
form in the Bible itself?[20]

Some post-Christian feminists like Mary Daly have
declared Christianity too thoroughly rotten to be sal-
vaged.[21] Christian feminists find their position ambiguous. Much of the Bible and nearly all of Christian
tradition is deeply infused with beliefs and practices
oppressive of women. It is especially difficult for
evangelicals to have their Bible and their feminism too
without being more modernist than their view of scriptural authority allows.[22] Many liberal feminists are
candid enough to say that the norm is "whatever contributes to the liberation of women." If the Bible
contributes to the full realization of the humanity of
women, well and good. If not, only what is in harmony
with that norm will be retained. Modernists applaud that
procedure, although the liberation of women is not the
whole or sole content of saving truth.

Rosemary Ruether uses the "prophetic-liberating
tradition" to judge everything else in Scripture. She
finds an egalitarian motif that stresses justice and
fulfillment for all as an undercurrent and as a "re-
pressed tradition" in the New Testament. This cornerstone
becomes the basis for a critique of patriarchy and is the

clue to a normative Gospel centering on equality, mutuality, and deliverance from all systems that exalt one group over another.[23] Christianity in none of its forms, however, can be regarded as absolute or final. Other ancient religious and modern secular traditions can also inform feminine consciousness. The final or culture-transcending norm for all religions, cultural traditions, and philosophies is "whatever is liberating and fulfilling for women" within a vision only partly derived from Scripture. She uses a criterion arising in contemporary consciousness to criticize all traditions. She acknowledges that the Bible and Christian history are dominated by patriarchy. Since she regards as authoritative in Scripture only what meets her own critical criteria, I call her in that regard a modernist. Taking into account all that she says, she appears to be suspended ambiguously between liberalism/neo-orthodoxy and modernism.

Elizabeth Schüssler Fiorenza is closer to a modernist perspective. She positions herself between the neo-orthodox essence-accident scheme of Ruether and the post-Christian philosophy of Daly.[24] Nevertheless, she appears still to espouse a notion of biblical truth and revelation that defines the Gospel for everybody.[25] She goes behind the texts to locate communities of faith and practice whose ethos becomes the norm of all traditions, including Scripture. She finds in early Christian history groups who practice a liberating, equalitarian religion of mutuality and justice -- a women's church whose praxis is a discipleship of equals. By recovering what has been obscured by the dominant patriarchal traditions, she locates something normative incarnate in history. She finds it in a religious movement loyal to Jesus, the founder and exemplar of the faith. How does she know that it is the liberating-equalitarian-mutuality ethos that is truly definitive of ecclesia? Her modern feminist consciousness tells her so. She recognizes that the Bible is predominantly sexist in its textual expression.

Her claim, of course, is that women's equalitarian church embodies the truth, the way, and the life exemplified in Jesus and his earliest disciples. In that sense she is "liberal" in the tradition of Adolf Harnack, who identified the "essence" with its original formulation in the historical Jesus. How sure can we be that any contemporary reconstruction of Jesus is reliable enough to make such a claim? Can we deny that this may be another idealized and modernized Jesus mistaken for the real one? Whether Jesus' calling forth a discipleship of equals involved a self-conscious attack on patriarchy as defined by a present-day critical feminist outlook is contestable, as she notes.[26] It is arguable that the egalitarian motifs in early Christianity are best understood in eschatological and ecclesiastical terms. They do not necessarily imply imperatives for reforming the existing secular social order. And does it not require a considerable imaginative leap to identify a small sectarian-utopian-eschatological community in the Roman Empire with the situation of women, especially white, middle-class, affluent ones, in the United States today?

To maintain that a critical feminist consciousness calling for full equality of the sexes in every aspect of secular and church life is a valid modernizing of the praxis of Jesus and of some early Christian communities is one thing. Modernists applaud that move. To claim that this contemporary outlook is identical with the liberating-equalitarian tradition in the New Testament is something else and not beyond question. Why not say that

we appropriate from the Christian past only what is best
and worthy of preservation? Why worry whether we have
discovered its foundational heart and soul? It is important, of course, to get the history of the early church
correct for its own sake. Would it matter normatively
whether there ever was a women's church existing as a
discipleship of equals surrounding Jesus? This is a
different question from whether or not such a church was
a historical fact. For Ruether and Schüssler Fiorenza,
then, Scripture is authoritative only in so far as it
exhibits or conforms to the standard dictated by a modern
critical feminine consciousness. They do not hesitate to
reject outright anything that does not pass this test.
The functioning norm for them is defined in the light of
present-day reason and experience. Else how would they
know to recognize those elements that are liberating for
women as the real Gospel when they find it Scripture or
in early Christian practice? Yet they claim they are not
inventing the content and norm of religious truth but
finding it in Jesus and thus in the Bible or in early
church communities.[27] Mary Daly stated the implicit logic
of much liberal feminism in saying that she is a feminist, whether Jesus was or not.[28] That is a modernist
principle. Liberals, however, want their feminism and
Jesus too.[29]

Sheila Greeve Davaney maintains that Ruether,
Schüssler Fiorenza, as well as Mary Daly, apparently hold
on to a correspondence theory of truth, at least for
their own positions. Yet they otherwise recognize the
conditioned nature of all human thought and social practice.[30] All three assume that "what is liberating and
fulfilling for women" is the operating norm for judging
all traditions past and present. They also profess that
truth so measured puts us in touch with Ultimate Reali-

ty. For this reason Davaney contends that they have failed to carry through the full implications of a modern historical consciousness. Such consciousness recognizes the relativity of all human thought whatsoever, not excluding feminist or any other kind of liberation theology. If this is the case, they are not modernist as defined by the pluralist, relativist, and pragmatic outlook advocated on these pages.

Trying to find texts and/or principles that make sexual equality appear to be the real biblical view is unnecessary. Feminists don't need the Bible to tell them they are equal with men. We rightly reject those passages that teach subordination. Why should we take so much comfort in the few that do teach equality or use feminist images for God? Besides Paul may have only meant in Gal. 3:27-28 that women and men, slaves and free persons, are equal in status before God. He may not have implied that equality is a principle for organizing secular society. At the same time, the New Testament proclaims that eschatological redemption is available to men and women alike. Many New Testament writings assume slavery and the subordination of women (Ephes. 5:21-33, 6:5-9; Col. 3:18-25; I Tim. 2:11-25; Titus 2:5; Philemon; I Peter 2:13-3:7). Unless we are prepared to argue that these views are justified contextually, we have to say that the Bible is wrong on those points. In any case, the social situation of early Christians -- an underclass of apocalyptic sectarians devoid of political power -- differs far too much from that of contemporary Americans to make direct identity plausible. Women are equal with men, and a sexually one-sided view of God is inadequate for today, whether the Bible agrees or not.[31] Truth as we judge it is what operationally matters. In the last analysis we determine what is authoritative in Scripture.

Whatever in Scripture appears to be either untrue, immoral, or irrelevant, we reject (or ignore), whether we are fundamentalists or modernists.

In short, much that is compelling in contemporary theology is in agreement with the modernist outlook. (1) Weakness appears in the aspiration for a public theology that can be both biblical and acceptable to the secular consciousness of university elites with broadly effective results. The aim is commendable. However, no consensus exists about biblical religion in the church or about reason and reality in the university. Hence, no generally productive consequences necessarily follow from the program of public theology. All useful conversations between theology and other accounts of the ultimate facts are local, particular, and aim at some temporary practical accommodation. No global prescriptions defining the task of theologians in relation to the methods and conclusions of other reasoning professionals will find universal acceptance today. (2) The other shortcoming appears when theologians identify their normative belief systems with the universal Gospel defined by Scripture or Jesus. It is time to give up the search for the essence of Christianity or at least to forego the claim of having found it. Modern theologians always manage to interpret the essential tenets of Scripture in ways that do not offend their own secular consciousness and their denial of supernatural phenomena. Both these deficiencies spring from overconfidence in the power of theological reason to find something universal, or at least objectively reliable, either in revelation or in reason to which the weary soul can repair amidst the confusions and calamities of the modern world. We have to be more modest and particular in our efforts and settle for something less than certainty. Pluralism and relativism, if taken with the seriousness that many contemporary theologians themselves initially recognize, will push theology toward a new modernism.

THEOLOGY AND THE ACTIVITY OF GOD

Difficulties arise also with respect to the reality and activity of God. Speaking of the acts of God in nature and history -- central to the Bible -- has been problematic since the Enlightenment. The assumptions underlying classical theology scarcely allowed room for human actions that originate novelty.[32] Nor do human actions set the course of history in a fashion not overruled by the sovereign will of God. Nothing determines matters of fact and destiny in the final analysis but the omnipotent divine will. Moreover, belief in miracles gave genuine substance to the notion of "the mighty acts of God."

Liberal theologies for the most part gave up the idea of supernatural intervention. Liberalism was bound to ideas of a law-abiding universe and thus lacked the idea of miracle. By emphasizing the immanence of God, they saw in the course of nature and history evidences of divine aim. The liberal view identified the providence of God with a general purposive dimension in things. The idea that God did specific things on particular occasions, like rolling back the waters of the Red Sea or raising the dead, disappeared. Also, the fact of human autonomy in originating events required the cooperation of humanity to bring about the gradual coming of the kingdom of God on earth.

Neo-orthodoxy substituted transcendence for liberal immanence but retained respect for scientific ways of accounting for events in nature and history. Thus, miracle played no more role than in liberalism (with a few exceptions like Barth).[33] Neo-orthodoxy spoke of "the mighty acts of God" but required heavy use of paradox, myth, symbol, and what amounted to double-talk to make it work. Langdon Gilkey demonstrated that in many cases reference to acts of God, by which connection was made with biblical thought, was brave rhetoric well-nigh empty of content. It was certainly not what Calvin had it mind![34] Since both liberal and neo-orthodox theologies made a place -- as orthodoxy typically had not -- for human freedom as the originating source of novelty and thus of the direction of world history, ideas of providence and eschatology became problematic.[35] It was no longer clear how God's will could be accomplished in all things if human acts set the course of history or if contingent events occurred in nature. Of course, one can always appeal to mystery, asserting that God is somehow ruling in all things although we don't know how. Liberals had confidence that the spirit of Jesus would gradually rule human motives. Progress in kingdom-building was expected, although World War I dampened the optimism of most. Neo-orthodox views of human sinfulness had no such confidence and looked, as Reinhold Niebuhr did, beyond history for the full reign of love and justice. Even then it would require a fresh and presumably unilateral coercive act of God to bring heaven into being. In that sense Niebuhr was orthodox.[36] Generally, however, he was liberal in not believing that God did particular public and visible things here and now. Rather God is the Ultimate Source and End of all things who judges, forgives, and guides human actions. History in its concreteness is the product of human choices and deeds.

In contemporary thought equally formidable problems exist, if present-day thought intends to re-present biblical modes of thought. Process theology by using the technical vocabulary of Whitehead can say precisely how

God is active in every event. However, divine activity lacks the irresistible efficacy that both the Bible and orthodox theology asserted without hesitation. Moreover, God's power to overcome evil is limited, requiring human cooperation to make it effective.[37] The process model is more respectful of human freedom and expresses the creative-responsive love of God more credibly to the contemporary mind than classical thought. Nevertheless, it is a departure from notions of divine sovereignty found in the Bible and orthodoxy. Hence, it strains the point to insist that the result is a mere "re-presentation" of that ancient witness. That miracle is accomplished only by proceeding as if what does not fit the contemporary model is not essential.[38] Moreover, in its rationalistic and boldly speculative varieties, the claims of process thought to know so much about the inner workings of God are overconfident. The purists among main-line process thinkers promise secular skeptics that if only they will buy into the metaphysics of Whitehead, belief in a robust biblically compatible theism will become credible. Unfortunately, the difficulties posed by taking Process and Reality literally are no less forbidding than those associated with belief in the God of the Bible, except that Whitehead is himself a modern who rules out supernatural divine interventions.

Liberation and eschatological theologies speak of God as the liberator of the oppressed. Yet non-conservative exponents perpetuate liberal and neo-orthodox modes of thought with respect to the priority given to science in explaining the causality that works in nature and history. Thus, they too reject miracle in the old-fashioned sense, except for the resurrection of Jesus. Langdon Gilkey has shown how dubious are the efforts of Wolfhart Pannenberg and Jürgen Moltmann to establish the historicity of the resurrection on grounds of a modern rationality.[39] Such arguments, by and large, convince only those who need no convincing. John Cobb confesses perplexity to know what Moltmann means when he speaks of an ultimate liberation at the consummation.[40]

Liberation theologians do not generally promise the oppressed that a new deliverance from the Pharaohs of today will be accomplished by divinely-sent plagues and wonders similar to those that occurred at the Red Sea. They also give status to human freedom and activity as the real creator of structures of oppression. Thus, it is not clear how God acts to overcome such structures. Presumably God does not interfere with natural law and must work through human freedom, at least here and now. Divine persuasion generally is not effective in securing release of captives from Pharaohs, especially in the short run. Moltmann teaches that God acted supernaturally to raise Christ from the dead as a foretaste of a future supernatural act at the consummation when the world will be made whole. In the present, believers live in memory and hope between these two mighty acts and expend themselves in love to bring about justice and reconciliation.[41] No promise of supernatural help in the present task is offered. God's action in the present apparently consists in inspiring believers through the power of divine promise to liberate the captives and to heal the wounds of the afflicted. Liberation theology is often not precise about how the acts of God and the acts of people are related. Whatever role the Holy Spirit plays does no violence to natural law. Thus, there is vagueness about what is meant with respect to how God liberates as something other than human beings doing God's will in bringing about gains in freedom and equality. Do they, indeed, mean something

other than that? God has acted and will act in the
structures of cosmic and historical events. Now God acts
through the promise of future deliverance to generate
militant hope and action to emancipate the captives.

James Cone admits that black theology has no answer
to W. R. Jones' question as to why blacks in America are
still oppressed after all these centuries, if God is the
Liberator.[42] Is it fair to make strong assertions about
God's liberating action in history and then appeal to
special revelation when empirical evidence does not
confirm the claims? Granted, all theological and philosophical outlooks can only be validated by internal
criteria. But where is the locus of meaning? If it is in
heaven beyond history, then the program of black theology
would appear to be compromised if not vitiated. If it is
primarily in this life and history, then verification has
to be made in terms of historical facts and possibilities. If he refers to the abolition of slavery and the
gains of the civil rights movements, he is still talking
about partial and ambiguous liberation. How long, O Lord,
must we wait (Hab. 1: 2-4)?

When he refers to the Christ-event as the paradig-
matic embodiment of God's liberating activity, present-
day history is abandoned. The world is, of course, the
arena of liberating human action inspired by God's past
acts and by eschatological hope. What for the Christian
is evidence in events here and now that liberation is
occurring by divine action? Appeal to a supernatural
cosmic event in the past not accessible to general
criteria of worldly reason puts the argument on a different plane of reality. In this case Cone has to show that
concrete worldly history has not been put aside.

If the appeal is to the facts of history, then cross
and resurrection must exemplify and symbolize patterns

of suffering and triumph that illuminate the course of empirical human events. That does not appear to be Cone's approach. Rather he suggests that the resurrection -- a unique rather than a representative event -- is a mighty act of God that proleptically discloses the meaning of history and its final destiny. In the light of this mighty act of God, the oppressed live in hope while undertaking their own liberation sustained by the promise of what is to come.[43] The oppressed live between two supernatural events -- the resurrection and the second coming. In the present they cannot account for the seeming contradiction between the affirmation of a Loving and Omnipotent Liberator and the misery of God's chosen.

Most Christians probably have lived and died by some such faith. But is this view adequate to the secular, social, historical focus that Cone makes central? He does say that the final test of a theology is its power to lead the oppressed to strive for their own liberation. Measured by this pragmatic, empirical, and relativistic standard, Cone's theology will, of course, be judged adequate for some people and not for others. By the same token, Jones's black humanism, which Cone rejects, would have to be judged successful to the extent that it inspires engagement with the forces of oppression.

At times he explicitly identifies God's acts with human acts that overcome white racism and, indeed, with black history, black culture, and black experience. Liberating deeds of blacks are God's deeds. Certainly a more complete ontology of events is required if we are to understand what this identity of divine and human acts means. He notes the risk of pantheism.[44] But pantheism usually means an identity or unity of all finite being and events with the divine. Is it, then, an attribution of double causation of the same event in every respect? Is it a doctrine of "real presence," so that human acts become divine acts when they are liberating? Or is it a doctrine of occasionalistic incarnation so that liberating acts are both fully human and fully divine? Most likely it translates into a notion of God using the hands of the oppressed to do the divine work. In Cone's text the claim is merely asserted without further interpretation.

Finally, what can it mean when Cone speaks of God as "struggling," when his God is the omnipotent Lord of history?[45] This is language usually employed by those, like myself, who affirm a finite God. If God chooses to be weak in history and let the oppressed remain in bondage, this qualifies the liberation theme. Is God honoring human freedom by not immediately overruling sinful acts? In this case, God is not struggling but merely living out the divine choice not to interfere. Moreover, it does not fit with the Exodus event in which God interfered with human freedom and nature all over the place. And how can God both honor freedom and be the Liberator who negates sinful human deeds? These are not problems merely for Cone but for all who speak of God acting redemptively in history to do specific things.

Other liberation and eschatological theologies have similar difficulties. The early Jürgen Moltmann spoke of the new age as creatio ex nihilo by the God who acts from the future.[46] The promised fulfillment in no way depends on human action or on potentialities within the historical process of worldly events. Yet believers in the promise expend themselves in liberating acts of love for the oppressed. Here he sounds like Calvin, for whom service of neighbor springs from the redeemed life as acts of grateful obedience. He sound less like Rauschenbusch or some of the Latin American liberation thinkers. For them, socially transforming love is the means by which believers cooperate with God to make the kingdom real. He interprets history, not by an empirical analysis of its facts and possibilities, but in terms of a divine promise to perfect the world. This pledge must be received in faith beyond any power of worldly reason (i. e., the modern scientific-secularized consciousness) to validate. At the same time, the encounter with the risen Christ provides believers with an interpretation of world history. With it they can contend for the truth against the rival faith of the modern secularist, who rejects law-transcending events as impossible or at least as unreal. Hope stands in contradiction to present experience. Only in the eschatological future will faith be vindicated. This reliance on a special set of Christian facts and on faith in a divine promise given from beyond history is not a way of believing that appeals to an empirical, naturalistic modernist. For the latter, reason must be in conformity with experience here and now and not in contradiction to it while waiting in hope for an eschatological verification of belief.[47]

The "mighty acts of God" theme, prominent in neo-orthodoxy, is subdued in much feminist theology. The theme of liberation for the poor and oppressed, however, is central. Liberation appears mainly to mean the transformation of individual and communal life that results when believers begin to live out the imperatives of the "new creation." This happens here and now in response to the divine promise of a new order present, coming, and to come. How, if, when, and where the biblically promised ultimate consummation is to be concretely enacted is often left vague and undefined. The strongest note is that eschatological salvation began in the words and deeds of Jesus and continues now as a present reality. The not-yet implied by the absolute consummation to come from and in the future by the action of God is not absent from all feminist writings. Yet the major theme is a call for the present transformation of church and society. The question of how God acts among us, except as an immanent power and presence to energize and inspire us to liberate ourselves and others from oppression is not usually specified with precision.[48] Feminist theologians in the mainline process school, of course, employ the metaphysics of Whitehead to indicate technically how God works in the world.[49] However, the notion of a God who only persuades means that the redemption of history depends on human cooperation. This theme rejects a fundamental attribute of the biblical God whose Word, when uttered, is irresistibly and effectively enacted from creation to consummation. Hence, process theologians must be put in the modernist camp. Yet they like to emphasize how biblical they are.[50]

Many of the same problems can be found in present-day thought as were present in neo-orthodoxy. Frequently interest in such technical problems -- what Reinhold Niebuhr called "the niceties of pure theology" -- is lacking. The result is that brave talk about the liberating God and of liberating acts of God threaten to become rhetoric. Often such speech has little specifiable or precise content in relation to the events of world history, at least of the kind that newspapers report. Even among theologians who do work at the problem technically, the main result is to demonstrate how difficult the issues are. Contrary theories eliminate each other right and left. It is well-nigh impossible to get agreement about the matter.[51] Once (1) the notion of divine determinism is surrendered and (2) human freedom is made the source of history's content and direction and (3) a law-abiding concept of finite reality is espoused, it becomes extremely difficult to specify what can be meant by God doing particular things in nature and human events. To forego that option and identify the providence of God with a general outworking of purpose in and through the whole network of finite events may be a theological necessity. I agree that it is. However, it hardly qualifies as a restatement of biblical doctrine except in some attenuated sense.

In summary, whether we examine the question of the authority of the Bible or inquire into theological language about the reality and activity of God, severe problems arise. Those who would be modern and biblical are in danger of betraying one interest or the other. It is time to give up the pretense of merely re-presenting some vital core of biblical thought, some universal Gospel, in contemporary terms. A need exists for an empirical theology that makes its concepts clear by reference to experienced events within the context of a candid pluralism and relativism. Hence, I call for a new modernism for the present-day world. A pragmatic, empirical approach leading to a form of naturalistic theism has much to offer in the current search for a theology that is both credible and useful. The roots of this outlook can be found in a group of American theologians who did their work in the first third of this century and who have long been forgotten by all but a few of us.

THE SHAPE OF A NEW MODERNISM

The call is not for a reproduction of the old modernism of Shailer Mathews, Shirley Jackson Case, Henry Nelson Wieman, and others. The summons is for a new modernism that shares some but not all of their assumptions. Neo-modernism must come through and not around neo-orthodoxy, for example. The optimism about history and human possibilities some of the earlier modernists espoused must be rejected on empirical grounds -- their own standard. The tragedies and absurd evils of everyday common life, the threat of nuclear destruction and of ecological catastrophe, the poverty and injustices endured by the wretched masses of the earth, as well as the ambiguous character of history generally require a realism absent in the more sanguine outlook of Mathews. Chicago modernism in the 1920's was, in some ways, the last gasp of the Enlightenment. Their too unambiguous hope in the blessings science would bring and their too easy resolution of the threats and terrors of existence cannot be our stance. Freud, Marx, Nietzsche, and Kierkegaard must inform us so that we can get past the illusion that we have no illusions. They were more confident (or ambiguous) than we ought to be about having the truth or at least the best means to secure it. Essential, however, is a realistic hope that a better society can be achieved as human beings respond with justice-producing actions to the gift and promise of divine purpose ingredient in nature and life. For modernists old and new this hope must be grounded in the real potentials of actual history.

No detailed interpretation of the assumptions and procedures of the Chicago modernists is needed here. This essay agrees with them at least in the following particulars, although they may require modification or reformulation.[52] Shailer Mathews is my primary point of reference.

1. Religion, whatever else it may be, seeks to relate persons and groups salvifically to what they regard as ultimate in their cosmic environment.

2. Christianity is a social movement belonging to general world history and of Western civilization. No special or supernatural assumptions are needed to explain its origin or development. Its center is the way, the truth, and the life incarnate in Jesus of Nazareth.

3. Doctrines interpret the religious experience of the Christian community and function pragmatically to serve the spiritual needs of people. Belief systems are relative to the socio-cultural setting in which they arise. They change as one "social mind" (Mathews -- a set of assumptions that define the mentality of an epoch) is succeeded by another.

4. Based on a study of the Christian movement in its socio-historical environment, the function of theology is to discover relevant values within this history and to restate them in a conceptual system that is appropriate for the prevailing "social mind." Central to this way of understanding life are the methods and conclusions of the empirical sciences.

5. The Bible is neither the norm of universal truth, nor does it contain such a criterion. It is a valuable source of insight that provides continuity with the Christian past. The truth and worth of its teachings, however, must be judged by their capacity to meet human needs as they are felt and understood today. Whatever in the Bible assists persons to relate redemptively to the Creative Cosmic Processes and to achieve fullness of life is to be appropriated. What does not serve this function is without authority.

6. Doctrines of God are not literally true. They do, however, define relations between persons and whatever created them. They are historically conditioned conceptual formulations that function pragmatically to facilitate saving relationships with the Ultimate Environ-

ment. God is the name for the creativity in the cosmos upon which human beings depend for their origin and destiny.

Modernism is primarily a stance and a method, not a body of theological doctrines. Other modernists will come to different conclusions from those presented here. I propose to formulate a new modernism in the spirit of Shailer Mathews. No attempt is made to resurrect his own thought. Important are his assumptions regarding the relativity of Christianity and of the conceptual frameworks that support systems of theology in a given cultural epoch. Equally significant are his theistic naturalism, his empiricism, and his pragmatism. Doctrines are tested by their power to relate persons to God in salvific ways. In order to do so, they must be credible as measured by the convincing conceptual assumptions of the age. They must be relevant to felt needs and experiences of people in a given situation. All this, of course, must be determined by some interpreter, making pluralism inescapable. Much of the best of contemporary theology continues or revives or is analogous to some of the earlier modernist themes.[53] Yet Mathews and company are seldom given any credit.[54]

THE MODERNIST AS CHRISTIAN BELIEVER AND WORLDLY SELF

Two facts about human existence must be taken into account by any responsible theology: the connectedness (1) of individuals with communities and (2) of present life with the social and historical past. Individuals are members of communities. Individual identity is also social identity. I _am_ an American. I _am_ a Christian. We are members one of another, organically related each to the other. As creatures of nature, we are the eventual product of processes that occurred in the deep interior of stars billions of years ago. As creatures of culture, we are formed by language, by ideas, by cultivated modes of appreciation and aesthetic response, and so on created over thousand of years by millions of human beings.[55] Hence, we are not autonomous units but selves organically connected to our past and to our contemporaries.

Seldom do any of us believe anything that has not been taught by others. Originality does flicker now and then as some genius or some ordinary soul stumbles upon neglected insight or even discovers something new. Nevertheless, we all have to decide or at least confirm for ourselves what we will believe and practice. We do so in fear and trembling but sometimes with certitude born of experience. It may be in our suffering and in our dying that our solitariness is most evident. "You gotta walk that lonesome valley; you gotta walk it by yourself. No one else can walk it for you. You gotta walk it by yourself." Yet even when we suffer and die, our solitary reflections usually reproduce what we got from others.

Apart from a past that lives on in us today we have no identity and nothing to guide us. We are rooted in and shaped by religious and cultural traditions that have taught us how to think about important matters. That wisdom is to be honored, for it is the bread that has nourished us and can continue to do so. Christianity itself is relative to Western civilization. It is one religious trajectory among many. Hence, the modernist is willing to go "beyond dialogue" (Cobb) and become open to saving truth in Buddhism and other world religions. The result may be mutual conversion and creative transformation toward ways of thinking that transcend the vision of any historic faith. Given our rootedness in a particular history, we are most likely to find the most effective resources for living and thinking in our own past.

Against this background we may note that a modernist Christian has a self-conscious identity as both a self in the world and as a believer in the church. These two identities overlap and interpenetrate. Together they constitute the personhood of one thinking, feeling, acting subject. As a theological modernist, my ruling identification is as a self in the world. I can to some extent subject my present beliefs to critical analysis and, if persuaded to do so, change my mind. But I can do so only with the conceptual tools, visions of reality, and value systems my religious and cultural past provides.[56] Obviously one of the primary traditions shaping my life is the Bible as it has been interpreted through that segment of the Christian community that constitutes my own past. Within these constraints it is to the truth as I see it that I am committed. Hence, it is only as I determine that what I confess as a Christian is worthy of belief and that what I cannot help but affirm as a human being is in some deep sense Christian that I unite my identities as "self in world" and "believer in church."

RELIGIOUS BELIEF AND TRUTH

Insights from Scripture and Christian tradition may prove to be more true to life than some prevailing cultural assumption soon contradicted by events. Historic faith and present-day reasoning test and transform each other in a continuing dialectic. The weakness of modernism is that it may neglect the deeper insights of the Christian past out of enthusiasm for the ruling fashions of the present. It is always in danger of sinning because of its easy virtue in courtship with the age. Wise discernment, precious and rare in all theological parties, is needed to recognize what is germane to what under which circumstances. No fail-safe method exists to save the orthodox from foolish devotion to the mistakes or anachronisms of the past. No magic method can safeguard modernists from being seduced by the novel enthusiasms of the present. Nevertheless, credibility and saving potential as measured by persons and groups here and now are the final appeals. Traditions, including the Bible, contain various and conflicting strands of "truth." Some present interpreter must choose what is normative for today.

No fail-safe method exists by which we can be saved from conflicting or perverse interpretations of religious truth. Entire communities embodying traditions that are hoary with age can perpetuate error for centuries and resist new truth and higher morals for indefinite periods. Reliance on a special hierarchy, alleged to function by divine authority direct from Jesus, offers no infallible guide to belief and practice. The Pope of the Roman Catholic Church in the name of God pronounces women unfit for the priestly office on the basis of reasons so flimsy that they can only be regarded as defensive of privileges and of traditions completely out of touch with contemporary reality. The moral absurdities taught by official doctrine with respect to birth control are rightly refuted by the common sense of ordinary Catholics. It took the Episcopal Church in this country until 1977 to come around to the position that women may be licitly ordained. These are churches that value communal tradition and stress the authority of the whole community of believers over the centuries.

Individual prophets may be more clear sighted than communities. Yet eccentric individuals claiming to be acting on God's immediate mandate can stray into bizarre territories that boggle the imagination of the sane. Individual Protestants interpreting the Bible for themselves have produced a bewildering variety of sects, denominations, and independent congregations following their own insights allegedly on the authority of the Holy Spirit. The sad fact is that no error-proof method exists either in the interior of exceptional individuals or in the tradition of communities with centuries of practice and multiple procedures for testing what the saints are permitted or required to believe or do.

No matter how we arrive at our convictions, we can never be sure that our affirmations correctly describe what is objectively the case. No way exists to test conclusively whether there is any correspondence between belief and reality when speaking of God. A pragmatic approach to truth is preferable. Practical adequacy in interpreting the whole range of experience is the best we can do. That test does not yield theoretical absoluteness. If being a pragmatist means never having to say you are certain,[57] the modernist is at least relieved of that burden.

DOCTRINAL DIVERSITY AND THE UNITY OF THE CHURCH

A modernist position can be further clarified by examining more fully the nature and function of doctrines. George Lindbeck has recently posed these issues in a fresh and provocative theory.[58] For him becoming a Christian is like learning a language or being socialized into a culture. Its peculiar rules must be learned. Its own internal practices must be personally appropriated. Christianity teaches us how to think and live and is thus prior to us, shaping us and determining how we shall experience the world and God. The church properly uses the changing world-views of succeeding cultural epochs to interpret and proclaim its internally determined message. It does not reinterpret its witness in accordance with culturally-generated ways of thinking and forms of life for the sake of relevance. A deeper and longer-lasting pertinence is achieved by being true to its own speech. Church interprets culture, not the other way around. Contrary to the "experiential-expressive" model in which religious experience is foundational and conceptualizing is derivative, the "cultural-linguistic" model specifies that the rules and practices of the culture/language/religion are prior. Experience is derivative and conceptualization conforms to the rules of the given tradition, although experience in turn may modify the inherited faith.

Surprisingly, in what appears initially to be a conservative approach, great diversity in the propositional content of theology is allowed, contrary to what a "cognitive-propositional" model would permit. Doctrines must conform to the vocabulary, grammar, logic, and rules of the language/religion. These forming determinants do not prescribe what is to be said concretely or propositionally. They only regulate the kinds of truth claims that can be made. That some propositions may be true in the sense of correctly pointing to or properly signifying objective reality is possible. This apparently is a matter of conviction and decision on the part of particular persons and groups beyond the power of the theory itself to adjudicate. As Lindbeck expounds the rules, tritheism, docetism, and Arianism would be excluded in developing doctrines of God and Christ. Correct trinitarian and christological doctrines could be stated either in the vocabulary of Greek metaphysics or in Kantian, Hegelian, or Whiteheadian terms. The essential requirement is that monotheism, the full historicity of Jesus, and utterly maximal claims about Christ not invalidating monotheism be preserved.[59]

This view of doctrine is useful in facilitating ecumenical reconciliation without capitulation. Diversity of doctrinal expression may represent legitimate ways of instantiating the governing rules under different circumstances. Carrying this out, however, requires a complex "taxonomy" of doctrines distinguishing between what is essential, unconditioned, necessary, and permanent in the witness of the church and what is accidental, conditioned, contingent, and changeable. It is even possible, given all the combinations, for a doctrine to be "accidentally necessary." Given agreement on the classification, explicitly conflicting conceptual formulations can be accommodated within a deeper unity, since the competing doctrines may conform to certain regulative principles.[60] I agree with Lindbeck that the persisting pattern may, in some respects, be more fundamental than particular conceptual expressions. Identifying these patterns or specifying the rules can be illuminative and useful. Moreover, Lindbeck has provided a way to allow for historical relativity in the propositional content of doctrines and yet preserve constants, continuities, and abiding points of reference necessary to Christian identity and authenticity.

The fundamental difference between Lindbeck and myself is that he assumes that the norm of theology is "intratextuality." This principle requires conformity to the ways of thinking and forms of life intrinsic to the Christian story to which Scripture gives witness. Lindbeck assumes an inner logic and structure to the Christian phenomenon in history statable in regulating principles or rules (though not in specific cognitive propositions) that give direction to doctrinal construction. He offers something comparable to specifying an "essence of Christianity." Likewise, in his own way, like

Barth, he is a theological positivist who insists that Christianity is what it is as a given reality in history. As such, we take it or leave it. Or we receive it in faith as a gift that irresistibly evokes our acceptance. Preserving Christian identity is his primary motive, although his faith is that only authentic Christianity is genuinely relevant.

The modernist, on the other hand, takes a stand in the present as a self in the world and seeks for a way of intelligent practice that is most conducive to the increase of value -- human, non-human, and divine good. She/he is committed to preserving only what is deemed worthy of belief in the historic tradition and especially in Scripture, not some assumed essence or permanent given or set of rules, however defined. Moreover, modernism is committed to a Christian outlook only because it is unsurpassed and probably unsurpassable as a guide to life. The modernist insists that what presents itself as saving truth today is historically continuous with something deep and vital learned from Christ and the apostles.[61]

Of less importance is a different way of formulating the elements that enter into a comprehensive understanding of doctrine. (1) We must look behind the rule-embodied, propositionally articulated doctrines of the Christian community to a history of religious experience that they express. It was the religious experience of Israel and the church that gave rise to doctrines and their justifying rules. If this is not, in fact, the deeper truth, it is certainly a fundamental and correlative one.

(2) Any historic experience of God occurs to people who think within some culturally shaped scheme of interpretation. Religious experience is always, and can

only be, elucidated in the language, categories, understandings of reality, and operating assumptions available
to a given individual or community from a given religious
and cultural past. Conceptualization of the reality and
nature of God always reflects some background theory.[62]
As I have said elsewhere, the logic of faith (acquired
belief) interacts with the logic of experience (life here
and now) in the continuing life of a religious community
to create the history of doctrine.[63] Which comes first or
is logically prior? Surely we speak of a mutually
dependent and dialectical relationship between inherited
theory and present experience. It is impossible to go
back to some initial encounter with God logic¯ly and
temporary prior to some received framework of interpretation. Nor can we conceive of some conceptualized religious vision antecedent to a history of experience in
individuals and communities. Religious experience and
theological interpretation are dialectically interdependent and mutually constraining.

(3) Doctrines serve a practical function by organizing belief and practice in accordance with a Christian
vision of life. The final test is whether they facilitate
saving relations between persons and God and lead to the
increase of justice, joy, and human good.

In short, three dimensions of doctrine come into
view: the experiential, the interpretive-propositional,
and the pragmatic. Doctrines must be plausible and
relevant to life as judged by contemporary individuals
and communities. It is not possible to define rules of
the game to which everyone would agree. We seek primarily
for a form of intelligent practice even where intellectual agreement about what is means and requires is
lacking. I am less concerned than Lindbeck to get us all
together by some formula that interprets the nature of

doctrines. This is doubtless connected with my Baptist appreciation for individual and congregational freedom to seek the mind of Christ as the Spirit leads here and now. Freedom in the Spirit has a tendency to increase diversity.

Lindbeck's proposal contains complexities, possible confusions, ambiguities, and disadvantages as do alternative proposals. He readmits under a different rubric all the old questions about unity and variety, universality and particularity, permanence and change, essence and accident, appropriating novelty without loss of identity, accommodating diversity that preserves continuity, form and content, and so on that the church has always struggled with.[64] The bottom line is that individual believers and particular churches have to decide all these issues for themselves.

MODERNISTS AND LIBERALS

Liberalism in theology is an attempt to come to terms with the modern world. Harry Emerson Fosdick described the liberals of his generation as standing between the fundamentalists on the right and the humanists on the left. The fundamentalists, he said, thought that if you changed astronomies, the stars would be lost. The humanists concluded that there were no stars and never had been. Liberals believed that the stars were still there, as they always were. Astronomies must change as knowledge advances. Abiding stars, changing astronomies -- that is the metaphorical clue to much liberal methodology of the last century and a half.

Behind the rise of liberal theology lies the discovery of the historical nature of reality, perhaps the most important intellectual legacy of the 19th century. The universe has come to its present state through a long process of development, passing through many stages along the way. Nature evolves, said Darwin. Human societies and human thought unfold over time, said Marx and Hegel. Even God has a history, said Whitehead. The consequences of thinking of reality in historical terms are enormous. History produces a variety of specific patterns of thought that come to be and pass away. Two fundamental assumptions follow that are crucial for theology. (1) All social and conceptual systems are human constructions, historically relative and culturally conditioned. This holds as well for the Bible. Its message is expressed in categories peculiar to a particular time and place. (2) A wide gap exists between the world view of the Bible and that of the modern world.

Historical relativity posed problems of enormous difficulty for the notion that there is one abiding Gospel, a universal message, "the faith once and for all delivered to the saints." Put otherwise, how can a Bible written in the language of an ancient culture provide an absolute revelation of God valid for all cultures? Liberals believe that the only way you can be a Christian is to make some sort of distinction between stars in the heavens (the everlasting Gospel) and the astronomies on earth that describe them (particular culture-bound theologies). The cosmology of Genesis, the ritual procedures of Leviticus, and the code of household duties in Ephesians do not belong to the universal Gospel. The effort to identify the abiding elements in Scripture took many forms. Some sought for a the vital core or essence that transcends all cultures, enabling it to speak to every historical situation when translated into the appropriate thought forms. Some looked for the existential meaning found in biblical mythology. Others looked for the major motifs of the Bible as a whole and so on.

This procedure made it possible to have historical relativity and a Gospel for all times and places. The fundamental motifs remain the same although expressed in a variety of languages and conceptual schemes. What would otherwise be incredible or morally embarrassing could now be relegated to the historically conditioned vessel that contains the everlasting Gospel. A great deal of effort during the last 150 years has gone into the search for this universal something that constitutes the abiding stars as distinct from changing astronomies. Endless unresolved arguments were predictably forthcoming. Unfortunately, while there was agreement that something is of permanent significance, no one was able to say what it was in a way that commanded universal assent. Nevertheless, this way of retrieving the Gospel made it possible for liberals to be "serious Christians and intelligent moderns" (Fosdick). In short, then, one widespread response to the threat posed by historical relativity was to make two claims. (1) It is possible to identify the original witness of faith and to make a distinction between content and form, between essence and accident. (2) Once the Gospel treasure has been identified as separable from the earthen vessel that contained it in its primitive and normative form, it is possible to reincarnate the Gospel in some prevailing "social mind" (Mathews). The evangelical liberals and neo-orthodox theologians, generally speaking, took this approach, as do a variety of black, feminist, liberation, and process theologians today. This is the moderate way of being liberal.

Other theologians, recognizing the difficulties of discovering amidst all the variety and change some one definitive essence of the Gospel, followed the "history of religions school" in identifying Christianity with its developmental history. It is nothing other than whatever it has been as a religio-social movement or has now become. Nevertheless, while rejecting the idea of a normative essence of Christianity, Shailer Mathews, for example, struggled to find some continuities and con-stants among the changes. He wanted to identify them so they could be restated for a scientific-democratic age as pragmatically effective guides to life. Henry Nelson Wieman made an appeal, not to the essence of Christianity or of the biblical message, but to "the best."[65] The best is to be judged by its conduciveness to the increase of human good. Scripture is valuable and authoritative today because it has much to teach about achieving a saving relationship with the Creative Purpose at work in the cosmos. This is the radical or modernist way of being a liberal Christian.[66]

The thesis of this book is that we need to take the more radical stance. The situation today calls for the development of a new modernism. We should give up the notion of an identifiable something that specifies what the one and only Gospel is. Our appeal must be to what in Scripture is convincing given our particular stand-point as modern people informed both by Christian tradition and secular culture. Two clarifying comments are necessary. (1) Scripture is authoritative in so far as it offers a compelling way of believing and living -- and only for that reason. What is most excellent in Scripture is not only supremely but perhaps unsurpassably good. It is the source of the most persuasive vision of life available to us in the world's inventory of religi-ous possibilities. That is why we are committed to it. That is what makes us Christians. (2) We must take responsibility for deciding what in Scripture is worthy of belief today. All such judgments are relative to our own social location, interests, needs, life-history, and general outlook on things.

It is not often put it this way, but the moderate way of being liberal has a point of identity with fundamentalism. Fundamentalists appeal to an infallible Bible located in the original manuscripts. The older evangelical liberals gave that up but found a religious absolute in the historical Jesus. The neo-orthodox theologians also abandoned the infallible Bible but replaced it with a universal Christ-event. The difficulty with identifying something absolute, universal, and culture-transcending is that once we try to say exactly what it is, we reintroduce the very relativity, particularity, and culture-boundedness we were trying to escape. Neither the historical Jesus nor the Christ-event is accessible to us as an uninterpreted reality in itself. It is well and good to point to the historical Jesus or to the incarnation of God in Christ and say, "There, right there, teaching and healing by the Sea of Galilee or there on the cross, that's what I mean; there is the Word of God in flesh and deed." To interpret what that Word is, means, says, and requires of us can only be done using human words that reflect some background theological theory.

Nevertheless, the search for something objective and reliable beyond the feeble, shifting opinions of theologians tossed to and fro by many winds of doctrine is important. Undergirding this quest are two fundamental convictions: (1) The Christian Gospel is something definite that appeared in human history, although its boundaries may be hard to draw. It has its own identity. (2) Whatever the Gospel is, it is defined by the biblical witness to Jesus as the Christ, although in one sense Mathews is right in saying that Christianity is what it

has become.[67] If you want to find the Gospel, look in the
Bible. Pointing to Jesus rather than to Socrates or
Buddha or Marx identifies us as Christians. Unfortunately, once we get specific about what it is that is concretely defined in Scripture, we can only provide a
particular, historically relative account that is one
among many.[68] That the Christian vision is a historical
reality objective to us and located in its original form
in Scripture is clear. Any attempt to say what it
normatively is introduces somebody's theological theory
for which only relative validity can be claimed.

We deal here with a subtle but crucial point. Many
liberals of the moderate stripe acknowledge relativity
and plurality. Yet they often claim that their reconstructions are not better for some purposes in their
opinion but superior as an interpretation of the Gospel,
truer to the original one and only real thing, the
genuine article objectively considered. Maybe what seems
to be theological hubris is outward exuberance that
obscures inward humility. Their books often give a
different impression. Frequently, two things are implied:
"My theology is one more feeble attempt, destined to pass
away." And, "I have seem more deeply into the one and
only true Gospel than those who disagree." The result is
a subtle ambiguity that needs to be exposed. The modernist is determined to say one thing: "My theology
expresses the best vision of life I have been able to
find so far, and its roots are in Scripture."

Today we must acknowledge pluralism and relativism
more radically than have most liberals. We must take our
own finiteness and historical particularity with full
seriousness. It is hard to resist the temptation to play
"At last, we've got it." This theme could be illustrated
over and over: "Now we know what that elusive essence is.

Now we have discovered what the real Gospel is, maybe for the very first time since Jesus left the earth. It is, of course, defined in my theology better than it is in yours. My Gospel is identical with the Gospel or at least closer to it than yours." We should have learned by now that any attempt to state what the Gospel uniquely and objectively is tells us as much about the interpreter as it does about the Gospel. The only alternative to relativism is to claim a privileged status for some contemporary way of believing that, despite all, is the real truth, the Gospel that Jesus himself taught and lived, or at least better than the alternatives.

So far the moderate liberals might agree. The modernist draws a further implication which may mark the parting of the ways. The pragmatic, relativist, pluralist modernist goes on to say that functionally we become the authorities when we get down to specific cases of doctrines and morals. The Bible says a lot of things but means very little for what we are to believe and do until somebody interprets it. Once that happens, we have one more particular, historically relative theology. We should acknowledge that and quit claiming some identity between our outlook and biblical truth as such. No one allows the Bible to teach as the authoritative Word of God for today what is strongly believed (for whatever reasons) to be either untrue or immoral. Hence, the modernist abandons the attempt to define the essence of the Gospel, what true biblical faith is. There is no objectively existing vital core of Scripture, just as there is no human face inside in a huge chunk of granite waiting to be chiseled out. At any rate, recovering it is conceptually impossible for history-bound creatures. Since we cannot agree on what it is, it is not much help to us merely to know that it is really there. William

James reports giving a set of random numbers to his students. They came up with all sorts of patterns that some vehemently claimed to find right there in the numbers themselves! The Bible is not random in its configurations, but every attempt to discover an internal essence is an imaginative construction. This is not to deny that one can locate motifs that add up to a Gestalt. Every attempt even to do that is infected with the relativity virus.

At this point, the modernistic liberal goes one step further. The modernist has a self-conscious identity as a contemporary person in search of truth about life and the way to salvation. It is only because the Gospel presents itself as the best available candidate for the role of truth-telling about human existence and its possibilities that it is of existential interest anyway.[69] Put most pointedly, the modernist is not primarily interested in the truth or essence of Christianity but in the truth about life. The Christian tradition is of concern because of its power to illuminate the meaning of this human pilgrimage as that can be judged by our own reason and experience here and now. At the same time, the modernist would not bother to claim continuity with Christian tradition if what is appropriated from that treasury is not seen to be deeply embedded in the biblical witness and not incidental or peripheral to it. The vision of God and salvation found in the Bible is not only supremely excellent, but it appears to be unsurpassably good. By way of contrast, the liberal tries to stand with one foot in the Gospel and one foot in the modern world. However, in attempting to stand on the Gospel foot, one cannot sever connections with the contemporary foot. Hence, no interpretation of the Gospel

can have independent or autonomous footing but always
reflects the social location of the interpreter.

We see through a glass darkly as creatures shaped
by the time, place, and circumstances of our lives. Does
this not leave us without a firm foundation on which to
stand as we contend against the principalities and powers
of darkness? No, I think not. Seeing through a glass
darkly does not mean that we cannot see at all. It does
mean that we need to move back and forth between two
modes of life that should not be confused with each
other. In one moment we will be passionately committed
to what we presently believe to be true, right, and good.
We will fight for it in all appropriate ways. In the
other moment we will engage in disinterested reflection
in which we will open ourselves to the possibility that
a greater and deeper truth waits to be found. We will
subject our beliefs to questioning and earnestly seek to
find the better way. We can only do that, of course, by
assuming some ideas while testing others. Yet when the
time comes to do something, we will act in the sincere
conviction that the best we know up to now is the truth
that will make us free. When the time to testify comes,
we will give witness to what we are compelled to believe
and argue for what we cannot deny, cross my heart and
hope to die. I call this alternation between passionate
commitment and detached reflection living by the warm
heart and the cool head.

In summary, in order to deal with historical
relativity, liberals tried to identify something universal in Scripture that could be distinguished from the
particular world view in which it was expressed. However,
every attempt to express the unique faith once delivered
to the saints turns out to be particular and relative,
one interpretation among many. Hence, plurality and

relativity undercut the original project of preserving
the one and only true Gospel. Here enter the modernists,
who insist that what is crucial is not the preservation
of some ancient tradition but the achievement of salvation here and now. They agree that saving truth is found
in the Bible. Their modest aim, however, is to make a
local and presently compelling interpretation of Scripture that provides us with our best hope for now. That
is enough. It must be, since the alternative is fruit-
less. Liberals frequently reject no less and affirm no
more than modernists do. Whenever they come across
something in the Bible they don't like, they deny that
it belongs to the essence. Modernists don't play that
game anymore. They reject the effort to overcome relativity by claiming that our Gospel is the Gospel.

A wider point needs to be made here. Theologians
frequently claim their version of the Gospel escapes
relativity better than other interpretations. A further
assertion is that while all historical religions and
philosophies of life are relative, the Christian Gospel
is just plain true. Our outlook on life corresponds to
reality. We believe this because it provides a pattern
that makes sense of our experience. Therefore, we say not
simply that it is coherent and compelling for us but that
it is true for everybody whether they recognize it or
not. This is a neat trick. It amounts to saying that we
escape relativism because we just do. Since the Gospel
is justified by our criteria, we declare that it corresponds to reality.[70] Verbal victory is illusive.
Believing something strongly does not make it true. Why
do Christians think their belief is exempt from the
relativity they otherwise attribute to all human constructions of reality? The modernist refuses to get into
that quagmire any more.

Kaleidoscope comes from two Greek words meaning "beautiful form." The same pieces of glass produce a multitude of pretty patterns depending on how the instrument is turned. Does it make any sense to say that one of them is more right than the others? Doing theology is like playing with a kaleidoscope. We all read the same Bible and refer to the same classical texts from Tertullian to Barth. Many beautiful forms have been produced from Nicea to Trent and from Calvin and Luther to Tillich and Tracy, Cone and Cobb, Ruether and Suchocki. Which of these delightfully colored arrays of brilliant arrangements is the right one? The Bible is a kaleidoscope. Which beautiful form is seen depends on how it is turned. It is the same Bible, but we produce a bewildering variety of images, alike in many respects, different in a lot of others. All have common colors, and the arrangements are often only slightly at variance from others. We are Christians because it is the biblical kaleidoscope that we play with rather than the Buddhist or humanist one.

Subtle issues arise. Since nearly all modern Euro-American ethical and religious philosophies have some connection with the Jewish-Christian past, could not even Marxists and secular humanists claim to be preserving the highest and best of the Bible? Can a line to be drawn that excludes anyone from claiming to be a Christian? Formally, one can say that the requirement of being a Christian is to confess that Jesus is the Christ or that the Bible contains the norm of religious truth. Yes, but what does that exclude in terms of content of belief or moral practice? Some Nazis, slave holders, KKK members, haters of homosexuals, racists, torturers of heretics, fanatics, zealots, and lunatics of all sorts ancient and modern belong to the company of those who confess Christ as Lord. If we take Jesus' own criteria, we may get different results than if we depend on the creeds and the theologians to write the rules (Lk. 10:25-37; Mt. 5:1-10, 7:15-23, 25:31-46). Some Marxists, atheists, and humanists may show mercy, seek justice, and produce more fruits of faith in daily living than do orthodox believers. The problem has no definitive solution. Two points may be relevant. (1) Many lines of inclusion and exclusion can be drawn specifying who real Christians are. In every case, somebody has to draw that line on the basis of principles that can claim only relative validity. Theologians who want to be Christians always establish boundaries that include themselves in. Hence, a generation ago Christian atheists taught that "God is dead." (2) Practically speaking, there comes a point at which persons and communities feel so remotely connected to biblical authority that they self-define themselves out of the Christian circle or are indifferent to the issue.

Modernists can be identified in three ways. (1) They feel deeply their rootedness in the Christian past. That identity matters but not ultimately. Salvation is the ultimate concern, not being Christian.[71] (2) They claim that what they preserve is not incidental or peripheral to the biblical witness but important and basic to it. (3) They continue to work out their own theologies in deliberate conversation with the Bible and Christian tradition. Their main departure from liberal Christians is that they see little profit in arguing about the form and content of a universal something that constitutes the one and only essential Gospel of Jesus and the Apostles. Also, they more self-consciously identify themselves as modern persons seeking fulfillment of life and are Christians for that reason. Liberals want to be Christian

and modern in an equal and primary sense. Thus, they
argue endlessly and inconclusively about what that
requires of them and others. Modernists are content to
say that what they believe is the best they know up to
now.

CONCLUSION

To conclude, modernists continue to look to ancient
Israel and the early church for a saving Word. We are
Christians because it is to that tradition we turn, are
compelled to turn, have no choice but to turn and return
to, to argue with, to revise, to doubt and to reject, to
transform and reinterpret, to be judged and transformed
by. Looking elsewhere has not yielded so rich a harvest
of wisdom. We confess Jesus as the Christ because he has
disclosed grace and truth. We read the Bible as Holy
Scripture because of its unexcelled power to illumine a
way of living that promises to make real the beauty and
the goodness that life -- the gift of that Ultimate
Mystery -- offers.

THE OUTLINE OF THINGS TO COME

The following chapter will set forth a theory of
knowing. I affirm a form of intentional realism that
seeks to discover the way the world is. Yet all we can
achieve with respect to the big questions is a relative
perspective that functions pragmatically. The primary aim
of thought is to enable us to cope with life satisfactorily. That is why we seek to know the world as it is.

Chapter III will offer a polemic against the
classical theism that has dominated the Western Christian
tradition. The traditional theodicies will be criticized.
An alternative centering around the notion of a finite
opportunistic God will be set forth.

Chapter IV will develop the category of life as a
key to understanding the evolutionary process in its

forward advance. This will be related to some of the some current issues in biological philosophy arising out of the scientific understanding of evolution and the nature of life. Finally, a doctrine of God will be developed in some detail. It will amount to a version of naturalistic theism in the tradition of process theology.

ENDNOTES

1. Liberal is used with two standard meanings in theological literature. (1) Sometimes it refers to the 19th and early 20th century movement in theology that followed Protestant orthodoxy and preceded neo-orthodoxy. (2) At other times it refers to non-conservative or non-orthodox or modern theologies generally. In this second sense evangelical liberalism, modernistic liberalism, neo-orthodoxy, and a variety of contemporary theologies -- revisionism, liberation theology, eschatological theology, process theology, post-liberal theology, etc. -- are all liberal. They agree in calling for a reformulation of all orthodoxies in the interest on being credible to the scientific-secularized consciousness of the modern world that includes taking historical relativity with deep seriousness. Later in the chapter I distinguish between the moderate way of being liberal (2) and the radical way of being liberal that I call modernism. The context should make it clear when I am referring to liberalism (1) and liberalism (2). For a distinction between evangelical and modernistic liberalism during the first third of this century, see my The Impact of American Religious Liberalism. See also my Systematic Theology, pp. 21-27, 411-442.

2. See Kenneth Cauthen, The Impact of American Religious Liberalism; Langdon Gilkey, Naming the Whirlwind, pp. 31-145.

3. See Cauthen, The Impact of American Religious Liberalism, chapters 8, 9, 10. See also Creighton Peden, The Chicago School.

4. Ibid., chapter 12. See also Gilkey, Naming the Whirlwind, pp. 73-106.

5. Neo-liberal perhaps fits even better those who were closer to the older liberals, such as Daniel Day Williams (and other process theologians) and Robert Calhoun.

6. For a brief account of theology since 1960, along with references to the relevant literature, see my Systematic Theology, pp. 21-27, 411-442; see also, Langdon Gilkey, Reaping the Whirlwind, pp. 109-238.

7. See Gayraud Wilmore and James Cone (eds.), Black Theology; Cone, A Black Theology of Liberation; and Deotis Roberts, Liberation and Reconciliation.

8. See his Theology of Hope.

9. See John B. Cobb, Jr., A Christian Natural Theology; Cobb and David Griffin, Process Theology.

10. The standard source here is David Tracy, Blessed Rage for Order.

11. David Tracy does not speak of recovering the "essence" of Christianity, but he does refer to the "meanings" found in the tradition or "the central motifs" or "central meanings" or "basic meanings." Ibid., pp. 17, 34. This sound pretty close to "essence."

12. Like so many contemporary efforts, David Tracy in Pluralism and Ambiguity succeeds better in describing the problem than in resolving it. Circles of interpretation overlap, and by being mutually open to transformation, we can enlarge our circles, but even the best success of "the analogical imagination" can never unite the centers of our interpretive circles at a single location.

13. The recent works of Gordon Kaufman are a good example of this. See his The Theological Imagination and Theology for a Nuclear Age. Sallie McFague's Models of God and Rosemary Ruether's Sexism and God-Talk should probably be included here as well, as well as Elizabeth Schüssler Fiorenza's In Memory of Her and Carter Heyward's The Redemption of God.

14. The early Tracy stresses the universality of principles of right reason, while the later Tracy emphasizes the particularity represented in stubbornly conflicting traditions of thought. Others have noticed this too, including William Placher, Unapologetic Theology, pp. 154-159. In Blessed Rage for Order, he comes close to an old-fashioned natural theology in his claim that an appropriate transcendental or metaphysical philosophy can establish the necessary presuppositions of all thought and experience whatsoever. See pp. 53-56, 146-171. Moreover, reason can point to signals of transcendence in experience that point to a divine dimension to reality. See pp. 91-118. In The Analogical Imagination and Plurality and Ambiguity the historicity and relativity of thought are more prominent. Yet the denial of an absolute standpoint, as well as confidence that theology can stake out public claims, are present over the whole period. Only with great reluctance, one surmises, does Tracy give up on the idea that right reasoning can lead us into the truth. Yes, but alas, when

are we reasoning rightly about God? Who is doing it? We
cannot be sure.

15. For a comparison of revisionist and post-liberal
theologies, see Placher, Unapologetic Theology. I discuss
Lindbeck later in this chapter.

16. Typical feminist texts are Rosemary R. Ruether,
Sexism and God-Talk; Marjorie Suchocki, God, Christ,
Church; and Letty Russell, Human Liberation in a Feminist
Perspective.

17. See Wilmore and Cone (eds.), Black Theology,
pp. 620-622, and Cone, God of the Oppressed, pp. 138-194.

18. James Cone, A Black Theology of Liberation,
pp. 35-39.

19. See God of the Oppressed, pp. 16-107, and A
Black Theology of Liberation, pp. xxi-xxii.

20. Cone can be read differently perhaps, i. e., as
a thoroughgoing relativist, agnostic before the ultimate
mysteries who confesses his own faith on the basis of
undeniable conviction yet without being able to prove its
objective truth. See God of the Oppressed, pp. 102-107.
That theme is present. Yet the philosophical skeptic is
finally overcome by the Christian believer who cannot
doubt that faith arises in a genuine encounter with a
Living Word, an Other, a Liberating Subject, who calls
the oppressed to claim their destiny as free subjects. The final, stronger theme is that faith grasps or
is grasped by Reality, yielding not simply subjective
confidence but objective truth. Or so I read him.

21. See Gyn/Ecology.

22. Letha Scanzoni and Nancy Hardesty are evangelicals who state that "any teaching in regard to women must
square with the basic theological thrust of the Bible."
All We're Meant to Be, p. 20. But they seem quite timid
in saying that a given passage is just plain wrong rather
than merely needing a contextual interpretation that
makes it say something worthy. The resort to "the basic
thrust of the Bible" as a norm opens a very wide door
that allows the interpreter considerable latitude in
defining acceptable biblical doctrine. The tension
between appealing to specific texts, when good ones are
available for our purposes, and resorting to "the basic
thrust of the Bible," when they are not, poses a crucial
methodological problem in both liberal and evangelical
theologies.

23. Sexism and God-Talk, pp. 12-46.

24. In Memory of Her, pp. xiv-xxv, 1-95.

25. Ibid., pp. 30-33.

26. Ibid., pp. 105-159, 140-141.

27. It is of interest that Schüssler Fiorenza finds in Ruether (as well as in Letty Russell and Phyllis Trible) a neo-orthodox procedure of finding a canon within the canon, a universal essence of the Bible or Christian faith that can be distinguished from its time-bound form and accidental features. See In Memory of Her, pp. 14-21. Her criticism of this procedure is telling: it abstracts from history an idealized pattern that is used to criticize the specific content of faith and practice and, in effect, to claim that the underlying essence of the tradition is different from its actual existence. But is that not that to play tricks with history? Unless Schüssler Fiorenza herself is saying merely that an equalitarian church actually existed and that women today can be empowered by identifying with and continuing that ancient minority tradition, then she is not entirely unfree from that tendency herself. I hear her saying that the discipleship of equals is not only fact, it is also normative for the Gospel by the Gospel's own internal standards.

28. Mary Daly, Beyond God the Father, p. 73.

29. Numerous complex and subtle issues arise here. They might well claim that they did not invent the norm they employ but rather found it in the tradition and just recognize it as what is truly valid in it. Yet the tradition contains much else besides, which they reject. How is it that they make normative precisely what coincides with what a critical feminist principle requires? They can hardly claim that what they make normative in the tradition is what is explicitly normative in the Bible or the early church, since both admit that patriarchal and oppressive motifs are dominant. Certainly what is not dominant in the tradition can be made normative for us. Yet how can they claim that something not dominant in the tradition is definitive, not merely for us, but for the tradition itself? One might, of course, maintain that the implicit norm of the tradition itself really did require equality, mutuality, and universal justice but that the dominant interpretations of the community of faith failed to see that what they most deeply believed undermined the patriarchy they practiced. But that seems strained. Hence, while Ruether

and Schüssler Fiorenza may have arrived at what they accept as normative as believers who have been informed by the Christian past, it would nevertheless appear that a modern critical feminist consciousness is determinative, regardless of how they learned of or were convinced by the norms explicit and implicit in that consciousness. It is in that sense that I suggest that they accept only what is best in the tradition, whether or not it is dominant in or definitive for the tradition. They must forego any attempt to claim that what they take as normative for present-day believers simply re-presents what is self-defined in the Bible as its essence. Even if Jesus himself turned out to be another patriarchal male, they would have to reject him too. That is the logic of the matter, although they are convinced that Jesus is on their side, or they are on his.

30. See Sheila Greeve Davaney, "Problems with Feminist Theory: Historicity and the Search for Sure Foundations."

31. On one occasion, Bernard Loomer looked up after reading a sentence from the paper he was presenting and said, "As the Bible plainly teaches." He looked down, paused, looked up again, and said, "I don't know where, but it does." He looked back at his paper another time, paused, looked up once more, and concluded, "Well, if it doesn't, it ought to." Now there's a modernist after my own heart!

32. See Langdon Gilkey, Reaping the Whirlwind, pp. 159-187.

33. See my Systematic Theology, pp. 132-162.

34. Langdon Gilkey, "Cosmology, Ontology, and the Travail of Biblical Language," in Owen Thomas (ed.), God's Activity in the World, pp. 29-43.

35. For an excellent discussion of history and providence in modern Protestant theology, see Gilkey, Reaping the Whirlwind, pp. 209-238.

36. See The Nature and Destiny of Man, II, pp. 287-301, and Faith and History.

37. See, for example, David R. Griffin, God, Power and Evil, pp. 251-310.

38. Schubert Ogden, The Reality of God.

39. Langdon Gilkey, Reaping the Whirlwind, pp. 361 n35.

40. "It is not clear, at least to this writer, whether Moltmann believes the promise will someday really be fulfilled, whether he thinks it may be fulfilled, or whether his concern is entirely for the meaning of life here and now in light of the promise, so that the question of its actual fulfillment in the future does not arise." John B. Cobb, Jr., Process Theology as Political Theology, p. 69. My reading of Moltmann is that he thinks the promise really will be fulfilled. See Theology of Hope, pp. 15-22, 216-229, 288-91. Delwin Brown, To Set at Liberty, pp. 113-121, and Langdon Gilkey, Reaping the Whirlwind, pp. 226-238, also read him as referring to an objective fulfillment, total and complete, on the very earth on which Christ was crucified. I agree with Cobb, however, that he is not always clear.

41. Jürgen Moltmann, Theology of Hope, pp. 288-291, 325-338.

42. William R. Jones, Is God a White Racist? For Cone's response, see God of the Oppressed, pp. 138-194.

43. See Wilmore and Cone (eds.), Black Theology, pp. 620-22, for a brief summary of his conclusions about these matters.

44. A Black Theology of Liberation, pp. 10, 30, 64.

45. God of the Oppressed, p. 194.

46. See his Theology of Hope, pp. 15-36, 139-229.

47. I have been much helped by Langdon's Gilkey's interpretation and evaluation of recent European eschatological theologies. See Reaping the Whirlwind, pp. 226-238. Cf. my Systematic Theology, pp. 392-398.

48. See, for example, Rosemary Ruether, Sexism and God-Talk; Carter Heyward, The Redemption of God; and Letty Russell, Human Liberation in a Feminist Perspective -- A Theology, The Future of Partnership, and Growth in Partnership.

49. See especially in this regard Marjorie Suchocki, God, Christ, Church.

50. Process theologians can hardly claim to be reproducing the essence of the biblical witness, unless it came be shown that a motif so prominent throughout the

Bible of a God who acts unilaterally to bring about any
divinely desired result can be so fundamental, frequent,
and unchallenged and yet not belong to the essential core
of its teachings!

51. See Owen Thomas (ed.), God's Activity in the
World.

52. See my The Impact of American Religious Liberalism, pp. 147-168, 188-206; my introduction to Mathews in
the reprint of his Jesus on Social Institutions that I
edited, pp. xi-lxxii; Kenneth L. Smith, Shailer Mathews:
Theologian of Social Process; William J. Hynes, Shirley
Jackson Case and the Chicago School: The Socio-Historical Method; and Harvey Arnold, Near the Edge of Battle,
1866-1960; and Peden, The Chicago School, pp. 12-23.

53. For essays that indicate how profoundly an acute
awareness of pluralism and relativism informs contemporary theology, see The Myth of Christian Uniqueness: Toward a Pluralistic Theology of Religions. The
essays by Gordon Kaufman and Langdon Gilkey express ideas
close to mine. See pp. 3-15, 37-50. See also, of course,
David Tracy, Plurality and Ambiguity, although his points
of reference in terms of a solution are quite different,
but we both agree, along with many others today, that
open-minded conversation between competing theories of
the true and the good leading to mutual transformation
of perspectives moving toward a consensus of warranted
belief and a corresponding effective praxis is our best
hope.

54. The naturalistic theism recently espoused by
Gordon Kaufman interprets the reality of God in terms
similar to those proposed by Shailer Mathews. Both
connect God closely with the complex of natural forces
that gave rise in the evolutionary process to human
life. See Kaufman, Theology for a Nuclear Age, pp. 30-
46. Nowhere do I find a hint that Kaufman sees the
connection.
Years ago I was amused to find a passage in Eustace
Haydon's The Quest of the Ages (1926) describing the
pragmatic, secular, technologically-oriented age that
could have been lifted bodily and placed in Harvey Cox's
The Secular City (1964) Nobody would have known the
difference! How many American theologians were aware of
any continuity? Think also of the similarities between
the theological debates of the 60's around the secular
challenge and the discussions among the Chicago theologians in the 20's. They even had their own "death of God"
theology -- and its refutation -- right among themselves.
selves. There were differences, of course, most of them

related to the importance of Nietzsche, Camus, Sartre, Heidegger and others in the latter-day obituaries.

Not long ago I heard a prominent historian of American religion remark that developments in the Chicago school were interesting, but then he wondered if they were really doing "theology." His comment got a big laugh. John Cobb, to his credit, gets the Chicago school into the picture in his discussion of recent political theology. See <u>Process Theology as Political Theology</u>, pp. 19-43.

55. It may be objected that despite my professed adherence as a process theologian to the social character of human existence, I have presented Christian theology in highly individualistic terms. Has not the reality of the church as a distinctive community of faith existing as the living bearer of the Christian treasure through history been obscured and down played? Has not theology in this presentation become an activity of individuals with a Christian heritage seeking a credo for themselves rather than a specialized activity of the community designed to preserve its identity amid changing circumstances by testing its present message against its own internal, historic, and unchanging norms? Is being a Christian defined in terms of loosely connected individuals with similar religious commitments rather than as living out the shared vision of the Christian community? Doubtless, this leaning is present. This is a likely tendency of an individualistic Baptist with sectarian roots who is generally suspicious of established traditions. (Those familiar with the Myers-Briggs inventory will not be surprised to learn that I am an INTJ.) I do admit that the bottom line is that "you gotta walk that lonesome valley, you gotta walk it for yourself; nobody else can walk it for you." Even then, however, we do so having been shaped, formed, and destined by the communities to which we belong.

56. David Tracy makes this point profoundly in an impressive display of scholarly overkill in <u>Plurality and Ambiguity</u>.

57. Jeffrey Stout, <u>Ethics after Babel</u>, p. 297.

58. George Lindbeck, <u>The Nature of Doctrine</u>.

59. But how far are we to go with this? Can two doctrines both instantiating the same rules or formal pattern yet be so far apart in conceptual and propositional content as to constitute different religious visions, so that to call them both authentically Christian and thus at one with each other approaches ludi-

crousness? Would Lindbeck allow both Anselm and Mathews into the ecumenical consensus of allowable doctrines regarding atonement? For Mathews Jesus illustrates a right adjustment to the purposive evolutionary process that produced human life. He was faithful to the death to his conviction that love guides the cosmos. His resurrection meant only that by his own right adjustment to the personality-producing cosmic activities, he triumphed over the maladjustment of others. Mathews sees himself as giving a contemporary version of doctrine that obeys the formal rules or patterns that the major historic doctrines have. Yet the propositional content is far removed from anything Anselm or Irenaeus or Luther would have recognized.

At this point a crucial question arises with regard to what constitutes an instantiation of the governing rules? Lindbeck requires that maximal claims not invalidating monotheism be made about Christ. The Chalcedonian creed in asserting that Christ is "fully God" carries maximality to the maximum! Mathews developed a pragmatic-functional view in which Jesus reveals God and illustrates the way of salvation, but is not literally God, i. e., deity was not fully and wholly present in Jesus. Yet in some Ritschlian-like sense, Jesus as the supreme disclosure of the way of salvation has the value of God for us functionally. Pragmatically, Jesus is the focal point of an effective and true revelation of God and the facilitator of a right adjustment to God. Mathews sees his view of incarnation and atonement as preserving in a pragmatic-functional outlook the same formal patterns that were operative in previous ages of Christian thought and in Scripture. In his own way, he is making maximal claims about Christ. Would he qualify by Lindbeck's version of the right rules? (1) If so, the original question reappears. Is any conceptual claim valid, no matter what its content is regardless of how far out and bizarre, as long as the formal patterns are exhibited? Can form and content be totally separated? Are there any restraints of form on content? Is it a matter purely of form and not of content in any sense? Or must form and content both be included somehow in judgments about what is authentically Christian? (2) If Mathews' formulations do not conform to Lindbeck's rules, then do we need some other or better way of thinking about the nature of doctrine so that the Chicago modernist could be included within the Christian consensus? In order to do embrace all these doctrines, do we not need to go beyond the "cultural-linguistic" approach to a "pragmatic-functional" understanding of doctrines that Mathews and I espouse that can accommodate relativity and pluralism within a framework of loose rather than strict historical continuity?

60. Indeed Shailer Mathews pointed to certain constants and continuities in the Christian tradition in a similar fashion though in different language. In investigating the history of Christian doctrines about God and Christ, he found a set of recurring patterns whose propositional content differed from age to age as one "social mind" replaced another. He suggested that Christ has been seen in every epoch as accomplishing by divine initiative whatever is necessary to reconcile God and humanity. Christ's work makes forgiveness morally legitimate as determined by acceptable contemporary social practices. Atonement theory illustrates Mathews' conviction that theology is "transcendental politics." Anselm, for example, used patterns from the medieval feudal system to show how unequals could be reconciled by appropriately "satisfying" the offended honor of the higher party. This social paradigm is then applied to the God-humanity relationship. The New Testament uses imagery from the sacrificial practices of Israel to show how Christ secures forgiveness by being Priest and Sacrifice (Hebrews). See his Atonement and Social Process. Likewise, I have identified trinitarian and christological patterns basic to Christian thought that reappear, thus providing continuity over the centuries. A trinitarian pattern for thinking about God and a christological pattern involving unity of personhood and duality of nature, role, or function seem to arise inevitably and necessarily from the inner logic and structure of Christian thinking. These patterns, however, are expressed within doctrines that exhibit great diversity of propositional content. See my Systematic Theology, pp. 104-127, 164-166, 225-229, 240, 259-262, 402-409.

61. "Loyalty to Jesus" was, for Mathews the principle of continuity. Whether this is the best way to put it is arguable, but he was willing under this rubric of loose continuity to allow a wide latitude of doctrinal content, even wide enough to include his own naturalistic, empirical pragmatic functionalism. Lindbeck would too if Mathews obeyed the right rules. Mathews does practice "Christological maximalism" in his own terms, but do his terms meet Lindbeck's interpretation of that rule that requires that "every possible importance is to be ascribed to Jesus" that does not compromise monotheism"? Mathews finds in Jesus the supreme clue to God, maybe even "the highest possible clue" (Lindbeck), but he does so in a purely functional but not ontological sense. I have the impression that finally Lindbeck would be a more strict constructionist than Mathews, but maybe he is radical enough to embrace even purely functional doctrines. But, in any case, I affirm that a pragmatic-functional approach to doctrine is more capable of

embracing the extremes of conceptualizing displayed in Christian history with less strains that threaten self-destruction and fewer complications than his cultural-linguistic theory. See The Nature of Doctrine, p. 94.

62. This is the burden of Wayne Proudfoot in Religious Experience.

63. See my Systematic Theology, pp. 402-409.

64. See, for example, the complicated "taxonomy of doctrines" he elaborates requiring distinctions between unconditionally necessary permanent doctrines and conditionally essential ones. Conditionally essential doctrines are subdivided into the permanent and temporary, and temporarily conditional doctrines are classified as either reversible and irreversible. See The Nature of Doctrine, pp. 84-88. Won't we all have a lot of fun fighting about which teachings fall under which category? It may be useful to do so, but fight about it and disagree we will. Is it really worth the effort to make all these detailed and precise classifications? Perhaps a theologian thoroughly committed to finding the maximum amount of doctrinal agreement might. Maybe the difference here is that Lindbeck is a Lutheran, while I am a loose Baptist!

65. Henry Nelson Wieman, The Source of Human Good, p. 268.

66. For an elucidation of this, see my The Impact of American Religiou Liberalism.

67. A set of very difficult problems arises here. One could argue that whatever deviates from the original defined in the New Testament is no longer Christianity but something corrupt and false. One could argue that the primitive expression has no privileged or normative status but is simply the beginning of what can only be defined by looking at its total history. Moreover, we are to examine its existence and refrain from making any judgments about essence. One could argue that Christianity legitimately develops from its origins into something mature, so that later versions contain novelties and variations that nevertheless are not only continuous with its beginnings but are authentic even essential to its true nature. An so on the interpretations might go. I am enough of a classical Protestant to think that the original witness does have a privileged status, so that any versions that cannot be rooted in motifs central and not merely incidental or peripheral

to Scripture (What does that mean?) lose claim to authenticity. Yet I also argue that the intent is not to preserve Christian truth or some original essence but to find the truth about God and life. A modernist is a Christian only because he/she believes that something central to Scripture is also definitive of abiding or at least compelling religious truth.

68. I shall argue in a later chapter that the same problem faces science. It is well and good to claim that the objects dealt with in scientific theory are real, but once an effort is made to say precisely what it is that is real, historically-developed, culturally-produced descriptions framed in concepts, laws, theories, words, etc. come into play. There is no way to present the thing in itself as an uninterpreted reality. That something is real in the spatio-temporal region being observed or talked about is one thing. To say what it is that is really there in that place doing just that introduces human language and theory for which only a relative but pragmatically sufficient claim can be made.

69. Reinhold Niebuhr once said that he was a Christian by a process of elimination. No other option interpreted human existence, its predicament, and its possibilities as persuasively, he said.

70. For an example of this claim, see William Placher, Unapologetic Theology, pp. 123-137.

71. Here I differ from Paul Tillich. He says that a Christian is one for whom the content of the Christian circle is a matter of ultimate concern. I say that salvation is the ultimate concern. Being a Christian is the way to salvation. See Tillich, Systematic Theology, I, pp. 8-11.

Chapter II
A WAY OF KNOWING:
SEEING THROUGH A GLASS DARKLY

An English cab driver reported to T. S. Eliot that he often had celebrities for passengers and told the following story. "A while back I recognized Bertrand Russell. So I said to him, `Sir Bertrand, what's it all about?' And, you know what, he couldn't tell me!" The cabby may not have realized it, but it is not only Bertrand Russell who suffers from this disability. No philosopher knows "what it's all about." More precisely put, no human being knows for sure what the ultimate facts and meanings are. Philosophers have no privileged insights, only more sophisticated ways of talking about things.

The philosophical enterprise of epistemology is a failure. The Cartesian experiment to discover some indubitable foundation of wisdom only produced another series of arguments in modern thought about the method of knowing. Today philosophers debate all the old questions about what we can know and how we can reliably come to know it. Experience is so variously interpreted that the word is hardly usable as a common coin of communication. Science -- often thought to be the supreme method for discovering what is genuinely the case -- offers a sequence of interpretive schemes. Science is one more historically relative approach to reality. It provides no way to overcome the relativism that otherwise pertains. Pluralism and relativity mark human attempts to state where the universe came from, how it operates, and what it all means. No way can be found to overcome the human predicament of not knowing for sure how accurate our reality-portrayals are. More importantly, we are quite limited in our ability to overcome the destructive conflicts between groups that keep the ground red with blood and hearts full of hate.

A major effort of the day is to find a way "beyond objectivism and relativism,"[1] No one knows how to convince everybody else that her/his proposal is best. Some philosophers and theologians appear still to be playing "At last, we've got it." For those in a more modest mood, conversation among representatives of conflicting visions in the quest of a consensus of warranted assertions -- the new definition of truth -- is among the more popular remedies currently advertised. Others have given up and urge that all we can do talk with each other and do the best we can by whatever available methods will work in given situations.

If the assessment given is accurate, some form of skepticism and relativism follows. Is not skepticism self-refuting? If the skeptic's assertion that we cannot know anything for sure about ultimate matters is true, it is false. We can presumably know one thing to be true, namely, that nothing can be known with certainty about final facts. The skeptic's claim stands in the unhappy position of being false if it is true. Presumably the skeptic could not be certain about uncertainty without being certain about a lot of other things too. Hence, skepticism as a doctrine may be self-refuting. However, the smart skeptic will not propound skepticism as a theoretical proposition known to be true. She/he merely says, "I am not sure we can know anything for sure about the big issues of life and destiny, even whether skepticism is justified. Nevertheless, we can commit ourselves to the best we have discovered up to now."

Similarly, it is argued, the notion that all points of view are relative implies that relativity as a point of view is relative too. Perhaps, but the statement that all philosophical systems are relative may have a different epistemological status than particular outlooks themselves. Even if there is one and only one true religion and morality, it is reasonable to remain skeptical about attempts to state what that one truth is. Moreover, if relativity only means that what we are justified in believing depends on our location in a particular culture at a specific time,[2] it is a defensible doctrine.

Beyond the quick kill of logical absurdity, the practical objection to relativism is the fear that doubt about the objective truth of beliefs will lead to a decay of moral seriousness and finally to nihilism. I don't believe this necessarily follows. I love my children, promote a liberal social agenda in politics, work for the relief of hunger, and so on because these things are important to me and are worth doing. I cannot do otherwise. Any lack of moral heroism on my part is not due to my relativism. If one of my children needed assistance, I would provide it without even wondering whether the cosmos or God or whatever laid this obligation upon me in some absolute fashion. It never occurs to me to worry about relativism when I send a check to the American Friends Service Committee. Nor would conversion to any form of objectivism necessarily make me a better person. I suspect it is the same with other people. What matters is that beliefs and values are operative within us, that they are important enough to us to generate action, and that we are open to change when a better interpretation comes along. Belief systems and moral commitments develop in us through socialization, experience, and choice to form character that determines how we will think, feel, and act. One can hate suffering and injustice as one construes them without having either the illusion or the certainty that Reality approves. If moral commitment decays, it will be for reasons other than an intellectual persuasion that beliefs are relative to time and place. Moral complacency exists among persons committed to notions that objective truth is available. Despair and nihilism accompany loss of meaning and purpose in living. Relativists may find life overflowing with possibilities for good and be motivated by love to seek justice for all, while recognizing that their theories about ethics may not correspond to universal cosmic patterns. The worst evils spring from lack of regard for other people, often as a consequence of certain life histories. These deficiencies are not the necessary product of skepticism about the powers of reason to determine with certainty the ground of meaningfulness and purpose in final facts. The relativist can believe strongly what is personally convincing, workable, or necessary for worthwhile existence without attributing absolute merit to ideas and ideals.

Consider Proposition A: Gratuitous cruelty is wrong. Six possibilities come to mind:
1. I know that Proposition A corresponds to reality.
2. I believe that Proposition A corresponds to reality.
3. Proposition A is worth believing because living by it is better for everybody on every count. Maybe that's

what truth means. I am deeply committed to it as a
guiding value.

4. Proposition A is a warranted assertion, where war
ranted means compelling to me and to those communities
of inquiry whose conclusions I trust.

5. Proposition A seems to me valid because of 3 and 4.
Nevertheless, since I am a relativist and have no
certainty that Proposition A corresponds to reality,
the logical implication is that I should be indifferent to acts of cruelty, since relativism a.
necessarily in theory or b. eventually in practice
leads to moral nihilism.

6. Proposition A is false, unworthy of belief, and offers
no advantage for anyone anywhere ever.

Under 1, the grounds for certainty would need to be
stated. Whatever underlies the alleged knowledge can only
produce various degrees of subjective confidence. But no
degree of subjective confidence can guarantee correspondence of theory with reality. Hence, I hold that 1 is
that form of 2 from which all doubt has been excluded,
nothing more. As a pragmatic relativist, I affirm 3 and
4. Since I am skeptical of claims of apodictic certainty
about matters of morality, the grounds for 1 amount to
3 and/or 4. But 3 and/or 4 only banish effective doubt
and persuade the will toward assent and thus lead to 2
or obliterate all qualms and produce 1. They do not
guarantee correspondence of theory with reality. Both 2
and 1, then, become the practical equivalents of 3 and/or
4. Truth-as-correspondence-with reality objectivists,
truth-as-warranted-assertion objectivists, and pragmatic
relativists would oppose 6 and all of its milder versions. What do 1 and 2 have that guarantee anything
useful not possible for 3 and 4? Nothing, so far as I can

tell. I do not believe that 3 or 4 necessarily or eventually in theory and/or practice lead to 5.

Respect for life in all its forms, confidence that existence is worthwhile, and, above all, dedication to finding and living by those beliefs and values that lead to the most satisfying life for all under conditions of justice as we can best discern it -- these are the requirements of sustainable moral existence in concert with others, in my opinion. Dogmatism, absolutism, arrogance, fanatical devotion to parochial ideologies, certitude that ones own views have unique value or special divine sanction -- these are the enemies we ought to fear and oppose most. Popes, preachers, politicians, priests, and professors who know that they know the secrets of the universe -- these are the disturbers of the peace most likely to sanction violence done to others in the name of absolutes.

All this leads me toward a pragmatism that seeks ways of conceptualizing the world that aid in coping with life in practical ways. The aim of thought is to help us get into satisfactory relationships with the world. The function of reason is to promote the art of life.[3] This requires, among other things, the need for a coherent way of understanding that makes sense of our experience and provides a guide to what is worth living for. Of utmost importance is the necessity for lived out commitment to what is believed to be true, right, and good, even though we "see through a glass darkly" (St. Paul). The best that can be attained by human reflection is a perspective on ultimacy not a set of truth claims that tell us with certainty what reality is in and of itself. We need some way to organize and unify our experience and to work out practical living arrangements with others in the light of some meaning-value scheme that is experientially workable and existentially satisfactory. The aim of life is to seek happiness for all under conditions of justice in light of the best we know up to now. I offer one more relative, fragmented interpretive scheme, one among the many.

THE KNOWING PROCESS

Knowing involves an interplay among three factors:

Reality

Experience   Interpretation

Initially, reality means "what is actually the case, objectively there in fact." Experience means "what happens in and to or by the agency of human beings as registered biologically in their bodies and/or perceived, consciously or unconsciously; life as lived and felt." Interpretation means "linguistic description and explanation constituting the theory formation by which the world is constructed and articulated; everything contributed to the knowing process that is not a part of the immediate natural perception of human organisms." Conventionally, it can be put this way:

OBJECTIVE   SUBJECTIVE

Reality   Experience

                                  Interpretation

Objective in tendency means here "independent of the subject, determined or at least contributed by the object, what is there, whether experienced or experienceable or not." Subjective is bent toward "occurring within or received, constructed, or otherwise contributed by the experiencer." These distinctions are abstractions from a stream of unified processes useful for analysis but misleading if the mutual dependence and the flowing of each into the others is obscured. Each can serve, on occasion, as a complete epistemological reference by embracing the others. When we see cars moving down the street, watch a loved one die, determine that a disease was caused by a virus, appreciate the beauty of the sunset, confess the goodness of God, etc., alternately we can say:

> we are in touch with reality;
> reality is being experienced; or
> experienced reality is being interpreted.

Conceivably, something may be real that is not knowable by human beings. What counts for us, however, is what is experienced and experienciable, directly or indirectly, now or later. What is experienced matters much, but prior to or apart from interpretation may mean little, except for whatever value attaches to sheer perception, awareness, and sensation as such. An indissoluble connection exists among reality, experience, and interpretation, yet each also has a relative autonomy. Neither can be wholly reduced to the others, nor can they be fully separated except abstractly for purposes of analysis.

We (I do anyway!) have an incontrovertible and ineradicable confidence that we live in a world that is prior to and independent of our experience of it. I believe that events occurred before I was born that my parents have told me about. Similarly, I believe that events are occurring now to other people in other places that I may learn about later. If my consciousness disappeared tomorrow, the universe of such happenings would otherwise still exist. Experience is real and is of reality. In the most comprehensive framework that includes all experiencing of all experiencers past, present, and future, experience is reality, i. e., the only reality that matters. Yet experience as pure perception or consciousness logically prior to interpretation, while full of content, is relatively low in human meaning. This is certainly the case when compared to the culturally enriched mode of interpreting experience made possible by historically-created ways of constructing the world.

The human epistemological predicament is that we have no infallible way of accurately separating out these three elements. Nor can we precisely identify what contributes precisely what to our complete inventory of beliefs in each of the relevant spheres in which the question arises (scientific inquiry and religious experience, e. g.) We only know reality as experienced and interpreted. But what is real in and of itself in relation to what we experience? And how does interpretation shape or determine what is real as experienced? We go around and around. All we have is the connectedness of the three. Attempts to define, identify, and locate each in relation to the other are caught up in a circular process that cannot be fully transcended in order to provide a final resolution. No supreme court can be appealed to, since all judges are themselves immersed in the same predicament and circularity. Hence, we can never be sure how successful our efforts are.

The aim is to understand and cope with reality, but our only access to the real is what I shall call "interprience," i. e., interpreted experience. We know the world as experienced and as interpreted. However, all elucidations of experience transpire within the framework of our inherited language and our accepted cultural traditions as they are embodied concretely in particular elucidators. What we bring linguistically and conceptually to an experience partly dictates what we will be able to see before we even look and inevitably shapes it when we do. At the same time, however, experiences new or old may alter the interpretive order. Creative imagination moves back and forth between settled interpretive schemes and fresh perceptions, on the one hand, and between familiar experiences and novel interpretive schemes, on the other hand. We are neither frozen into established ways of explicating experience nor entirely free from them. Hence, while we are constrained by what we have come to believe already, from whatever sources and for whatever reasons, we are not enslaved by this fact. We may, however, have blind spots. Reality as experienced and interpreted -- that is what knowledge is all about. The search for truth is an adventure of hope without finalities or absolute certainties.

THE ANATOMY OF EXPERIENCE

Experience is not a passive receiving of data from outside. Perception itself is the organism's power of grasping or feeling of its surroundings for the sake of promoting the art of living. Experience is the active engagement of a living subject with the environment. It is first of all an emotional affair -- terrifying and fascinating, pleasurable and painful, threatening and promising, enjoyable and ecstatic, dull and boring, dreadful and miserable. Experiencers have intentions, interests, and goals. They initiate purposive action and respond to objects and the initiatives of other subjects. Knowing, feeling, and choosing are ingredients in the commerce of experiencing agents with what is real, i. e., with what has power to affect them. Subjects engage the world with intent to overcome obstacles, solve problems, and to achieve ends.

Experiencing is in the most comprehensive sense but another name for living. It is the inner, subjective reality of the comprehensive process that is life. Knowing facilitates the thoroughly practical affair of living as a process of actualizing the potential for

enjoyment given with the gift of life. Even contemplation
is not a purely disinterested entertainment of realities
and possibilities without practical consequence but an
enjoyment that contributes to fullness of life. Knowing
in human beings is continuous with that practical engagement with the world that makes up the experience of
animals rooted in instinct, habit, innate intelligence,
and learned savvy.

Briefly, the underlying cosmology that supports
these views is that nature is one complex flux of life-
like events all taking account of (experiencing, prehend-
ing, responding to, having a perspective on) each other
in an dynamic, ordered but not fully harmonious whole.
Human beings are members of this community of perceivers
uniquely gifted in taking account of, and in developing
linguistically sophisticated perspectives on, their
surroundings.

PRAGMATISM AND REALISM

Throughout this chapter I recognize the partial
legitimacy of both pragmatic and realist interpretations
of truth. On the one hand, in the knowing process the
final reference is always to experience and to its
interpretation. More precisely, truth ultimately has to
do with the relationships between some ideas, other
ideas, and the sum total of experiences. To say that
something is real amounts to the claim that competent
experiencers have had, are now having, or could have
certain ideas or experiences. Whatever is real (that
matters) can affect us in some way. As William James was
fond of saying, reality is what it is "known as."[4] The
crucial question is what practical difference it makes
in our experience whether we hold one belief or another.
If no practical experienceable difference ever arises
from affirming A rather than B, the dispute is futile,

a waste of time, irrelevant, even meaningless. Truth is the so far verified or well-established in quest of the potentially verifiable, where satisfactory workability in the totality of experience is the final test of all claims.

On the other hand, reality is prior to our experience of it. Reality is determinative in some sense of our experiences. To some degree reality is manifest in and to experience. This implies that the content, the sequences, the connections, and the entire pattern of relationships that constitute our experiences detect and reflect what is going on in the world itself. The reason we experience water boiling minutes after it is put on a hot stove is that a causal connectedness inheres in reality that is determinative of our perceptions. The reason I feel pain when I place my finger too close is that the stove is hot. Hence, truth is not first of all about me -- my ideas and my perceptions -- but about the world. Experience is of reality. We experience things a certain way because the order of nature is a certain way. Hence, reality is antecedent to and independent of our experiences and our interpretations of it. Truth is description adequate to realities, an account of how things really are or can reasonably be believed to be, not merely a survey of what practically works for us.

The pragmatist in me latches onto the fact that reality for us is what we know it to be and thus forgoes any reality claims that are not, in some sense, experience claims. The realist in me locks onto the priority and independence of reality in relation to experience. Depending on which of these perspectives becomes the organizing center, a pragmatist or a realist interpretation may follow. Each perspective is partially valid but incomplete without the other.[5] Hence, something like the following conversation takes place in me between the pragmatist and the realist.

Pragmatist. We can only say what is real in frames of reference that are contained within the realm of interpreted experience. Reality for us is what we know it to be, taking into account the totality of its experienceable effects on us.

Realist. Reality is what it is, entirely apart from our knowledge. Truth is a portrait of what reality is, not a description of the order of experience.

Pragmatist. Granted we would not know the world the way we do if reality were not as it is. The point is that what it is means what we experience and interpret it to be. We can never overcome that epistemological predicament to know unexperienced, uninterpreted reality. What could that even mean?

Realist. Nevertheless, when we say that dinosaurs roamed the earth long before any human beings were present, is it not the case that the beings referred to were real, although we did not experience them? If the creatures indicated by that term really did live, eat, breed, and die in such a fashion that what is meant by the words we use did actually happen, our statements are not about our experience but about dinosaurs. If that is what and all that correspondence to reality means, aren't the statements true?

Pragmatist. That only means that if we had been there as observers certain experiences would have occurred to us. Otherwise, what is meant by saying they were really there? Tell me what they are apart from experience that we could have had of them.

Realist. No, the important point is that those experiences would reveal that the dinosaurs were having certain experiences.

THE IMPORTANCE OF THE CONTEXT

The reality-experience-interpretation connection is indissoluble. Human beings seek beliefs and theories that correspond with, i. e., correctly interpret, reality. In some limited contexts where particular gross facts are involved, such truth is attainable if we specify what we mean. For example, when the specific background, identifications, locations, time frame, and definitions are supplied, a statement like "The broom is in the hall closet" is sufficiently precise in meaning that it can be said to be literally true or false. It can be shown conclusively to be so. If the broom in question is in the bedroom closet, the statement is false. If it indeed is in the hall closet, the statement is true. Our common sense conviction is that the term "broom" stands for something not us, i. e., not wholly reducible to some phenomena occurring in the consciousness of the speakers. It has a kind of independence in the spatio-temporal realm as an molecular entity whose existence continues when no human being is observing it.

Of its _thatness_ we are confident. We can point to it, hold it, and otherwise locate it for others and say, "This thing right here is `the broom.'" Its _whatness_ is a more complicated matter. We are caught in a circularity of words and a web of experiences. The epistemological predicament is that we can never say _what_ it is without reference to some background assumptions and some level of what in a broad sense can be called "theory." First of all, there is the word "broom" and its equivalents in other languages. Some languages may not even have an exact or similar word for a thing used to sweep with. One might describe it as a stick with long straws strapped to it, but that does not quite convey the meaning of something used to sweep with for cleaning purposes.[6] Such a simple word has a history in the English language (of which I am almost totally ignorant!) related to a group of people, their interests in ridding something of dirt and dust, succeeding versions of this implement, etc. The use of the term carries with a nest of assumptions, interests, associations, and the like. Witches ride them, for example. We learn the word as children without knowing much of the history of the word or the technology. When the question is raised, "Where is the broom?" we know what is meant (once having identified which broom is being spoken of), and we know how to settle the issue of whether it is or is not in the hall closet. Yet it does not make much sense to say that it is a broom apart from human interests, words, linguistic history, and so on. What that thing there is in and of itself apart from the human convention of naming it a broom is hard to say. Both the pragmatist and the realist seem to have a point here.

In ordinary language within relatively simple circumstances such as this, a correspondence theory of truth works quite well, if we say precisely what we mean by it. But what is it that corresponds to what? Strictly speaking, it is a correspondence in the minds and experiences of the particular people involved in certain restricted circumstances. The correspondence is not as such between the word and the object in the world of nature as a connection existing independently of human speakers and writers. The correspondence is between certain ideas, words, meanings, and descriptions, on the one hand, and certain experiences of the intended object.

In the background is the unspoken assumption that when the word "broom" is uttered or written, it refers to that thing "broom" that we hold, point to, or otherwise specify as the referent to be associated with the use of the term. "Broom" when uttered or written brings to mind and is connected with the "thing." The word stands for the object. These meanings, associations, and references are common in the society and thus can normally be assumed, enabling speech that, apart from exceptional or marginal circumstances, causes no misunderstandings among those who share this particular linguistic and cultural tradition of using "brooms" to "sweep." The connection between "word" and "object" is in the minds of the beholders, although there is some-thing really there, a molecular entity, a contortion of space-time in a locatable region existing as a focus of matter-energy -- or something -- that is not reducible to ideas or impressions in the minds of the speaker. What the "broom" really is in itself, well that brings on a lot more talk. Referring to it as a molecular entity occupying time and space involves another set of cultur-ally created meanings with a history and does not at all indicate what it objectively is, except by agreement that these words are an appropriate way to refer to whatever detectable goings on that are in present usage called molecules. Any correspondence that exists is strictly speaking in the minds of speakers and writers, although associated necessarily with something out there in the real world. Meanwhile, if we do not press the meanings beyond "When I say this (the word `broom'), I mean that (the object `broom')" and follow through similarly or appropriately with all the other terms in the sentence, we should have no difficulty in holding a correspondence theory of truth.

With regard to the simple matters of everyday life, then, the relations among reality, experience, and interpretation give us little difficulty.[7] Unfortunate-ly, not all disputes are as easily understood or resolved. Hence, we need to distinguish between different contexts within which the question of justification is raised. Take the following sentences:

(a) This sack of salt weighs twenty pounds.

(b) The causes of the French Revolution were X, Y, and Z.

(c) God is one substance existing as three persons.
This list could be lengthened indefinitely in ways that would doubtless show a startling variety in the kinds of statements that make up the conversations of daily life. In ordinary language, at least among contemporary Americans, every one of the terms and meanings of (a) is such that agreement about its truth or falsity could be secured within margins sufficiently precise for practical purposes.

The situation with (b) is much more complicated.[8] Each of the alleged causes (X, Y, Z) would likely be controversial as well as complex and not subject to the kind of precision of definition and testing that is possible in (a). Yet we speak of persons, events, and relationships that in principle were publically knowable at the time and that are now accessible to historians within limits. Propositions about these events are testable in ways that (c) is not. Yet a notion like "the French Revolution" is a high-level abstraction whose meaning and whose location in time and space involve complex judgments that are highly controversial. Was it one event or a complex of occurrences or both? When did "it" begin and end? And what does "cause" mean when applied to historical events? Statement (c) requires even for its intelligibility a set of beliefs and assumptions specific to a particular historical tradition. This is true also in (b) in large measure, but (c) is even more complicated. It hardly makes sense to speak of verification outside some circle of believers with a shared set of metaphysical assumptions who further agree on what counts for and against the assertion. Christians themselves form many circles of interpretation and come to many conflicting conclusions about the matter, not to mention atheists, Buddhists, and logical positivists. Justification of belief takes on many meanings with differing possibilities of achieving assent depending on the claim being made. Universal assent on ultimate matters of fact is no guarantee of truth that corresponds to reality. At some point, we begin to deal with claims about matters of fact whose truth is not certain, allowing only for varying degrees of adequacy for understanding and coping, depending on the context.

Yet theories about God that cannot be verified with certainty may have important for consequences for living. In agreement with William James that differences that make no difference in life now or later do not matter, we may safely ignore those that do not.[9] Theoretical and pragmatic considerations are relevant to the testing of theological claims. Based on prior learnings and theories, present beliefs are in part tested by the consequences of living as if they were true. What we seek is a way of intelligent practice based on theories that both satisfactorily interpret and unify our experience and that teach us how to come to want and to get what we would want if we fully understood the ends and obligations that maximize happiness under conditions of justice. This does not mean that religious beliefs should not be tested theoretically in terms of their appropriateness to our best interpretations of reality. It only means that all such validation is internal to the point of view being verified and thus relative and perspectival. The appeal may be to public evidence and criteria in principle available to all, but all judgments thus derived reflect particular readings of the situation.[10]

EXPERIENCE AND INTERPRETATION

Experience and interpretation are interdependent, each requiring the other for its full reality and definition. Perceptions without concepts are blind. Concepts without perceptions are empty. Language articulates and canalizes experience into a body of concepts that organize our intellectual world. Experiences overflow concepts and escape full conceptualization. Yet imaginatively created concepts may enable us to grasp elements in experience that would otherwise go unnoticed. A system of ideas constituting a paradigm provides a framework within which particular experiences are organized into larger articulated generalities that may embrace ever enlarging ranges of data. Such a working paradigm provides understanding and practical guidance until anomalies force a revision more adequate to the facts and to the network of logical connections that unite them into a coherent body of theory. Williams James says, "Experience, as we know, has ways of boiling over, and making us correct our present formulas."[11] It is sometimes difficult to know when a paradigm needs modifications within its foundational assumptions and when its inadequacies are so serious as to require a new organizing center.

Intense experiences generate in us a profusion of data -- thoughts, feelings, evaluative responses, vivid sensations, vague apprehensions, etc. -- that overflow our linguistic abilities to canalize. The interpretive system may suffer from data overload beyond our capacity to assimilate into our presently existing fund of conceptual capital. We know more than we can say. As Bernard Meland says, "we live more deeply than we can think."[12] We are aware of being in touch with more than we can process. Experience outruns our capacity to appropriate and articulate. The experienceable is more than the expressible. Even for those gifted in its use, language is a crude instrument for elucidating what is felt in all its dense, rich, complex, thick, flowing, variegated, multiform concrete fullness. All articulation abstracts from this whole by making use of some linguistic expressions that channel into more definite, more precise, more discrete patterns what in actual experience is a less discriminated totality. This is the case even if we think of speak or even feel in imaginative metaphorical terms rather than in more abstract concepts. What is felt at once as a multiform and variegated totality must be expressed bit by bit. Not all that is contained in awareness is ever articulated. Much remains around the edges that is vaguely felt in ways that defy accurate formulation into expressible content, while even the center overflows the abstracted articulated content. Finally, language itself embodies culturally preformed conceptions about the world in its way of grasping/ shaping reality that may inhibit or even falsify experience as well as elucidate it. Minimally, any language and every language will give form to experience in its own peculiar fashion. The bare data that we actually see and feel are linguistically and conceptually molded by the tools we use to elucidate them. Hence, the instruments themselves play a role in determining what is real for us as well as providing the only means we have for saying what we have come in touch with.

One side of the story, then, is that overflowing experience is partially distilled into more discriminated or articulated knowledge by language. The other side of the tale is that previously acquired interpretive schemes enable us to make sense of present experience. A person totally ignorant of Christian theology would not understand what is going on while observing what is said and done when bread and wine are being consumed during a communion service. Certain of the traditional phrases might even suggest cannibalism! The participating believer knows or has beliefs that give form and substance to the transpiring ritual by clothing with deep meaning and feeling what otherwise would remain blank or merely strange. But there is much more to it than that. Possibilities and expectations based on acquired theory enable us to find what we had not seen before. It is frequently the case that we cannot or do not experience what we do not believe is there. It might be present in the experienced data waiting to be found but missed because attention was not attuned to locating it.

Examples of all these processes are numerous in scientific inquiry. Scientists searched for decades to find the neutrino postulated by theory and were successful only after constructing elaborate equipment which provided the required observational confirmation. The opposite case occurred when a new theory supposing the existence of positrons enabled observers to review data that had been scanned for years only to discover that the elusive little entities had been showing up all along without being noticed.[13] Newtonian theory was quite successful in predicting planetary motions, except that the orbit of Uranus was irregular and not accounted for. Was the theory wrong? An auxiliary hypothesis presupposing that an unknown planet was causing disturbances in the movement of Uranus led to the empirical discovery of Neptune. Newton's laws were intact. Later, however, when a similar prediction was made to account for deviations in the perihelion of Mercury, no previous-

ly hidden planet was found. Instead, Newton's ideas prov-
ed to be at fault. Newly produced relativity theory was
able to account for the observed discrepancy.[14] Nature is
subtle, almost appearing to play hide and seek with its
investigators!

The experimental seeker in science and religion has
to say two things: "If I hadn't seen it, I wouldn't have
believed it" and "If I hadn't believed it, I wouldn't
have seen it." Previously developed theory determines
what constitutes evidence and thus what will count as an
explanation of fresh or novel experience. If I get sick,
I may conclude that the local witch doctor has cast a
spell on me. Or I may accept my Harvard-trained doctor's
verdict that the malady is caused by a virus. At the same
time, new observations may upset existing doctrine.
Galileo's telescope gave him fresh data that required
modification of the received notions about heavenly
bodies.

Unfortunately at a given moment it may be impossible
to make a rational, i. e., rule-governed, choice between
competing "paradigms" (Kuhn)[15] or "research programs"
(Lakatos).[16] Theories have been held to be true when no
experiential confirmation was yet available. Likewise,
a prevailing paradigm has persisted tenaciously in spite
of ever more threatening anomalies. Both moves may be
justified at times. One can never be sure. Moreover,
scientists have sometimes reacted defensively, even
vehemently, when new theories have been proposed that
might supplement cherished ones (especially if they have
authored the threatened hypothesis!). This despite the
alleged openness of science to the new if it is better.

If these difficulties exist in science, it is no
wonder that religious people are tenacious in defending
traditional views facing possible refutation by reason

or experience. Fundamentalists are ingenious in accounting for apparent contradictions, errors in matters
of fact, morally embarrassing precepts, and other
complications that threaten the dogma of biblical
inerrancy. Science, historical criticism, common sense,
notions of cultural relativity and so on have not
expunged belief in an errorless Bible. The comfort of
infallible authority, the power of tradition, and other
needs beyond the ken of doubters enable learned as well
as naive believers to hold on to some form or biblical
inerrancy in the face of seemingly overwhelming evidence
to the contrary.

Disputes about the reality of God are even more
difficult to resolve. No crucial experiments are available. Belief in the omnipotence, supreme goodness, and
infinite wisdom of God persists in the face of the
absurdity, suffering, injustice, and the gigantic
miseries and heart-breaking tragedies that curse the
creatures of earth. Numerous appeals are available to
protect the central hypothesis. When all else fails,
resort to divine mystery and human ignorance can indefinitely preserve faith in God's unqualified power and
goodness in the presence of enormous evils. It cannot be
demonstrated that such faith is erroneous or irrational.

Political ideologies can have so much power over
persons that they will rationalize the cruelest of events
and deny the most compelling evidence rather than
surrender the dogmas that have nourished them. Theories
in all the sciences, as well as interpretations of
history, may have a similar hold on searchers after
truth. Metaphysicians and social theorists, as well as
scientists and theologians, may be ideologically moribund
in the face of devastating evidence that would ruin their
favorite conceptualities. Arthur Koestler, looking back

on his communist years, said, "My Party education had equipped my mind with such elaborate shock-absorbing buffers and elastic defenses that everything seen and heard became automatically transformed to fit the preconceived system." Karen Horney reflecting on her devotion to psychoanalytic views spoke of how "the system of theories which Freud has gradually developed is so consistent that when one is once entrenched in them it is difficult to make observations unbiased by his way of thinking."[17] As the popular song says, "knowing when to hold'em and knowing when to fold 'em" -- that is the question. We all live by faith when truths of broad generality are being sought. But faith need not be blind or merely arbitrary.

Knowledge emerges, then, in the dynamic interplay between experience and interpretation. Each confirms, corrects, expands, transforms, limits, and completes the other. In this process habitual modes of perceiving, believing, feeling, and valuing culturally and personally acquired are sustained, modified, abandoned, or replaced in the search for ever more adequate styles of understanding our existence and coping with its perils and promises.

If experience and interpretation are mutually dependent, how can any priority be assigned to either? Without experience, there is nothing to elucidate. Without elucidation, little in the way of definite or organized meaning, knowledge, or belief arises. Vague apprehensions of mysteries unplumbed may, of course, constitute a kind of knowing beyond conscious clarification. But naked feelings or perceptions yearn for articulation into conceptual, or at least metaphorical or symbolic, form. Each such interpretive scheme needs to be ordered in relation to the rest of interprience, in so far as that is possible. Even if we assign a relative priority to experience, that does not alter the dynamic process whereby our feeling of the world is rendered into the clarity of conscious articulation by the total structure of meanings and evaluative schemes. In the sequential movement, fresh perceptions confirm or disturb our acquired and habitual modes of thinking and valuing.

KNOWING AS A FOUR-FOLD PROCESS

Immediately arises a whole set of more specific issues pertaining to the nature of the knowing process itself with special regard to the filters that screen reality as it is experienced. Four elements enter into the experience-interpretation-reality relationship:
(1) our perceptual equipment as creatures of nature that determines what and how we apprehend [the perceived],
(2) our given conceptual equipment as members of some linguistic and cultural community that further deter-mines, shapes, distorts, or otherwise patterns what can and does enter into experience [the perceived as con-structed],
(3) the historical and cultural traditions that have shaped us and our communities since birth as we have appropriated and transformed them into our own personal conceptual system [the constructed as interpreted][18] and
(4) the individual and communal interpreting we do of experience thus constituted that confirms what we previously held or is imaginatively reinterpreted into a novel scheme [the interpreted as reinterpreted].[19]

Some further elucidation of each of these elements may be useful. (1) Human beings come genetically equipped with an evolved set of organs and neural structures that enable them to perceive the world. No inventory of pre-linguistic, extra-cultural perception is indisputably accurate, since we cannot infallibly distinguish the description and the elucidation from the whatness being described and elucidated. Language constructs even in representing. In fact pre-linguistic experience itself is already one kind of interpretation of the world. If, for example, our visual powers were magnified, say ten million times, our perspective on the world would be quite different and doubtless much less useful. Noting that, we may start with the five senses and a sixth sense involving value and quality discernment. Consciousness of sequences involving some comprehension of the connectedness of things and some awareness of causal patterns (stone hurting hand) and relationships are primal modes of comprehension. Those conjunctional and prepositional features of the world formalized in language are first perceived, thus requiring some linguistic articulation. Those arrangements suggested by such terms as "and," "by," "on," "under," "behind," "before," "after," "through," "in," "with," and "from," designate observed relationships among things.[20]

Trying to imagine what perception of an automobile would be were we adults totally lacking in language or prior experience is not easy. The object would generate a series of excitements and reactions in the eye and the brain resulting in visual perception.[21] Presumably we would see an expanse of colors in a three-dimensional region of local space and hear sounds if the motor were running. The sights and noise might excite some emotional response either positive or negative. Much more than that it is hard to say. Would we _feel_ curiosity, for example, even though we had no _word_ for curiosity? Could we think about what we were seeing and hearing? But how? With what? Definitely we would not experience "it" as a "car." Contrast this with the sight of the same object by members of a family viewing their new Buick for the first time. Innumerable thoughts and feelings would flood each of them, fed with all the cultural significance owning a car has for an American, plus all the personal meanings and practical implications for these particular individuals.

Physical sensations and sensory perceptions have some degree of autonomy and presumably would be felt as either neutral, pleasant, or irritating independently of linguistic abilities. They have an initial authority and constitute knowing that is direct, instantaneous, and incontrovertible. A sudden severe blow to the shin is felt as pain. The sight of the setting sun is felt as beauty in some primal sense that requires no words or thoughts. Sexual orgasm is felt as pleasure apart from any linguistic rendition. Yet the total meaning of these experiences requires connection with the whole of life as interpreted by an ensemble of habits and structures of thought and feeling acquired from infancy onward.

What about near death experiences of tunnels, lights, peace, and ineffable joy? Many who have had the experience do not doubt that their experience was of transcendental reality and not merely of internal processes. Yet who is to say whether or not the experience is the body's way of preparing the organism for death? If so, it is not necessarily a register of trans-biological realities, even if it is the occasion of a deep transformation of life. But it may hint of life beyond.[22] Such experiences need to be taken seriously and not dismissed summarily.

Religious experience itself constitutes a variation on this. Is there a sense of God or of transcendent reality or value in any form in the biological human prior to any contemplation aided by language or cultural traditions? What awareness or experience of God, if it is present, might mean is difficult to say. Schliermacher's "feeling of absolute dependence" introduces background terms, definitions, and a considerable interpretive framework.[23] The same is true of the witness of the historic religious traditions in their variegated splendor. For culture-bound persons and communities that natural capacity for apprehending the divine, if there be one, has become so overladen with historically produced understandings of God, the good, and the beautiful that the innate aptitudes and intuitions have been obscured. Regardless of what experience as experience contains, we cannot be sure that we are in contact with some transcendent, superhuman realm or being, power, and value. The claim that experience is of God requires a background definition of the very reality that experience itself is assumed to supply. Such assertions involve circular processes of reasoning. This does not necessarily invalidate the interpretation. It does mean that neither the interpretation nor the experience constitutes an absolute foundational starting point on which to build indubitable knowledge. Rather the experience and the interpretation are interdependent, mutually determining dimensions of the total interaction and its product. Hence, while basic aesthetic and religious data are immediately given in experience, their meaning and truth depend on interpretation.[24]

In short, this primal encounter with the world generates a thick, rich, dense, complex stream of rudimentary perceptions, feelings, and evaluations variable and shifting in content, importance, and intensity. Perhaps this flux contains its own primitive intelligibility uniting meaning and mystery that repetition and time would magnify and order. This plethora of data in the pre-cultural animal yearns for clarification that is provided by the remaining components of the knowing process.

(2) Language itself shapes reality or our perceptions of it. Speakers of dissimilar languages will, in part, have different world views because of their disparate modes of linguistically apprehending what they immediately perceive. A language itself is a historically developed interpretation of reality not a theory-free, neutral net in which the structure and content of the world can be captured. We speak here of the background shaping of perception and understanding imposed upon particular experiences by the very categorical patterns of the language itself that enable us to describe the world. This is a complicated topic in itself beyond the scope of the present essay. The fact itself -- widely recognized -- needs to be noted as contributing to the relativity of reality portrayals. Language does not simply express an experience; it contributes to the construction of experience.

(3) Culturally-developed traditions containing beliefs about and evaluations of everything of importance are acquired along with mother's milk in the maturation process. Experience is interpreted through these encultu- rated forms of understanding. Individuals may, of course, abandon or modify these inherited ways of thinking, feeling, appreciating, evaluating, and acting. Cultures themselves may undergo minor or major transformations of ideological consciousness. Nevertheless, the influence of socially implanted modes of grasping and constructing reality is deep, pervasive, and inescapable.

In no realm is this more evident than with respect to morality and religion. Ways of appreciating and appraising the paramount truths, the supremely good, and the sublimely beautiful reflect particular historic legacies that produce generation after generation of Buddhists in Burma, Roman Catholics in Spain, Southern Baptists in Georgia, and Muslims in Iran. Reflection upon this ostensibly should produce more humility and a greater sense of relativity than it does among Christians who somehow know that God has been revealed to them in uniquely normative and universal fashion in Jesus Christ and Scripture. The predilection to regard ones own spiritual inheritance as epistemologically privileged is well-nigh inescapable.

(4) Individuals, whole cultures, and subgroups within reappropriate, criticize, transform, gradually modify, radically reject, and otherwise indefinitely change or preserve what has been handed down from the immediate and distant past. Freedom as creative self-transcendence enables persons and societies to remake the past and create novel futures. Nevertheless, the stamp of our cultural rearing is difficult to erase. As Paul Tillich points out, atheism in the modern West is Christian atheism. Marxist philosophy of history is a radical transformation of biblical eschatology, and so on. Yet the future is open and indeterminate, waiting to be constructed and molded from the materials inherited from the past.

The boundaries between these facets of interprience cannot be precisely drawn. All are influenced or co--constituted by the mutual indwelling of each in all and all in each. Experience is so formed, conditioned, and even determined by the interpretive process that it is impossible with confidence to isolate (1) pure perception from (2) its reception, (3) its structuring and (4) reconstructing into the fullness of concrete belief. Nevertheless, neither dimension can be subsumed under some other category, since each has some relative autonomy. The dynamic interplay of all four create the perspective we have on things.

TRUTH-TESTING AND THE SEARCH FOR CONSENSUS

Knowing that all these elements enter into the process of knowing may set in motion critical and creative analysis that leads to some degree of transcendence over the constraints thus posed to the way in which reality is mirrored in interprience. But the circuits of perception, construction, interpretation, and reconception are so intricate and so mutually interdependent or determining that any conclusions reached about how things really are in the world must be held tentatively and skeptically.

Justification of points of view about comprehensive matters, such as the meaning of life or the reality of God, is internal to the perspective being tested. We can state criteria of verification within an intentional perspectival realism. A perspective must account for all the evidence relevant to the topic at hand. It must be internally coherent. It must further be consistent with everything else that is believed to be the case. Internal verification does not guarantee objective truth (correspondence of theory with reality). Crucial data may be lacking, or the available evidence may have been misinterpreted. Yet the whole as constructed may be, or appear to be, systematically consistent. If this is so, then surely we must turn to pragmatic criteria for the crucial testing. Put most simply, a theory is relatively adequate for now if it works, i. e., provides a way of understanding and coping with the world that makes it possible for us and others "to live, to live well, and to live better" (Whitehead). We may possess truth in the practical sense if it leads to the survival, enhancement, and

fulfillment of human and all life in the most universal
perspective available to us, which means at least the
earth in the present state of precariousness and promise.

Ah, but what is life-enhancing and life-fulfilling?
What does it mean to "live well and to live better?" At
this point, we are thrown back on some theory of life and
its true ends. What works is what saves. What saves
depends on a theory of salvation. That presupposes a view
of reality, goodness, justice, and so on. We cannot know
something is working without criteria of ends and
norms. We can, of course, learn, revise, experiment, and
grow in wisdom about life and what truly satisfies. The
experiment is a continuing adventure of theory derived
from experience seeking confirmation in experience crea-
tively guided by imaginative construction and reconstruction. Thus life proceeds in quest of the wisdom that
works in practice to save from destruction and to
maximize maximizing enjoyments punctuated by ecstasy.
Hence, even here we are involved in a circular, or
perhaps more accurately, a dialectical process between
theory and practice.

In this quest, can a way be found "beyond objectivism and relativism"?[25] Appeal to a particular communal
heritage is a form of social subjectivism in which the
tradition of some group is thought to provide escape from
the worst consequences of anarchic relativism. Traditions
even centuries old that have attracted millions of adherents need to be critically evaluated in the light of
present experience and belief. Widely advertised today
is the premise that ideal -- or at least free and sincere
-- conversation among conflicting parties may produce
ever widening circles of agreement. Theologians, philosophers, and concerned citizens open to mutual conversion

in the search for a better truth and not out just to defend a cherished ideology are our best hope.[26]

The overambitious project of Jürgen Habermas is only the latest attempt to suggest how right procedure can overcome conflicting belief systems.[27] Nevertheless, his "ideal speech conditions" may play a limited heuristic role. Essentially, the idea is that the quest for legitimate rational consensus requires the opportunity for unlimited conversation among free and equal, sincere truth-seekers. All parties must be unhampered by systematically distorting influences from oppressive power or dogmatic devotion to some unquestioned ideology. Assuming these conditions, the inquirers under the constraint of all appropriate rules of evidence and logic will be persuaded only by the "unforced force of the better argument." This proposal is too optimistic. It assumes a rational structure that all ideally competent and sincere parties can finally discern when systemic distortions to insight are removed. Part of the argument is about what constitutes the "better" argument. While he grants that the ideal requirements are counterfactual, he nevertheless presumes (or once did) an ideal or transcendental pattern in reason and reality that enables communities of inquirers to achieve consensus eventually. The finitude of human reason under conditions of historical existence produces too much plurality of belief to be fully overcome through conversation no matter how ideal.

The same criticism can be made of Charles Sanders Peirce, to whom Habermas is indebted.[28] He asserts that reality is what an ideal community would ultimately agree to. Truth and reality are identical, not immediately or in particular reasoners, but at the end of a consummated quest of rational inquiry that achieves consent from all parties. Peirce has a pre-Kuhnian view that scientific theories will eventually converge on one universally compelling set of theories. This is in no way to deny that limited success may be achieved in finding common ground and in overcoming some of disagreements that separate persons and groups in warring camps. Nevertheless, even when consensus is reached on the basis of a theory that truth is what we are warranted in believing, belief can still be wrong. Reality transcends even justified belief, i. e., the best we have been able to discern up to now.

It may help to think of cultural, philosophical, and religious systems of truth and values as forming circles, each with a center defining its presently compelling core convictions. Over time both the centers and the content of specific circles, whether of individuals or groups, may change. Even radical transformations may occur. New centers come to define fresh paradigms. Many of these circles overlap considerably, some more that others. None may be totally outside each other, i. e., constitute incommensurable perspectives. Each circle has sources and norms of truth peculiar to itself. We can hope that honest conversation among dedicated truth-seekers under achievable conditions of fruitful discourse may result in greater overlapping of conceptual circles. Increasing ranges of agreement on matters of common practical concern may occur. That all circles can ever finally converge into a single space with an identical center is unlikely, where the great issues involving vital interests are concerned. More important is that tolerable and non-destructive modes of accommodation and cooperation be achieved under mutually acceptable conditions a-mounting to some form of approximate consensual justice. More generally, in the present global scene we may hope that the necessities of survival may lead to enough practical agreement on values and strategies to enable the human race to escape nuclear destruction and ecological catastrophe.

What this means for Protestants and Catholics killing each other in Northern Ireland or Jews and Arabs hating each other in Palestine is hard to say. Where justice issues are involved, mere conversation is impotent apart from action that transforms or realistically offers hope for change in the conditions of life in which the conflicting parties exist. Unless mutual security, mutual justice, and mutual hope for the future precede and accompany or at least promise to flow from dialogue, talking will not get us very far. We all love peace, for example. Most of us love other things more -- territory, ideology, nation, material goods, rights, power, money, prestige, honor, race, ethnicity, privilege, freedom, equality, opportunities, security, respect, justice, even God, and all sorts of other good, evil, and ambiguous things. When the values we cherish more than peace are threatened, we fight. What good is it to agree that peace is desirable unless the other ends that the disputants want more are provided or otherwise dealt with? Liberation, reconciliation, justice, and opportunities to pursue happiness in acceptable ways as the parties themselves conceive these are the pre-requisites or co-requisites of the edifying conversation relevant to mutual creative transformation.

Moreover, since historical conflicts are filled with ambiguity and entail right versus right, the contending parties must appropriate the history of the other along with all the concomitant feelings and memories. This opens the possibility that, in mutual suffering, forgiveness, and reconciling love in the presence of the tragic dimensions of existence, healing may gradually come. Unfortunately, the goals of competing groups are so mutually exclusive, the human capacity for transcending past beliefs and commitments so limited, and the whole human enterprise so fraught with complexity and ambiguity multiplied by human insecurity and selfishness (or at least a limited faculty for altruism) that the quest for justice and intellectual harmony is slow, painful, and restricted. Can racial justice come to South Africa in any foreseeable future without violence in which the white minority is coercively deposed? Philosophers must be on guard against confusing seminar discussions about intellectual disputes that have little practical consequence for the participants with the situation in the wider world of human commerce, often splattered with blood and epitomized by the conflicts between Jews and Arabs in the Middle East.

CURRENT CONTROVERSIES IN THE PHILOSOPHY OF SCIENCE

Since science has been the enterprise most cherished in the modern world as the source of reliable knowledge about the nature of things, it will be useful to conclude this chapter by examining some issues in the philosophy of science. What does scientific inquiry tell us about the world? Do theories describe, represent, or any some way correspond with reality? Or should we concentrate on their practical value to enable us to do desirable things? Is there a purely rational method of discovery, or do personal choice and commitment play a role in deciding between theories? Working scientists get on with their daily work. The philosophers among them cannot agree about the nature of scientific knowledge or of theory change.[29]

A revolution has taken place in the philosophy of science in the last generation. The idea that from clear and reliable foundational observations bodies of increasingly accurate theories can be accumulated that either are true or progressively approach the truth about the world has gone with the wind. A brief accounting of this revolution leads to a consideration of current issues.

Mary Hesse characterizes this reorientation as a "turn from logical models to historical models."[30] The outmoded view assumed an external world that in principle could be exhaustively known through scientific inquiry. Observations of things can be captured in theory-independent language. On the basis of these observations a set of propositions or theories can be developed that stand in a one-to-one relationship to the world. Theories are true if they conform to the facts and false if they do not. The facts include unobservable entities or properties and events in the past that can be inferred from observations. These hidden facts are described in theories based on what is observable. The scientist stands apart from the world and comes to understand it as an objective and dispassionate knower. This view of science involved three assumptions: naive realism, a universal scientific language, and a correspondence theory of truth. All three have been subjected to damaging criticism.[31]

Since an indefinite number of theories can in principle account for the observed data, inferences from observations to theories cannot be made logically conclusive. It is impossible to prove that a given theory is uniquely true. A great many could be true. Theories are underdetermined by data. Nevertheless, it was generally assumed that a set of "coherence conditions" (Hesse), such as simplicity, consistency with other theories, plausibility in the light of general presuppositions about space, time, causality, and matter, etc., would take care of this difficulty. "Accumulating data plus coherence conditions ultimately converge to true theory."[32] This formula runs into two problems.

1. All observations are theory-laden. Observation statements must be stated in language that divides up the world in certain ways. In particular, classification seeks to express natural kinds. All pre-scientific or intuitive classifications are not reliable. To depend on science for these descriptive predicates involves a circular argument of the vicious sort. The movement from data to theory depends on observations that capture the world's own structural divisions, but the correct pattern of natural kinds depends on true theory. Without theory-free observations, it is impossible to move to theory not already prejudiced by the way the data is expressed.

2. In order to produce uniquely true theories, the coherence conditions must themselves be uniquely true. Unfortunately, every set of basic assumptions about time, matter, space, time, and causality have been overturned or could be in the future. The formal principles -- simplicity, fruitfulness, consistency with other theories, and the like -- come in various versions that have to be tailored to actual theories rather than the other way around.

Scientific Method and Theory Change

Philosophical debates about method go on endlessly without resolution. The history of science has shown than the hoped for convergence of theories does not take place. The epoch-making work here, of course is Thomas Kuhn's The Structure of Scientific Revolutions (1962). His well-known thesis is that scientific thought is not incremental, linear, and progressive in a simple, cumulative, evolutionary fashion. It moves through a series of paradigm shifts in which one explanatory pattern is replaced by another that may have radically different assumptions. Successive or competing paradigms may be incommensurable. These revolutions constitute changes in world-view. Reality is seen differently. In fact, "we may want to say that after a revolution scientists are responding to a different world."[33] What were ducks are now seen as rabbits. No end can be seen to the series of conceptual revolutions. Hence, with respect to the picture of the world provided by science, "all pretensions to universalizability and metaphysical necessity in what we can know must be abandoned. No actual theory at any given stage of development can be said to be empirically true in a strictly propositional sense."[34]

Imre Lakatos provides a quick review of the history of thought about theory change that leads toward a similar conclusion. According to justificationists, he says, knowledge consists of proven propositions. Classical empiricists sought this knowledge by basing their theories on a set of certain observations or hard facts, which by inductive logic produced the desired results. Classical rationalists sought certain truths based on experience, intuition, divine revelation and so on. With the help of logic this could be turned into a system of truth. Hence, enormous effort was put into saving a priori truths by the rationalists and to the certainty of an empirical base and the validity of inductive logic by the empiricists. Kantian a priori principles were overthrown by non-Euclidian geometry and non-Newtonian physics. Logical analysis showed that facts cannot prove universal propositions; nor can inductive logic add infallibly to empirical content. A group of Cambridge philosophers tried to show that while no propositions were provable, some could be shown to be more probable than others. Even this retreat from justificationism could not be sustained under the assault of Karl Popper. He argued that under very general conditions theories have zero probability. All theories, then, are not only unprovable but equally improbable.

Dogmatic falsificationists argued that while all theories were unprovable, they could be falsified by specifying what in a crucial experiment observations would refute them. Human beings propose hypotheses, nature disposes of them. Only those proposals are scientific that rule out certain observable states of affairs. Science advances, then, as theories are negated by the facts. Dogmatic falsificationism, however, rests on two untenable assumptions. (1) There is a clear dividing line between observation statements and theoretical propositions. (2) Proof of propositions can proceed from experiment or observations. Moreover, the demarcation principle that specifies that certain crucial observations can disprove theories is simply false. Theories are not necessarily abandoned merely because the facts contradict them. Even the most admired scientific theories exclude no observations. The observational anomalies can be accounted for by creating rescue hypotheses or simply ignored. Planets, for example, can be invented to account for deviations between observations and deductions from Newton's theories. "Scientific theories are not only equally unprovable, and equally improbable, but they are also equally undisprovable."[35]

In the light of this outcome, Lakatos offers his own conception of theory change and scientific progress. He proposes it as a revision of Popper in the light of Kuhn. The unit of assessment is not a single theory but a cluster of them being worked on by many scientists. Such an ongoing project constitutes a "research program." No instant rationality is possible. The evaluation of scientific theories requires decisions over a period of time among a series of theories. We speak of a critical, fallible, continuing process of choice between rival research programs. A progressive scheme will be ahead of discovery and observation. Progressiveness can be identified over time if each successive theory predicts novel facts that are corroborated by experiment. A degenerating program will invent theories to account for the discovery of new facts. It lags behind the empirical data and comes at last to be seen as bankrupt in comparison with its rivals that are growing in explanatory power.

As critics like Thomas Kuhn and Paul Feyerabend have pointed out, however, Lakatos' account is retrospective, not prospective. It can explain why successful programs or paradigms were judged to be progressive. He provides no criteria in the present that show decisively what are dead ends and what are open doors into the future. He gives little guidance for choice among competing theories or research programs at the moment. What appears to be a degenerating program may look progressive a quarter century from now.[36] Lakatos replies that he does offer criteria. The crucial point has to do with time limit. One can rationally hold indefinitely to a degenerating program. One should not deny the risks involved when a defended scheme is publically losing out to its rivals.

Nevertheless, it is impossible to make choice between competing research programs a matter of the purely rational application of logically decisive rules. Kuhn says, "There is no neutral algorithm for theory-choice, no systematic decision procedures which, properly applied, must lead each individual in the group to the same decision."[37] Even the same values (fruitfulness, simplicity, etc.) may be weighted differently. Hence, risky choices by individuals and communities of researchers are made in the presence of uncertainty. Such decisions involve the will and not merely the calculating intellect. Personal and ideological commitments may affect choices that nevertheless reflect reasonable judgement. The whole person is involved. While good reasons can be given, the abandonment of one paradigm or research program is more like experiencing a religious conversion than engaging in rational calculation or mathematical reasoning. Persuasion not proof marks the efforts of advocates of competing paradigms to convert each other.

I conclude from this that faith and reason are involved in science as well as in religion. Faith (choice not dictated by logically necessary considerations) is a component. No decisive theoretical or empirical factors dictate the one and only rational choice. Rational in this context can only mean competent persons having good reasons for affirming or doing something. What science does exhibit is growth in explanatory and predictive power, as well as in technological control. Here too similarities exist with religion and morality. Changes in cultural consciousness can with some confidence be said to be progressive. Paradigm shifts in moral and theological outlooks also occur. Not long ago some Americans defended slavery and opposed female suffrage on the basis of natural law and Scripture. No one who did so today would be taken any more seriously by most people than would the attempt to defend phlogiston theories in science. Calvinistic doctrines of predestination are largely abandoned. More humane views on sexuality, care for the mentally ill, and the like have grown stronger in the public consciousness.

While science is progressive in the sense that the line of theories exhibits increase in explanatory capacity, it is nevertheless historical, communal, and fallible. Philosophers of science do not agree on the nature of scientific knowledge. The debate over realism continues unabated with no resolution in sight or likely. When the community of the competent cannot figure it out after decades of intense debate in which numerous options have been suggested, one can only conclude that diversity of interpretation is inevitable given the complexity of the problem. The controversy evolves through stages punctuated by occasional revolutions of outlook with no cumulative movement toward resolution. Even the best present attempt to define the logic of discovery and the growth of scientific knowledge is itself a part of a continuing discussion subject to revision.

Realism, Relativism, and Rationality

Thomas Kuhn has portrayed scientific development "as a succession of tradition-bound periods punctuated by non-cumulative breaks." This, along with his notion that the "proponents of different theories are like the members of different language-culture communities," has raised the dreaded threat of relativism and irrationality.[38] He has been accused of reducing theory choice to matters better explained by social psychology or even "mob psychology" (Lakatos). One way to escape both the threat of relativism and of irrationality is, in spite of all, to see the movement of science toward a greater approximation of truth about the real world. Rationality and realism are the two chief issues in philosophy of science today.[39]

Realism is the view that the entities and occurrences described in correct scientific theories are objectively there -- real -- more or less in conformity with the description. Cautiously put by Ernan McMullin, realism asserts that "there is good reason to believe in the existence of entities substantially like those postulated by theories that have been successful over the long term."[40] No certainty is forthcoming, only "good reason" for holding that <u>something</u> is present not in exact conformity with but only "substantially like" what is postulated. A nest of difficulties beyond the scope of this essay fill numerous articles and books. Are realists in a dilemma? Sufficiently reduced to be defensible, are the realist claims worth the effort or of any practical utility? Sufficiently bold, are realist claims defensible or even intelligible? Exactly what is being claimed about the connection between theory/model and the actuality really there? What good does it do us to have confidence in the alleged unity? Why not be content with the practical consequences of theories and not worry about theoretical certainty and accuracy?

The arguments for realism are briefly:

(1) Theories from different sciences converge.

(2) Postulated entities can later be observed with new instruments.

(3) The best explanation of the continued success of a theory is that it fits the reality.

These considerations suggest the approximate likeness or connection between scientific description and the world.

The arguments against realism are:

(1) Well-established theories have been overthrown after long periods.

(2) Explanatory success does not necessarily justify belief in the truth of a theory if that means more than that it is predictively accurate.[41]

Various anti-realisms flourish.[42] A leading alternative to realism is some version of pragmatism.[43] Negatively, some pragmatists eliminate appeals to "the Philosopher" who knows about things like truth, reality, and the connection between thought and what's objectively there. These pragmatists deny that "the Philosopher" can put the world together as a whole and assign various truth-getting roles to the various disciplines that tell us about different bits of the real. Those so persuaded urge that "there is no global framework for a representation to world connection by which we can distinguish ideas that have real truth to them, in virtue of their connection to the world's own structure, from those that are called <u>true</u> merely as a courtesy, because of their conventional and practical acceptability."[44] Let us abandon both the quest for certainty about what is really there and theories about truth as impractical and unachievable. Instead, they urge us to view science as one more aid in helping us cope with life.

What good does it do us to have a theory about how statements match up with what the statements are about? Of what value is it to know that theories describe something really there? What matters is that theories enable us do things or do them better. Increased explanatory success can provide more and better things for better living -- that is the crucial point. Particular and tentative practical adjustments of scientific and other ways of knowing and dealing with the world, say religion, suffice without raising all the useless, irresolvable debates about different kinds of truth dealing with classifiable dimensions of reality. "Apart from some specific, local context of practical familiarity there simply is no way to decide which representations are connected to reality as opposed to being merely our own constructions."[45] What matters is the practical advantage all the instruments available to us provide, including science as a non-privileged member of the total ensemble of coping aids.

What is the fuss all about? Scoffers chuckle as they point out that realism offers no more than a desk-pounding, foot-stomping insistence that when science talks about electrons, it is the case that electrons are actually there, they really are, sure enough![46] That is about all it amounts to, really. Meanwhile, scientists go on about their work untroubled and unaided by this information. What seems certain is that there is no way to resolve the disputes. Realists, anti-realists, and those who declare themselves neither, argue endlessly in search for the right way to put it. An amateur may be excused for missing some of the more substantial points as well as numerous subtleties in the effort to sort out a few of the pertinent issues.

Pragmatists are on solid ground in recognizing the difficulty, if not impossibility, as well as the relative, if not absolute, non-utility of trying to identify what is real independently of human experience and conceptions of it. Hence, they flee from the desolate land of theory to the rich soil of practice and develop theories or non-theories about that. However, what is left unanswered is the question of the ontological status of whatever it is that we experience and know in practical ways. Scientists at least deal with data or phenomena, and they are not non-existent or unreal. The experienced is not reducible to experience.

When we do things with things, make predictions, exercise control, and otherwise solve problems or engage in other practical activities, we are not relating to, handling, manipulating, making use of nothing. As Ian Hacking says, "If you can spray them, then they are real."[47] For the pragmatist, then, what is the status in reality of what we come to know, react to, change, and otherwise use to cope with obstacles and achieve purposes? Within limits, could our theories be useful in practical ways if they were not true in some theoretical sense? The pragmatist may simply insist again that such questions merely waste time because they are both impossible to answer and totally irrelevant to getting on with life. We can understand how the realist might be unsatisfied with this reply and press the questions again for the sake of gaining understanding, which itself may be among the practical interests of some humans. Not only is rationality undercut or left incomplete, but without an anchor in reality pragmatism is on a slippery slope that leads into a dangerous forms of relativism and subjectivism.

Realists are on solid ground in their assumption that when we describe the world we are referring to something actually present and not merely linguistically and conceptually represented. Moreover, they are reasonable in thinking that the success of well-established theories over long periods of time in explaining, predicting, enabling us to do things with things, and so on suggests some connection between our descriptions and the described.

The problem arises, not in their belief in the thatness of the observed, detected, and theoretically postulated but in the precise description of the whatness of the objects thus linguistically represented. That something is there is undeniable and is hardly a matter of debate. What that something really is is more difficult. The whatness always is in some measure and in some respects conventionally designated, linguistically represented, theoretically constructed, and/or otherwise interpreted in terms that make a complete correspondence between our ways of speaking of the referent and the referent itself problematic. That gap cannot be totally closed it seems, although for practical everyday purposes it does not matter much.

The same point is made by recognizing the difference between a perception and an observation. A perception is the object's impact as registered in the perceiving organism. An observation is a statement that defines the content of the perception in language that interprets and so in part constructs the reality perceived in conceptual terms. Observation is a further selection and abstraction from the perception which is already itself a perspective on the world determined by the neurological equipment possessed by the biological organism. Hence, we do not passively grasp or receive the world's own structures that are then expressed in language that reproduces the prehended structures intact, so that the ontology of the language is identical with reality itself. Perception, observation, theoretical interpretations construct the world in ways that leave us unable to say what correspondence there may be between the propositions and the intended references in the world itself.

The reason is simple: our epistemological predicament is that we can have no access to a non-experienced, non-interpreted reality. We have access to the reality but only as experienced and interpreted. To say that the referent is there and real is one thing. To say what is real is another thing. We can only say, in the terms of William James, what reality is "known as." Reality, experience, and interpretation in indissoluble connection constitute the ingredients of our knowledge. It is reality that is experienced and interpreted, but it is reality as experienced and interpreted.

With respect to scientific theories Thomas Kuhn is surely right in denying "a theory-independent way to reconstruct phrases like `really there'; the notion of a match between the ontology of a theory and its `real' counterpart in nature now seems to me illusive in principle."[48] What the theory says and what the theory describes are both linguistic phenomena in the specific sense that we cannot say what is real independently of some linguistic representation of or theory about "it." The real as we identify it linguistically cannot be separated from that linguistic representation in order to compare it with that linguistic representation to see if there is correspondence. The referent is not available as such except as we can point to some concrete example or evidence of it and say "Here it is; this is it." But once we name it we have constructed it linguistically and theoretically at varying levels of complexity, depending on the referent.

Every linguistic identification is in part an interpretation. This may serve us well enough practically but leaves open a multitude of questions about what it really is. In some restricted sense it is what we say it is, in some cases at least, for all practical purposes. When we say that dinosaurs once existed, that the continents and the seas rest on massive, slow-moving plates, that stars are large masses of gas containing chemical elements like those we know on earth, there is a good chance that these statements are true, if we locate and limit the assigned meanings sufficiently at some gross level.[49] The issues are multidimensional and many-layered.

Realism and pragmatism are both on to something. Neither is invulnerable to attack at certain points. Neither is fully satisfactory. Perhaps the truth is somewhere between and beyond either. Hence, both realistic theories and pragmatic theories or non-theories of truth have partial validity and limited application. Each can be stretched to cover the whole of human inquiry and belief but in so doing becomes vulnerable to the searching criticisms of the other. With respect to science, for example, a critical realism can admit that we presently have only a partial perspective on the real while holding on to the hope that further inquiry may lead to fuller conceptions that more accurately correspond to what is really there. Faith must always bridge the gap, and faith always involves uncertainty.

Pragmatism can acknowledge that inquiry into certain realms may produce an enlarging body of coherent theory that adequately accounts for the evidence at the moment, thus giving the appearance of progressively describing the world as it is. It may insist, however, that no set of propositions can ever be known with certainty to correspond to reality. Moreover, correspondence to reality can only mean conforming to all expectations and meeting all tests under certain prescribed conditions that command agreement among trusted interpreters. In any case, the value in scientific knowledge lies in what it enables us to do or to better. We can have this benefit without believing that the models and propositions of science correctly represent something in the nature of things. The debates are interesting but unresolvable.

SUMMARY CONSIDERATIONS

The skepticism implicit and explicit in this essay is complete when the large issues of interpretation are involved. Even if it were possible inductively to build up a body of theory that (1) plausibly accounted for all the evidence, (2) was internally consistent, and (3) that connected experienced particulars with speculative generalities by a network of soundly constructed intermediate concepts, we could not be sure that the result was final or certain. Any number of possible theories might meet the same criteria. Even if we had in our possession a complete metaphysical vision correctly deduced from assumed first principles, we could not be sure that these a priori assumptions were sound. How could we be sure that they infallibly unite thought with being? Hence, neither empiricism nor rationalism nor any combination can provide a sure and reliable path toward systems of comprehensive truth that can be known with certainty to be true.

In short, no fool-proof method of contraconception, i. e., a sure way of preventing the birth of false theories about penultimates or ultimates, is available. No fail-safe procedure for truth control regarding interpretations of final facts can be invented. If somebody stumbled on one, how could we know that it was safe and effective? What we can do is to continue to work out ways of viewing the world from where we stand in our own generation as the inheritor of a long scientific, cultural, and religious tradition. We seek ways of understanding the world that are empirically and rationally compelling and that offer the best promise of increasing justice and happiness on this earth. We can engage in honest conversation with others in the search of greater consensus relevant to resolving the practical issues of life. We live in hope that such widening agreement can lead to the reduction of destructive conflicts and to increased human cooperation in the quest for justice and happiness on this fragile planet.

The chapters to follow offer a vision of life and its possibilities. The first step will be to set forth reasons for holding that classical Christian theism is inadequate for today. The last two chapters are essays in constructive theology. The result is a version of naturalistic theism centered around a view of a loving but finite God who works opportunistically to generate life and to actualize the potential for enjoyment in all living beings.

ENDNOTES

1. This phrase is, of course, the title of Richard Bernstein's influential recent book on the subject.

2. Cf. Jeffrey Stout, Ethics After Babel, p. 299. See also, pp. 82-105.

3. Cf. Alfred North Whitehead, The Function of Reason. See also my The Ethics of Enjoyment, pp. 64-79.

4. William James, Pragmatism, p. 45. He attributed the phrase to Shadworth Hodgson.

5. Cf. ibid., pp. 198-199.

6. Just out of curiosity, I reached for my dictionary and looked up the word. The first meaning is: "a sweeping implement consisting of a brush of twigs or plant stems on a handle." The American College Dictionary (1949).

7. Unfortunately, it is only in such relatively simple situations allowing conclusive agreement by a community of rational inquirers that the ideal speech conditions laid down by Jürgen Habermas can be fully successful. See Rick Roderick, Habermas and the Foundations of Critical Theory, pp. 81-87.

8. See David Tracy's discussion of the difficulties and complexities of interpretation, argument, and theory, starting with the old question about the French Revolution in Plurality and Ambiguity, pp. 1-46.

9. William James, Pragmatism, pp. 44-45.

10. Theology has many dimensions. I focus here on the reality claims made by theological propositions. The total task of theology also involves interpretation of texts, historical inquiry, making prescriptions for living, working, and worshipping (applying religious truth to life), and so on. Each of these tasks has its own aims, procedures, and criteria of truth and adequacy.

11. James, Pragmatism, p. 145.

12. Bernard Meland has made more of this effectively than most anyone else lately. See Fallible Forms and Symbols, p. 24.

13. See Holmes Rolston, Science and Religion, p. 10.

118

14. Ibid., p. 5.

15. See Thomas Kuhn, The Structure of Scientific Revolutions.

16. See Imre Lakatos, The Methodology of Scientific Research Programmes.

17. Rolston, Science and Religion, p. 11.

18. Compare these three elements with Mary Hesse's description of a learning machine that includes (1) empirical input from the environment that modifies the machine and is (2) represented in the machine by language programmed into it producing an initial classification of the received data and a set of observation sentences, followed by (3) theory construction guided by the requirement of coherence. She then notes how any mismatches between theory and data can then be reinterpreted until the best possible explication is achieved. This latter has similarities with my (4) to follow. See Revolutions and Reconstructions in the Philosophy of Science, pp. 125-128.

19. Cf. Nancy Frankenberry's discussion of Bernard Meland on this point. "Meland's Empirical Realism and the Appeal to Living Experience," in American Journal of Theology and Philosophy (May and September, 1984), pp. 117-129, esp. p. 118.

20. Cf. William Dean's discussion of William James on these matters in History Making History, pp. 102-105. See also James, Pragmatism, pp. 199-200.

21. I am inclined to accept the distinction Whitehead makes between "perception in the mode of causal efficacy" and "perception in the mode of presentational immediacy."

22. At least one process theologian thinks it may. See David R. Griffin, God and Religion in the Post-Modern World, pp. 97-98.

23. This is the convincing conclusion of Wayne Proudfoot in his important book Religious Experience.

24. This is the point I would make in regard to the powerful case Huston Smith makes for the truth and validity of what he calls "the primordial tradition." See his Forgotten Truth and Beyond the Post-Modern Mind.

25. See Richard Bernstein, Beyond Objectivism and Relativism, for one of the most influential statements of the problem in recent years.

26. David Tracy has worked at this as successfully as anyone in the theological community. His concept is that "the analogical imagination," by which we come to recognize the legitimacy of the other, can lead to recognition of fruitful similarities within differences that may yield some consensus of warranted belief. See The Analogical Imagination and Plurality and Ambiguity. Tracy, however, still operates under the assumption that a transcendental or metaphysical philosophy can establish necessary conditions for the possibility of existence and understanding. With Jeffrey Stout I am skeptical that such attempts are successful in establishing the basis for a public theology that yearns for universal cogency. Tracy himself recognizes that the historicity of knowledge provides the main basis on which his proposals are resisted. See Blessed Rage for Order, pp. 52-56, 63 n67; Plurality and Ambiguity, pp. 24-27; and Jeffrey Stout, Ethics after Babel, pp. 165-167.

27. See Thomas McCarthy, The Critical Theory of Jürgen Habermas; Rick Roderick, Habermas and the Foundations of Critical Theory; and Raymond Geuss, The Idea of a Critical Theory.

28. See ibid. See also, John E. Smith, Purpose and Thought.

29. See the following for an account of recent issues under discussion and the major positions taken: Nicholas Rescher (ed), Scientific Inquiry in Philosophical Perspective; Ian Hacking, Representing and Intervening; Arthur Fine, The Shaky Game; Mary Hesse, Revolutions and Reconstructions in the Philosophy of Science; Imre Lakatos, The Methodology of Scientific Research Programmes; Ian Barbour, Issues in Science and Religion; Holmes Rolston, Science and Religion; Thomas Kuhn, The Structure of Scientific Revolutions, and The Essential Tension; and Arthur Peacocke, Intimations of Reality.

30. Mary Hesse, Revolutions and Reconstructions in the Philosophy of Science, p. vii.

31. Ibid.

32. Ibid., p. viii.

33. Thomas Kuhn, The Structure of Scientific Revolutions, p. 111.

120

34. Hesse, Revolutions and Reconstructions in the Philosophy of Science, p. xii.

35. Imre Lakatos, The Methodology of Scientific Research Programs, p. 19.

36. Ibid., pp. 116-117.

37. Thomas Kuhn, The Structure of Scientific Revolutions, p. 200.

38. Ibid., pp. 208, 205.

39. Ian Hacking, Representing and Intervening, p. x, 1-31.

40. Ernan McMullin, "Explanatory Success and the Truth of Theory," Scientific Inquiry in Philosophical Perspective, ed. by Nicholas Rescher, p. 57.

41. Ernan McMullin, "Realism in Theology and Science: A Response to Arthur Peacocke," Religion and Intellectual Life (Summer, 1985), pp. 39-47.

42. For a brief account, see Arthur Fine, The Shaky Game, pp. 136-150.

43. For a brief description and defense of this way of looking at science, see J. Wesley Robbins, "Seriously But Not Literally: Pragmatism and Realism in Religion and Science," Zygon (September, 1988), pp. 229-245.

44. Ibid., p. 230.

45. Ibid., p. 233. Cf. Richard Rorty, Consequences of Pragmatism.

46. Arthur Fine, The Shaky Game, p. 129

47. Ian Hacking, Representing and Intervening, p. 22.

48. Thomas Kuhn, The Structure of Scientific Revolutions, p. 206.

49. Cf. Ernan McMullin, "Explanatory Success and the Truth of Theory," pp. 52-61.

Chapter III
WHY THE GOD OF CLASSICAL
THEISM WILL NOT DO

Modernism vehemently negates traditional theism. The God of classical theology embodies the sum total of all positive perfections. This is a being so great that no greater can be conceived (Anselm). Unsurpassable excellence requires that God be omnipotent, omniscient, omnipresent, eternal, necessary, absolute, immutable, and impassible. This list of attributes was affirmed by orthodox theologians from the second century onward. Along with these metaphysical attributes of Absolute Perfect Being, personal symbols derived from Scripture were employed as well. God is the Holy One of Israel --a sovereign moral agent, intelligent, wise, gracious, righteous, merciful, compassionate, and loving. This set of images points toward an Infinite Purposive Self with intellect, will, and even feeling.

The unquestioned assumptions of immutability and impassibility, however, required a symbolic rather than a literal attribution of process or change to the divine being. Hence, classical thought -- whether found in Augustine, Aquinas, Anselm, Luther, Calvin, or Zwingli -- spoke of a loving God who is not in the least affected by the suffering of the creatures. Fortunately for them, numerous strategies were available to escape the logical or moral problems this raised. The utter transcendence of Deity allowed theologians to convince themselves that this double-talk was not sheer contradiction or pure non-sense. The symbolic or analogical use of language enabled them to speak of the goodness and mercy of a Supreme Person with intellect and will, as the Bible required. At the same time they could appeal to divine otherness or the necessity of God's adapting the language of the Bible to our feeble intellects, and so on to avoid the plain meaning of some biblical passages.

Typical is John Calvin, who paused briefly to comment on the suggestion in Genesis 6:6 that God repented and in Isaiah 63:9 that God felt anguish. We "know," he says, that God experiences no such changes or feelings but "remains forever like Himself in His happy repose."[1] Whether the biblical idea of God survives in this rendering is open to question. Christians today who interpret God in more strictly personal terms and with love as the supreme attribute find classical thought on this point unacceptable. Contributing to this disavowal is a modern consciousness that takes time, change, and the emergence of novelty with utter seriousness. Is the notion of an eternal divine willing utterly devoid of temporality or process intelligible? Efforts to find a meaning of eternity beyond either mere everlastingness or absolute timelessness -- a view that both includes and transcends the passage of time -- are problematic.

This, however, is one of the lesser difficulties of classical theism as it developed from the second century onward through the eighteenth. The fundamental problem is that the outcome of the scheme devised by a God infinite in power, wisdom, and love is that the majority of human beings will spend eternity in torment. Generally, the idea is that those who end up in hell will be inflicted with punishments that range from mild to awful. The administration of just reward goes on forever. For those who taught predestination in the Augustinian sense, included among the damned are infants. Augustine is touched with enough pity to suggest that their punishment will be the mildest of all.

Surely a God who cannot or does not figure out a better way to run a world is either wicked or incompetent or both. The Calvinistic notion that God creates persons, causes them to sin, and damns the non-elect because they were voluntarily disobedient is reprehensible. It is shot through with enough logical and moral absurdity to require no further comment. The Arminian version that makes damnation a consequence of a freely chosen rejection of saving grace is only slightly less intolerable. And what about the saints enjoying the bliss of heaven? One standard view is that they rejoice at this marvelous exemplification of justice. Once convincing to a different mentality, such cruel doctrines cannot be part of the inventory of beliefs for the modernist Christian today.

Part of the problem, of course, lies within the Bible itself. The notion of the everlasting banishment of the wicked arose in the apocalyptic tradition. In an age dominated by psychological thinking, one cannot help but wonder at the motives behind this idea. Apocalypticism arose among oppressed peoples. It is understandable that they might imagine a resolution of history that gave their oppressors what they deserved. Did hatred of the enemy enter into the idea of everlasting punishment of the oppressor? A strictly moral interpretation of sinners, the idea that wickedness

justifies severe punishment, can certainly be found.
Nevertheless, even if one ignores the contradiction
posed by the idea of predestination, justice requires
only that the punishment fit the crime. An everlasting
hell is disproportionate to the evil deeds of even the
worst of humans, not to mention the damnation of non-
elect babies that Calvin included in the good news. The
claim that sin against an infinite good (God) warrants
infinite punishment sounds hollow today. It is, of
course, no comfort to liberal Christians to find the
notion on the lips of Jesus (Matt. 25:41, 46; Mk.9:48).
Even if responsible exegesis can turn "everlasting"
into "age-long" or "a very long time," the notion is
unworthy of a loving God.[2] Liberals usually manage to
reject this doctrine while otherwise treating Jesus as
the supreme authority in religious matters.

THE BANKRUPTCY OF TRADITIONAL THEODICIES

A final problem is raised by the problem of evil.
That God could be perfect in power, wisdom, and goodness is utterly preposterous in the face of the suffering, injustice, tragedy, misery, and absurdity endured
by so many of earth's mortals. It would be arrogant to
claim that the traditional view is contradictory when
measured by strict canons of logical necessity. My
agreement with the doubters is, first of all, a cry of
anguish from the heart. Of course, the sterner rationalists among the orthodox do not take that sort of
thing seriously. Apologetic theology can show that
classical theism is a logically possible outlook.[3]
Since Scripture gives a basis for positive views of
God, the only remaining challenge is the evangelistic
task of convincing skeptics that the received tradition
is true or is possibly so.[4]

Nevertheless, belief in an omnicompetent God of
boundless love is attended by as many difficulties as

is the notion of inerrant Scriptures. Defenders of traditional theism are no less ingenious in preserving the absolute flawlessness of God than fundamentalists are in defending an infallible Bible. Yet they are confronted with evidence no less damaging to their case.[5] Who knows whether these various strategies are successful in preserving the initial theory in the face of earth's giant agonies? Who can say whether deep religious needs forbid surrendering belief in the perfection of God despite earth's agonies?

THE DEFENSE OF CLASSICAL CLAIMS

Perhaps those who accept on faith the reality of an Omnipotent Love are wiser than the skeptics. That option is not available to me, for reasons that must now be given. In part, the outcome depends on the approach taken. I employ a method that seeks for the most persuasive and workable interpretation of the whole range of human experience. No theory about God in relation to evil is ruled out in advance. This may produce a different result from a procedure that begins with divine omnipotence and unqualified divine love as non-negotiable items of belief. While much latitude for creative thought remains, no resolution is allowed by orthodox thinkers that qualifies either the power or the goodness of God.[6] They had rather deny the reality of genuine evil.

The problem evil poses for classical theism can be put as a question regarding the compatibility of initial premises:

1. Divine Omnipotence

2. Unqualified Love   3. Genuine Evil

The standard objection is that it is logically inconsistent to affirm 1. the omnipotence of God and 2. the perfect love of God in the presence of 3. genuine evil in the world. It would appear that either

a. the power or the goodness of God must be qualified

or

b. the reality of evil must be denied.

Put simply, it seems that God either cannot or will not prevent or remove evil. To say that God cannot denies omnipotence. To say that God will not denies perfect love. The other alternative is to assert that no genuine evil exists, despite all the suffering and injustice in the world.

Two options are available. (1) One can assume all three premises and make appeals within that framework to show that no logical incompatibility arises. (2) One can modify one or more of the premises in the original framework and thus remove the inconsistency that would otherwise pertain. Many contemporary main-line theologians take the first way. A strong tradition in classical thought took the second option by denying the genuineness of evil. I also take way (2), but I surrender omnipotence in favor of a finite but loving God who struggles to overcome real evil. Let us examine the merits and the shortcomings of the appeals that are typically made in order to avoid surrendering either omnipotence or perfect goodness and without denying the reality of evil. The alternative of a good but limited God will be stated briefly and developed more fully in the next two chapters.

1. The Appeal to Mystery

Widely used is the appeal to divine mystery, human ignorance, and paradox.[7] Surely there is truth here. Hardly anyone outdoes me in stressing the limits of reason. I reluctantly embrace a pragmatism that gives up the hope of finding religious truth that can be known to correspond to reality. I settle for beliefs that co rently integrate experience and help us cope with life. Nevertheless, it always surprises me that theologians who seem to know so much about the ultimate realities otherwise suddenly become ignorant when they reach the theodicy question. Does it mean they are operating with contradictory premises? When is an appeal to mystery premature or invalid?

I propose that Reality is lost in mists of mystery; yet experience is infused with clues to final meaning. We need some hypothesis about the ultimate ground of existence to unify our experience, to make sense of life, and to give moral guidance. Failure to account consistently for evidence counts against the hypothesis. Orthodox thinkers may admit this, but they will not allow anything to count decisively against either one of the three initial premises (or at least not against omnipotence or perfect goodness).[8] Hence, they will push rational explanations of evil as far as possible but then appeal to mystery or human ignorance rather than qualify the basic hypothesis. The issue then becomes whether or not sufficient or irrefutable grounds exist for affirming or maintaining the initial premises regardless. I say there are not, one reason being the reality of massive real evils. If there are such grounds, it may be legitimate to mix rational appeals with a final resort to mystery.

2. The Appeal to Divine Punishment

A second appeal is that suffering is punishment for sin. The Bible contains both support and refutation of this proposition. What do reason and experience teach us? Certainly there are consequences of wrong human actions that often bring catastrophe upon the perpetrators. The wages of sin are often death or destruction or at least sleepless nights, a guilty conscience, and ill health. Those who live by the sword often die by the sword but not always. Yet frequently the righteous suffer and the wicked prosper (if fallible judgments of human beings have any validity at all).

Some have claimed that AIDS is a punishment for immoral behavior, presumably drug use or sexual activity among homosexuals. Yet AIDS does not discriminate between homosexual persons and heterosexual persons. The virus gets into the bodies of anyone when the circumstances are right, regardless of whether their behavior conforms to conventional standards or not. Babies are born with AIDS. Hemophiliac children can get the virus from tainted blood transfusions. Lesbian women, presumably as immoral as gay males in the eyes of the accusers, have a very low incidence. If sinners can prevent AIDS by using a condom or if drug addicts can avoid AIDS by using clean needles, does this mean that human prudence can outwit the judgment of God? Is it only ignorant or careless sinners who get punished? No consistent pattern can be discerned that makes any sense of the proposition that AIDS is a punishment for sin, even if one agreed that all homosexual acts are immoral. Some theologians in the South interpreted defeat in the Civil War as a punishment of God for sin, although slavery was not usually identified as the precipitating offense. The educational value of divine chastisement would seem to be limited by the remarkable powers of human rationalization!

The distribution of suffering only partially corresponds to the distribution of virtue. Misery occurs randomly as often as for moral reasons. It springs from so many sources that any systematic attempt to correlate suffering with sin is futile. At this point the appeal to mystery must take over. When difficulties are pointed out, we are confronted with the rejoinder that God's thought and ways are not ours. Well, all right, but if they are not, why not appeal to that fact in the beginning and not wait to spring it when experience fails to sustain the initial thesis? About all the claim reasonably amounts to is that some suffering may be divine punishment for sin even though we cannot tell for sure when it is and when it isn't. So reduced, this appeal does not go far in resolving the theodicy question.

3. The Appeal to the Nature of Finitude

A more successful and sophisticated appeal maintains that suffering is the inevitable implication of finitude.[9] Finite beings are by their very nature subject to disruption and destruction. As creatures of flesh, blood, bones, and nerves, we are necessarily subject to pain, accident, disease, decay, and death. Organisms are complicated systems of interdependent, mutually sustaining parts. Hence, they are easy prey to destructive forces within and without the body. The complexity of the brain necessary to sustain the higher human functions makes it extremely vulnerable to harm. Complexity and vulnerability are inseparable twins. The greater the complexity, in some situations at least, the greater is the vulnerability. The very structures and processes of the body that make possible enjoyment when they work right are the very structures and processes that cause misery when they go wrong. The fact that we are finite beings living at the intersection of a vast network of interacting causal chains means that something can go wrong. Consequently, we cannot have the possibility of good without the possibility of evil. In fact, the greater the possibilities of good, the greater are the possibilities of evil.

Moreover, in a law-abiding world made up of a plurality of relatively autonomous centers of action that make possible contingent events, disruptive inter-actions are bound to occur. Collisions are inevitable among different chains of causation. All this means that some outcomes will be undesirable from the standpoint of sentient creatures who are damaged by them. A huge boulder on a mountain side precariously balanced might be tipped over and set in motion when brushed by an eagle's wing. Rolling down the mountain, it might kill several animals and finally dislodge a bike rider and break his leg. Consequently, it would appear that even an omnipotent God cannot create finite beings capable of experiencing good without introducing the possibility of evil.

Could not an omnipotent God prevent the possibility of evil from being actualized and permit only those events which led to good? Maybe, but then another consideration enters. Perhaps God has good reason for not arranging the world so that only good actually occurs at every particular event. At this point, another appeal arises.

4. The Appeal to Excellence of Design

Perhaps some or all of those features of the world that introduce the inevitability of suffering are, on balance, really good for us. Consider, for example, the law-abiding character of nature. If we fall out a window, we may hurt ourselves because gravitation never takes a holiday. Without it, how could we keep our furniture on the floor? Moreover, the laws of nature make possible learning and the possibility of carrying out purpose. How could we build bridges or boil water for our coffee if there were no constants in nature? Pain is a warning system to alert us to danger. Human freedom is the source of much injustice and misery. Would we want freedom taken away? And so it goes.

If we really thought it through, would we change the way the world works? Would not any alteration in the basic plan make things worse? The most rational and optimistic even suggest that this may be the best of all possible worlds. If the optimist believes that this is the best of all possible worlds, then the pessimist is afraid the optimist is right! Many orthodox divines urge us to accept the good world that God has made and eschew unprofitable speculation about its relative merit.

The assertion that finitude is an inevitable source of suffering is powerful, whatever limits there may be to the claim. It would take a long time to sort out the wheat from the chaff. What it adds up to is this: Is this world in principle, i. e., in its basic structures and processes, equal or superior in excellence to any possible world? Is the way this world is made as likely or more likely to produce the greatest excess of good over evil as any world that God could have made? Of course, this world could be better in fact and detail if wiser choices were made and if the juxtaposition of events produced fewer accidents and tragic outcomes. It is quite possible, for example, that the AIDS virus might never have gotten into the human body if enough circumstances had been different.

What about the basic features of the world? Are they the best possible? The question cannot be answered with confidence, but some comments are pertinent. It appears that an either-or arises. Either God is not perfect or the world has a tragic dimension.[10] Suppose a world better in principle and in structure were possible. In this case God would appear to be imperfect, since God could not or did not want to create the better world. Now suppose a better world in principle and structure is not possible. In this case reality has an unavoidable tragic aspect. If this is the best of all possible worlds (in basic structure), then there

are cosmic necessities involved in creating finite
beings over which God has no control. These necessities
cause or permit every one of the enormous evils earth
has known. To state it in other terms, God cannot
create finite beings without introducing the possibility of horrendous suffering that will in all probability come about. Claiming that the risk is worth it
because of the good that can eventually be achieved
hardly takes away the horror of the alternatives: either no world at all or one that produces massive pain,
injustice, terror, and misery.

Even a perfect God, it seems, cannot create a
perfect world, that is, one filled with only goodness
and no evil. Yet classical Christianity has spoken of
heaven, a perfected world of finite beings who know
only joy and no pain or suffering. So is it possible
after all to have a finite world with no suffering in
it? But if heaven is possible then, why not now? Another either/ or arises. Either a perfect God can make a
finite world with no evil in it, or heaven is not
possible. Of course, God can eventually perfect the
world, some say, but not until this world with its sin
and suffering has provided the necessary pre-conditions
for the fulfillment of the divine aim. Irenaean and
free-will defense theodicies take this line. Are they
persuasive? Even if they are, does not the tragic
dimension remain?

Since many a slip of logic and meaning may occur,
the argument, at the risk of repetition, may be put in
a different way.

a. A God who is perfectly good would presumably
wish to create the best of all possible worlds.[11] (One
could, of course, argue that a free and sovereign God
could make any kind of world the divine will chose. It
might or might not be the best of all possible worlds

by some standards; it would just be the world God
wanted to make. Who are we to judge what a perfectly
good God would have done or ought to have done? Anyone
who find this line of thought appealing will find my
theology appalling!)

b. A God who is all-powerful (omnicompetent) would
be able to create the best of all possible worlds or
one that has no possible superior.

c. If this is not the best of all possible world
in the sense required, God must be lacking in either
goodness or power or both.

d. If this world is as good as any possible world
in its potential for producing the most good with the
least evil, then God confronts necessities that require
this design and yet permit massive suffering over which
God has no control. Hence, the world has an unavoidable
tragic aspect to it.

As far as the God of orthodoxy is concerned, the
distinction between the world in principle and structure and the world in fact and detail finally is indis-
tinct. This God not only initially designed the basic
framework of things but can prevent or cause particular
events here and now. For example, it would have been
possible for God to make a world without the smallpox
virus. Modern science has apparently stamped out the
disease. Has anything essential been lost from the
world? If so, we are back to recognizing that the world
is unavoidably ambiguous and more than a little tragic. If not, why did not God exclude it to begin with?
Assuming that the AIDS virus serves some good purpose
somewhere in creation, could God not have altered it or
the human organism so that it could do its job and not
kill people? To say that God deliberately allowed or
caused the AIDS virus to get into the human organism in

order to kill people is not a compliment to the Creat-
or.

But say the defenders of God's plan for the world,
had God eliminated some avowedly worst evil, we would
want the next worst removed and so on until only good
things were left. That would defeat the soul-building
purpose that evil serves. Thus, we have to live with
things as they are and trust that all will be ultimately well.[12] Surely an infinitely wise Deity would
know how much evil is necessary to accomplish the
desired end without permitting any excessive suffering. Besides the point is not what people want but what
is logically consistent with premises.

In addition to the four appeals already listed,
two others are especially noteworthy. Widely used by
contemporary philosophers of religion and theologians,
they have much merit. Neither, however, can justify the
ways of God to humanity with the success their sponsors
claim.

5. The Appeal to Human Freedom

The appeal to human freedom as a source of evil
not implicating God is made by practically everybody.
It has great merit. Much suffering and injustice are
caused by people acting irresponsibly. God is not
directly at fault. It is another thing, however, to
develop a whole theodicy around the theme. The free-
will defense is popular among some evangelical Christians as the main or sole justification of the ways of
God.[13] It is a modern form of an Augustinian theodicy
that suffers from some of its defects as well as bene-
fitting from its virtues. The basic idea is quite
simple. God chose to give us freedom. Freedom can be
misused and often is. Nevertheless, in light of the
good that is eventually to be achieved, a good that
could not have been brought about any other way, even

the worst evils will fade into insignificance. Proponents of this view must face the charge that this strategy makes suffering caused by sin only an apparent evil, since the freedom from which it springs is the necessary means to a good and justifying end. They reply that such horrors as the Holocaust are both genuinely evil and that they will be fully compensated for or at least lose their sting in the light of the glory that is to be revealed. This solution requires an wide appeal to divine mystery and human ignorance. Defenders of the view readily admit they do not know how it can be that some massive evils will contribute to the final good or at least be rendered innocuous by the blessedness of the life beyond.

This form of theodicy requires its adherents to say to many questions, "I just don't know." It also suffers from other defects. Leaving aside for the moment the question of whether God could create free beings who would always choose the good, four can be mentioned.

(a) The free-will defense accounts readily for moral evil (suffering springing from human irresponsibility) but does not account as easily for natural evil (suffering involving no human irresponsibility). Some suppose that Satan is responsible for many human ills. This possible explanation will get an approving nod from some, while others will find it improbable or even amusing.

A sophisticated hypothesis is proposed by David Griffin to show that some among what we usually regard as natural evils may, in fact, spring from the choice of sub-human creatures.[14] Its plausibility depends on the prior acceptance of Whiteheadian metaphysics. This will be a barrier for most, although not for me. If one, however, can believe that freedom (in Whitehead's sense) is found everywhere in nature, it can be argued that such trouble makers as cancer cells, the AIDS virus, and the smallpox virus are contingent occurrences and not a result of deliberate divine creation. Destructive organisms may have been produced by the cumulative acts of misguided "choices" made at the molecular or sub-molecular level. A series of such free acts could have resulted in the emergence of many evildoers in the long evolutionary process. Even so, not all natural evils can be accounted for in this way. Some, such as accidents, seem to be a likely feature of any world in which contingent events occur. More generally put, some suffering is deeply rooted in the very fact of finitude itself, given the presence of experiencing subjects. Anyway, the Whiteheadian God of Griffin is not the omnipotent God of orthodoxy that the evangelical proponents of the free-will defense presuppose.

(b) Freedom is made into an absolute or transcending value. No matter how much evil results from it, the method God had to use is cost-effective. Do no considerations whatsoever relativise the value of freedom? Is the prevention of no evil, no matter how enormous, worth the restriction of human freedom, no matter how little? Do not some values take precedence over freedom? Should I not restrict the freedom of my daughter in order to save her life when she is about to run in front of a truck to retrieve her beach ball? The reply that once God has given freedom, it must be allowed to take its course no matter what the consequence makes some sense, of course. Are then all miracles to be ruled out? And is there no point at which an omnipotent God might be justified restricting a little bit the freedom of a sinner about to perpetrate some monstrous deed? Is the freedom of the criminal to be preferred to the welfare of the victim? Always, without exception?

(c) Genuine freedom on the part of finite creatures limits the sovereignty of God in achieving a final victory of good over evil. If by freedom we mean the power to originate novelty, to set in motion a new stream of events, then God's power to control outcomes is dependent on human response to divine persuasion. Orthodoxy, of course, has always taught that God will at some time override human freedom and coerce the world into a perfect harmony. Augustine's view, widely honored in the classical tradition, was that "God judged it better to bring good out of evil, than to suffer no evil to exist."[15] It is not that sin and evil as such are necessary to the perfection of the universe, but souls with free will and the capacity to sin are, he thinks. Since in the next world the elect are finally made perfect by a fresh act of creative grace anyway, one wonders why it could not have been done to begin with. The argument that unabrogated freedom is temporarily necessary although it may produce horrendous evils but at the end can legitimately be overruled in order to guarantee the triumph of the good is weak and arbitrary.

(d) Freedom is not an unmixed blessing. Sometimes it is a burden. Often we have to choose in the face of anguished uncertainty. We cannot avoid choosing a way of believing and living; yet we cannot be sure our religious beliefs are true. We cannot always know what is right or best, even when we have the good will to do it. Moreover, many choices are ambiguous. Sometimes we cannot do good without doing harm. A soldier in a just war can preserve the rights and welfare of some only by killing others. Yet they may be as just and good as he/she. Again, some choices are fundamentally

138

tragic. Suppose two small children are caught in a burning house. The only parent at home can rescue one but not both. Choosing to save the life of one means choosing a horrible death for the other. If it be protested that the value of freedom, taking all considerations into account, far outweighs the disvalues, that may be true. But if a necessary or at least great good such as freedom cannot be had without its ambiguous side, then can we escape the conclusion that finite existence has a tragic dimension?

A final recourse of some sponsors of the free-will defense is that all a theodicy is required to show is that the orthodox hypothesis could possibly be true.[16] Since the belief in divine omnipotence and goodness is based on the Bible, it is sufficient for reason to demonstrate that evil does not necessarily contradict this affirmation. Of course, many theories about God and the world become plausible if you grant them enough initial assumptions. The question is whether another way of dealing with the problem might be equally credible and more explanatory of human experience than the free-will defense.

6. The Appeal to Divine Purpose

An influential theodicy more Irenaean than Augustinian has been proposed by John Hick.[17] Its essential point is that God has made the kind of world that will eventually lead to a community of persons who freely love God and each other. This will be the fulfillment of God's own purpose. The ultimate community will include all rational persons in a consummation so wonderful that the sufferings of this age will be justified. The world is a laboratory for soul-making. It was designed by God to fulfill this end. An initial epistemic distance (human ignorance and uncertainty) from God is required. So are perils, temptations, and snares that will surely lead to sin and suffering. The sojourners find their way toward God in this ambiguous situation despite mighty obstacles and in the presence of alternative ways of life. In the long run, perhaps involving many lives in successive worlds, the human pilgrimage will be consummated in a bliss so exquisite that the necessary means to its achievement will be exonerated. God's plan for perfecting moral personality through external challenge and internal choice is worth enduring the Hitlers and Holocausts, the diseases and disasters, the cruelty and the carnage, that inevitably occur on the road to heaven.

The virtues of this approach are substantial. Given the commitment to both omnipotence and unqualified goodness in deity, Hick's theory is probably as meritorious as any and more commendable than most. Nevertheless, weighty difficulties are present. His outlook, for example, is centered on the perfection of moral personality in human beings. One wonders, then, why an omnipotent God would choose to spend billions of years evolving a universe inhabited by persons only the last few seconds of cosmic time. He offers no compelling rationale for the existence of animal life or for the billions of galaxies that evolved for billions of years prior to the emergence of rational souls.[18] Non-human life is valuable primarily because of its contribution to God's purpose for humanity. Animal suffering is not redeemed eschatologically and so is left as a tragic necessity endured for human benefit. Leaving aside particulars, the fundamental question is whether the structures and processes of this world are the most desirable ones that an infinitely gifted deity could come up with to achieve the desired end of perfecting moral personality. Could the same goal be attained in a framework less likely to produce the massive evils earth knows? We cannot know for sure whether a scheme superior in principle is possible for a God with the unlimited talent assumed by Hick. My own hunch is that a God limited only by the laws of self-contradiction could devise a better world blueprint for producing saints than the present model.

Let us pause only briefly to ask whether Hick's definition of the end of life is self-evident. Perhaps virtue is the precondition for the realization of other ends, e. g., the fullest exercise of creative human powers in a community of free and equal persons. Suppose the aim of God is to maximize the enjoyment of experiencing subjects. Could it be that the self-actualization of persons experienced as happiness is the supreme goal for planet earth, an aim which also includes the fulfillment of the potential of all sentient beings? Is not animal life valuable in and of itself? Does the play of puppies or kittens require justification beyond the pleasure being enjoyed (by them, not by us watching them)? Given healthy bodies, a just society, and the opportunity to actualize the full range of human capacities that yield satisfaction, the union of each with others and with God in a community of universal love defines a worthy goal. Hick's own way of putting it is too narrowly moralistic or spiritual and much too anthropocentric. Is Hick's outlook on life too austere, too stern, too "puritanical," overly reactive to Hume's "hedonic paradise," too afraid of a simple, painless good time? Is he unduly dominated by the view that the worthwhile or normative ends of life require blood, sweat, and tears, can only be gained by hard knocks, struggle, and pain? My first visceral reaction to his proposal was: let us have less character and more fun! Some virtues are doubtless the prerequisite of the highest enjoyment in the long run. Nevertheless, some form of ontological hedonism may be as plausible a candidate as his spiritual perfection theory for defining the divine aim in creation. An alternative to his theodicy will emerge in these pages. Let us now examine his own proposal on its own merits.

The old question of whether God could make free, finite, rational persons who would always choose the highest available good is relevant here. A negative answer would appear to eliminate the possibility of heaven. Orthodox Protestant theology has taught that God will instantly perfect believers who die saved by grace but who are still sinners at various levels of moral achievement. Hence, following the last judgment heaven's party begins immediately with saints who are fully sanctified. They are presumably not able to sin or perhaps able to sin but not wanting to because they are perfect specimens of finite sainthood. In heaven, as traditionally conceived, natural as well as moral evil has been eliminated (Rev. 21). Thus, in the world to come God can by edict make heaven real by simply eliminating natural evil and by instantly sanctifying the as yet partially redeemed company of the saved. If heaven is possible then, why not now? Hick, of course, contends that orthodoxy is theologically unsound, lacking his insight into what is necessary if persons are to move by choice toward spiritual perfection. This latter idea has a distinctly modern and liberal tone and is of dubious scriptural ancestry.

The arguments of Anthony Flew[19] and J. L. Mackie[20] are worthy of attention despite all the attempts to refute them. They maintain that God could produce free, finite persons who would always choose the good. Obviously, much hinges on the meaning assigned to key terms like "freedom" and "morally good persons." Suppose we understand free acts to be expressive of character in the sense implied in Jesus' words that a good tree brings forth good fruit. Suppose we understand morally good acts to be those expressive of good moral character. In this case one might be free <u>metaphysically</u> to act contrary to the good in the sense of having the requisite powers to do so. Such a person would not be <u>morally</u> free to do so. I am capable, in the sense of possessing all the abilities necessary, to be cruel to my son. But unless my mind is destroyed by disease, drugs, or accident, I am not morally capable of doing harm to my son. Abuse would violate the love which determines how I freely act toward him. Moreover, I loved him and he loved me from the very beginning of his life or as soon as he was capable of response. No long period of struggle, pain, and disciplined "soul making" is the necessary means to a child's answering love to loving parents. In short, I am free in the <u>metaphysical</u> sense to choose alternatives that would be destructive. I am not <u>morally</u> free to do so. What higher doctrine of freedom than that do we need? What better love could God ever want from us?

Karl Barth holds a doctrine of God that follows this pattern. God always acts in freedom. God always acts in love. Freedom is never violated or suspended in God. Yet God's free acts are always expressive of love.[21] If we are made in the image of God, why could we not be made as free and loving beings who always express our freedom in accordance with our loving nature?

Suppose by "morally good person" we mean a rational self of wholly virtuous character. It would appear that God could create morally good persons whose freedom would always be expressive of their virtuous character. Such persons would always choose the best under the circumstances. The orthodox have to explain why this can be done in heaven but cannot be done now. One might, of course, do harm to another out of ignorance but not out of malevolence.

Hick agrees with Flew and Mackie that it is logically possible for God to make people initially so that morally good acts at the human level would always flow from good character. He argues, however, that the case is different if we speak of our relation to God.[22] It is not logically possible for God to design human beings so that they would inevitably respond to God in genuine trust and love. Such a response cannot both be forced and be free, be guaranteed and yet genuinely an act of choice. A post-hypnotic suggestion carried out by a patient would seem like a free act by the person doing it and to others. To the hypnotist the patient is a puppet or tool. If the post-hypnotic suggestion were that the patient should agree with the hypnotist on some controversial matter, the hypnotist would know that the agreement was not a genuine act of choice. God could make us so that we would give the appearance of loving God. It would seem real to us. God would know better. God wants a freely chosen act of loving response that might not have happened, not the equivalent of a post-hypnotic suggestion that is in fact determined in advance.

Surely this point fails. First of all, the analogy may not be proper. A post-hypnotic suggestion is a kind of irresistible compulsion, a manipulated response that comes from the outside mandating a specific act or a limited class of acts that may or may not correspond to the internal desires or will of the patient. This is not the same thing as a choice that genuinely expresses one's own internal nature. Good character only insures that whatever particular choices are forthcoming will all be good ones but does not dictate merely a particular act or limited set of acts. A good person may be quite creative, original, imaginative in choosing which specific deeds express her/his character. In any case, my impression is that even under the spell of post-hypnotic suggestion a person will not do anything that deeply violates his/her moral convictions.

Moreover, the distinction between a morally good act toward others and a religiously valuable response toward God is invalid. Actions springing from a post-hypnotic suggestion do not meet the highest moral requirements regardless of whether God or another person is involved. Whether God or a neighbor we treat properly knows why we are doing it is irrelevant. A good act is better than a bad act, whatever its motivation. A thoroughly good act toward either God or a neighbor must be freely chosen as an expression of our genuine intent. God knows what is in our hearts in self-neighbor relations just as much as in self-divine relations. Externally coerced goodness is inferior in either case. Hick's example only introduces confusion. It does not settle the issue or make his point.

Furthermore, we may ask what Hick wants or requires in this connection. His own view of freedom does not involve arbitrary choice unconditioned by moral character or anything else. He agrees that freedom means self-caused not uncaused. Unless choice were guided by some more or less consistent set of aims, obligations, and interests that define character, the acts of a given individual would be unpredictable, arbitrary, chaotic, and void of pattern.[23] That is not what experience tells us about the way people behave. When we are surprised by something our most intimate friends do, we conclude not that their choice exhibits an act of sheer will creatio ex nihilo but that we did not know them as well as we thought. Hick's own goal of the perfection of moral personality would not be possible of secure achievement apart from some notion that character determines choice. Otherwise the saints could at any moment choose something evil by merely deciding to do so. Hick presumably agrees with Augustine that in heaven the blessed ones have the capacity only to do good.

The persisting question is how this state is to be achieved, so that, once reached, it is reliable and permanent. What must be presupposed initially about human potential, inclination, predisposition, and tendency? Hick agrees with Augustine that we were made for loving communion with God and that we are restless until we realize this destiny. Some American neo-Calvinists argued that we inherit from Adam and Eve a nature that is corrupt in the sense that whenever we begin to make choices, they will inevitably be tainted with rebellion and disobedience. Is it not possible for an omnicompetent God to create us with an urge for righteousness and to provide us with unmistakable evidences of divine love such that when we begin to make choices, they will probably if not inevitably eventuate in love of God and neighbor? If that loving response is evoked and reinforced by the actual experience of God's own love, why should we doubt its genuineness as our autonomous act? Why should God be disappointed in it? The notion that an initial "epistemic distance" is required in an ambiguous setting in which God's reality and goodness are unclear is unconvincing. Certainly parents do not assume this in teaching their children to love them and others. Why should we assume it is necessary in God's economy?

Note further that Hick believes that it is essential to his theodicy that all persons eventually come by free choice to a state of perfect communion with God. Otherwise the sufferings of this age are not justified by the final victory. God's purpose fails. He works out an elaborate speculation about successive worlds of living and dying until God's persuasive love wins a free response from all. If we are free in Hick's sense (and mine), how can universal salvation be assured? He can never state with certainty more than a hope and a probability that all will eventually make the required decision. He cannot have it both ways. If all are free, what guarantee is there that all will finally freely respond with an answering love? Feeling the force of this objection, he meets it by admitting that universal salvation cannot be predicted as a logical necessity but only as a moral likelihood. While not an absolute inevitability, we can have practical certainty in the outcome. Nevertheless, even the possibility of failure is a flaw, if universal salvation is essential to his theodicy.

If everyone has sufficient time, opportunity, and ability to choose God freely in the clear light of known options and consequences, why is it so bad if they voluntarily exclude themselves forever from the blessed community? Assuming that God will never cease striving to win them, if they truly choose not to respond, then so be it. Is that not keeping with Hick's own notion that freedom once given must be allowed to flourish whatever the consequences? If he is so concerned that Hitler be free to create an Auchwitz on this earth, why does he fret over the possibility that Hitler might freely choose to remain in hell rather than share heaven with Jews? The reason is that God's plan would be defeated to the extent that any remain outside the gates of final blessedness. Is freedom to be taken with ultimate seriousness or not? Of course, we can sympathize with Hick's concern that all finally sit at the heavenly table. Can he have it all -- uncoerced freedom in human beings, the logical necessity of universal salvation, and the moral certainty of its achievement?

Hick needs to affirm that human nature is sufficiently inclined toward God and goodness to engender the likelihood that our true end will be actualized eventually. Yet it must undetermined enough that free choice is essential to actualize the desired outcome in a situation that could go the other way. If he stresses the initial built-in inclination to goodness, he may undercut the view of freedom he thinks essential. If he emphasizes the freedom to reject God and goodness, he cannot guarantee the universal salvation without which the purpose of God is defeated -- an alternative he is apparently not willing to entertain. God has made the world just right. There is enough freedom to assure human autonomy but sufficient predisposing conditions toward God to produce universal salvation with moral certainty. Well, then, why could not God see to it that there was just enough suffering in the world to perfect our souls without the excess that threatens to wreck his whole theodicy?

Hick admits that the greatest weakness in his approach is the excessive suffering, the inexplicable tragedies, the enormous injustices, the terrible waste, and the massive cruelties of life. It is an impenetrable mystery. Yet in a turn about that dazzles, he snatches a paradoxical rational victory from the jaws of defeat by absolute mystery. It is the very irrational, excessive, pointless, and mysterious character of suffering that enables it to do its job of soul-making![24] If suffering were justly proportioned, it would not call forth the virtues and efforts necessary to combat it. Only if it is not rationalizable can it be regarded as really bad and as capable of serving its soul-making purpose. Hence, reason succeeds after all in proving its case by showing that excessive evil is rational (i. e., reason can see that excessiveness is necessary) only if it is irrational (i. e., it defies reason's power to understand it). This is surely the location either of Hick's supreme triumph or of the total bankruptcy of his entire thesis.

Hick doubtless has a point in insisting that true virtue in loving God and others must develop in an environment with temptations, obstacles, and alternatives. I loved my two daughters and my one son the moment they were born. They loved me as infants. Our relationship deepened and matured as we experienced each other in a common history involving challenge, threat, pain, and sorrow, including the death of their mother from cancer. We could not have the relationship of deep love and trust that we have as adults apart from the experiences we have lived through. Wouldn't it have been better for all, including their mother, if she had lived past age fifty-five to enjoy them and they her? Can any kind of perfected future justify the tragedy of the moment, so that we sing through our tears, "O happy misery, O thoughtful Creator, to design these terrible sufferings for our eventual good!" The notion that premature and cruel death, hydrocephalic children, and starving children are necessary evils lovingly provided by an omnipotent Wisdom for some far-off perfection is offensive. While Hick might protest that no particular sorrow is necessary, he cannot deny that all miseries and injustices are unnecessary. Some set of events involving similar or worse experiences of suffering is essential, or the process cannot work, according to him. So he cannot get by with the evasive tactic of pointing out that some particularly gross and absurd evils might not have happened.

Let us grant that heaven in the richest fullest sense cannot be created instantly but can only be the outcome of a history of interaction between souls moving toward a perfection of mutual love. It is not at all clear that the requirements for developing spiritual maturity entail the harsh environment and stern circumstances Hick prescribes. His picture of the kind of environment that is likely to produce loving persons positively in tune with life and with God differs markedly from my own. He thinks that an omnipotent, all-wise, supremely loving God deliberately put a childlike human race in a threatening, ambiguous situation. Don't children need love from the beginning that is clear, consistent, and unconditional if they are to develop a sense of basic trust in life? Demonstrated, unmistakable love from the start tends to produce children who can themselves love others. The children who are not consistently and unambiguously loved, those who are loved and cared for one day and beaten and abandoned the next day, are most likely to become untrusting, insecure, and even violent adults who do to others as bad as worse as they were done to in their early years. Clear evidence that God is real, good, and powerful is more likely to produce souls fit for life in a community bonded by mutual love than an environment so threatening that self-regarding motives are readily understandable as prudent means toward survival and what meager fulfillment may be possible.

It is no surprise that the design of this world has produced just what it has -- sin, pain, suffering, injustice, hate, conflict, insanity, hydrocephalic children, cancer, religious doubt, and so on. Hick, of course, agrees so far. To claim that it is not possible or likely that trust in God and love of neighbor can develop without some such world conditions as ours embodies is outrageous. Consider the tragic trap that young Israeli soldiers and young Palestinians find themselves at the moment. They are destined to live in a situation they did not create and can hardly resolve. Their predicament is so full of contradictions that hardly any way of escape seems possible. No wonder Hick must allow the possibility of many worlds to come before heaven becomes real. Maybe with another kind of primordial world order, it might happen sooner. Isn't it remarkable that as much love, cooperation, and religious faith have emerged as has? When I confronted in a class in religious education in college the thesis of Horace Bushnell's Christian Nurture that children could grow up thinking of themselves as Christians and never otherwise, I was shocked. This principle of nurturing children gradually into faith contradicted the revivalistic pattern I had learned. Children are born innocent, the prevailing Baptist theology taught. When they reach the "age of accountability," their souls are in imminent danger. The stern passages in Romans can be preached to them. They must repent of their awful condition and be saved by grace, lest they risk judgment here and hereafter. You must be lost and in danger before you can be saved.

Hick's prescription is similar to this form of Baptist theology. The human race must be lost before being able to choose salvation. Otherwise, souls will be flabby, weak, pampered, and forever immature. Maybe Bushnell was on to something. Maybe if the human race were from the beginning subjected to loving nurture and instructed in the ways of God in a situation which challenged and tested but did not rip them to pieces with disease, pain, cruelty, violence, and premature death maybe, just maybe, they might grow up to live in love in vigorous maturity and never think otherwise. At least, this might happen much sooner that seems likely in Hick's soul-making laboratory.

If Hick is right in his assumptions, it is hard to escape a tragic sense about life, even given his optimism about an eventual perfection in the far distant future. The tragic implications are heightened by the fact that the world could contain even worse evils than it presently does! Is there any amount of suffering, any set of horrendous events of any magnitude, that Hick would consider as falsifying his thesis? Apparently not. I agree that life on earth has a tragic dimension. For Hick not even a God perfect in power and goodness can perfect the world except by using sin and suffering as instruments of grace. That is tragedy indeed! I believe that if God were indeed omnipotent love, this world could and would be much better than it is, much better.

Hick does not even avail himself of the option of claiming that the sufferings of this world are only apparently evil but not genuinely so, since they are the necessary means toward a good and justifying end.[25] Again, he wants it both ways. Suffering is not just apparently but truly evil. He also says that from the eschatological standpoint they are not "merely evil."[26] If the massive miseries we experience in the soul-making laboratory are regarded by us as only apparent evils, they could not serve the purpose of generating courage and compassion in combatting them. They must not be "merely evil" either, since they are justified only if they lead to an infinite and endless good in some far distant sweet by and by. Can he always have it both ways? This is typical of the way he dances and dodges, weaves and wiggles, to avoid the bullet damaging to his scheme. Can suffering be both thoroughly evil and to be fought with every resource at our command and yet not "merely evil" but in fact the necessary means for our perfection? Is this an acceptable paradox or a contradiction employed by a theologian?

Hick outlines an elaborate system in which he imaginatively creates all the conditions and possibilities that will make everything come out fine.[27] When all the claims are added up, does it begin to look like a Rube Goldberg invention? It gets terribly complicated. Is his case so problematic that it needs all the propping up it can get? Even then, he has to appeal to mystery at crucial points to make it work. Or, to change the image, his theodicy reminds one of all those adventure movies in which the hero has many close calls, escaping death by the narrowest of margins time after time. Yet we know that neither villain's bullet nor jaws of wild animals will defeat the good guy. All will turn out well. Everybody will live happily ever after. So Hick's proposal, by his own admission, faces many formidable difficulties. At every turn a new threat arises, each fully capable, it seems, of finally undermining the whole thing. Lo and behold, every foe is vanquished. At the end of his book, he still maintains, modestly to be sure, while wiping his brow from all the struggle, that his theodicy, bloody but unbowed, survives as a possible option for Christians. Surely we can grant him that. Perhaps all the difficulties might also motivate us to seek another alternative.

A CONTEMPORARY MODERNIST ALTERNATIVE

The world does not appear to be the deliberate product of an infinite rational intelligence. Reflection on the evolutionary process suggests that it is more like an experiment that does not know in advance where it is going. It pushes forward urged on by a Creative Eros that hungers to create life with its capacity for enjoyment. God works opportunistically in and through the constraints and possibilities of nature and the freedom of creatures. Hence, human beings are not the deliberate product of Divine Purpose but a contingent occurrence. Within this framework the ambiguities of life and the reality of suffering are interpreted differently from anything traditional theists have envisioned. God aims at the good but is limited in power. The Source of value, God cannot prevent the evils that occur. Creative Cosmic Purpose has the character of love and intends only good but cannot guarantee only good outcomes. God is the Great Adventure whose life is the evolutionary spectacle displayed on earth and in the surrounding planets, stars, and galaxies. God is the Fellow Sufferer, who in travail gave birth in hope to this universe of ours with its perils and promises. God is the Great Companion and Comforter who is with us and for us in our agonies and ecstasies. This version of naturalistic theism will be developed further in succeeding chapters.

A Playful Fantasy

For the moment, however, I do not want to argue my views against John Hick. I want to accept his assumptions regarding the nature of God and the divine aim in designing the present world. It may be useful and even a bit of fun to play with the central question: Could a supremely good, omnipotent God make a world designed to perfect souls but with no or less natural and moral evil? To begin with, let us make an inventory of the sources of suffering and evil. Next we can speculate about which of these sources might be eliminated without introducing undesirable features or leaving out some that are essential to the best of all possible worlds.[28]

NATURAL EVIL: suffering and injustice arising out of nature and the nature of things involving no human irresponsibility (the tragic).

Internal causes: original design faults and congenital defects or later breakdowns in organisms that lead to cal, mental, or emotional illness or premature death.

External causes: destructive intersections of relatively autonomous chains of events -- chance occurrences, accidents, disease, natural catastrophes, and the like.

MORAL EVIL: suffering and injustice produced by irresponsible human intention, choice, and action (the sinful).

Religious and quasi-religious or ideological fanaticism, absolutism, and idolatry arising from a mixture of pride, self-interest, insecurity, good intentions, culpable ignorance, and folly; deliberate harm to others; pursuit of self-interest with indifference toward consequences for others; unintended harm from avoidable ignorance or carelessness; and the like.

THE AMBIGUOUS: suffering and injustice comprising an inseparable mixture of good and evil involving a tragic (natural) element that even the purest of moral aims cannot fully overcome:conflicts among and tensions within values, inextricably intertwined virtues and vices, uncoordinatable just aims of interacting individuals and groups, mutually exclusive nature of choices, necessary connection between the achievement of greater good (more complex and intense harmonies and enjoyments) and increased risk of worse evil (more massive and acute suffering), the connectedness among human beings that unites our individual sorrows as well as our joys, and so on.

THE DEMONIC: an enslavement to evil powers originating in sinful choice but constituting a tragic dimensions for others who follow in time: destructive patterns and powers arising in the past, involving a complex inter-weaving of free choice and determination by causes and circumstances, that become embodied in individuals, in families, and in whole societies and hence get passed on through socializing processes into the life his-tories of persons and groups from generation to genera-tion to constitute a Gestalt of evil, that may or may not be consciously entertained, that cannot be over-come by simple rational, moral decision-making, and that may in a given situation be so effective as to render the capacity of contrary choice ambiguous or null and void, yet without precluding possibilities of future transformation.[29]

How many of these sources of suffering and injus-tice are removable without making things worse? An omnipotent, omniscient Deity could presumably create a world in which all persons have sound, fully function-ing healthy bodies. The natural order could operate in accordance with a "pre-established harmony" in which no harmful accidents or disease occur. Even so, it could have variety, complexity, plurality, transformation, evolution, change, and novelty. Moreover, this world could be populated with persons of perfect moral char-acter -- or at least with a dominating predisposition toward virtue -- designed to produce only good acts. They would live justly in society and in intimate bonds of harmony with family and close friends. Assuming that perfect or mature character cannot be created instan-taneously even by an omnipotent God, we could at least presume that God might provide initial irresistible prevenient grace and guidance. This would insure that virtuous deeds would be forthcoming until such time as experience provided the opportunity to develop the maturity characteristic of fully moral persons.

The desirability of the world so far described is dubious. It is an infallible cosmic machine operating harmoniously and thus lacking any harmful contingencies.[30] Human beings in this proposal may have the power of voluntary choice in that decisions flow inevitably from character aided by grace. It has not so far been established that such persons can be given the capacity of creative self-transcendence requisite to the power of contrary choice without possibly spoiling the scheme. Moreover, unavoidable ambiguity has so far been ignored. So has the question of whether it is mortality as such or only premature and tragic death that raises serious questions of evil. Finally, it has been assumed that a world without any suffering is the most desirable world. Is this necessarily the case?

We are seeking, of course, a model of the best of all possible worlds, or at least a world that is equal in excellence to any possible world. We also seek the most desirable world, i. e., one that contains no intense, unnecessary, or pointless suffering but yet provides the features necessary for justice, happiness, and the full realization of the human potential for loving union with God and other people. The most desirable world may not be a possible world, but it would include at least the following features:

1. sufficient constancy in nature to make learning and the effecting of purpose possible and sufficient contingency, chance, unpredictability, and surprise to make life challenging, adventurous, wild, and zestful and to provide sufficient risk and danger to promote

profitable learning, development of skill, carefulness, and responsibility;

2. persons with the capacity of self-transcendence [spirit], i. e., feeling, thinking selves with freedom defined as the metaphysical power of creative choice;

3. an environment with conditions and possibilities necessary to develop morally and spiritually mature persons with the virtues and capacities essential to a community united in the love of God and one another. A worthwhile world must surely include these three features. Can they can be incorporated without admitting into our imaginary utopia the possibility and high probability of suffering of indeterminate and maybe massive proportions? The issues become subtle and difficult at this point. Let us, however, proceed in fear and trembling but letting imagination run free.

A profound dilemma arises. The combination of constancy and contingency in nature and the ability of human beings to originate events and thus initiate novelty introduces the possibility of suffering and injustice. The design of a world with pre-established harmony was intended to prohibit this. To eliminate the constancies and contingencies of nature along with freedom in humanity takes away necessary features of a good world. It removes the conditions that are essential if people are to learn, to carry out purposes, to develop responsibility, and to grow into spiritually mature persons. Is this not to back into the point that Hick was making all along and to vindicate his theodicy after all? Perhaps, but remember Hick's God is omnicompetent. Can God overcome the dilemma and preserve the requirements of zestful, adventurous living as well as essential conditions for the development of moral goodness? Hick's answer is that God cannot. I am not so sure.

Needed is a world with sufficient risks, dangers, and threats of unwanted consequences to motivate learning and to promote responsible behavior. Also essential are safeguards that prevent lethal outcomes or consequences that are more severe than necessary. Positive payoffs for those who play the game of life correctly are perhaps even more critical. Would anything important for learning responsibility be lost if someone who fell by accident or carelessness into a fire were merely allowed to feel pain intense enough to be an effective deterrent? Is it necessary for him or her to be mortally burned or to suffer excruciating pain for long periods? After all, don't we learn not to hold our hands too close to a lighted candle by non-lethal but quite effective deterrents? Do we require dangers of killing ourselves or permanently rendering our bodies useless or racked with pain in order for us to learn caution? Will not lesser threats that are temporary but non-lethal serve the purpose? God could, after all, adjust the threat to each situation without killing or permanently damaging people.

Or perhaps we can learn from computers. Suppose we got an error message when we did something that if allowed to proceed would do great harm to us or to others. Suppose the world refused to function for us until we gave the appropriate or at least non-lethal responses or signals. This might be sufficient challenge for the conscientious. For the stubborn, God might use the harsher treatment advocated above.[31] An omniscient God could surely create and adjust a motivation system for each person in order to get the desired results. We are dealing with healthy persons sound in body and mind and with strong predispositions to love God and other persons. Hence, the constants and contingencies of nature would only be modified when necessary

to prevent suffering or to motivate learning and responsibility. Yet God could at every moment make essential adjustments for each situation to provide enough
danger and unwanted consequences to do the job. This
could be accompanied by fail-safe methods to prevent
the painful goads from permanently or seriously maiming
the population.

Let us keep in mind that so far we have been
talking about the interactions of persons with non-sen-
tient nature. If we move to the harm that persons do to
other people or animals, further considerations enter.
What are the conditions most conducive to the development of true virtue and genuine love? We begin with
persons born with high intelligence, a wide range of
creative capacities, sound bodies, and a set of predispositions toward harmonious relations with others. Such
persons have the potential in due time by God's grace
and goading of evolving with the right stimulations and
a history of learning experience into mature lovers of
God and neighbor. Put such persons in a challenging
environment, surround them with opportunities, and
provide them with training to develop their potentials
in a secure and harmonious setting. We might expect
them to grow voluntarily into creative, loving, mature
persons who find fulfillment in contributing to and
receiving from their companions. Surely challenges and
opportunities to develop fully the creative powers of
such persons could be provided by an omnicompetent
Creator.

Hence, my thesis is that

1. if you put persons into an natural environment
with dangers associated with consequences sufficient to
motivate learning and to make responsible behavior
essential to pleasant living, and

2. if you endow them with a strong predisposition toward virtuous character and a spirit restless for loving communion with God in a world designed to prevent accidents that produce serious harm, and

3. if they are given bodies, minds, and spirits with no design flaws in their original equipment and no susceptibility to disabling illness, a laboratory of soul-making would result. There could be learning, development, creativity, novelty, excitement, challenge, and growth sufficient for zestful, adventurous living without severe or long-term physical or psychic suffering or injustice. Why would not such a world provide a likely possibility that persons would eventually come to see the merit of a life of loving communion with God and neighbor in which virtue and fellowship with God are freely chosen for their own sake?

Let us grant that the creation and preservation of such an ideal universe would require constant miraculous acts of God and large doses of prevenient and sustaining grace. I do not believe that these arrangements would prevent the maturing of persons who freely and truly love God and neighbor. It might even facilitate it. It might not even require billions of years of cosmic evolution or innumerable lifetimes for genuine spiritual perfection to occur. Even if it did take a multitude of lives and deaths, stretching far into the distant future, this is the scenario required in the Irenaean scheme of John Hick as well. Unless it can be shown that the proposed substitute for finding our way to spiritual maturity will not work no matter how long a time we give it, why is it not to be preferred?

Yet four additional problems have not yet been sufficiently dealt with. A. Virtuous persons ordinarily will not harm other sentient beings knowingly. We cannot, however, rule out the possibility that persons with the power of contrary choice may be irresistibly tempted on occasion to use their creative abilities to take advantage of other people for selfish gain. In that case, one must presuppose that God will endow persons with the spiritual graces classical theology promised to the elect after death (the ability not to sin -- Augustine) or gave the angels who never fell into rebellion. Or the rise of bad intentions and actions could be accompanied with curative doses of temporary physical disablement immediately while super-naturally protecting the innocent from the consequen-ces of attempted violence and injustice. Is this not better than punishing the wicked forever after this life with no hope for their being redeemed -- the reigning eschatology of orthodoxy for nearly two thou-sand years?

Would not the latter course, if it were indeed necessary, obviate the development of virtue for its own sake? Would not people be good and do right to avoid punishment or to receive reward? This might be the case at first and for a long time. Yet would not the lesson be plain that freedom misused is futile, that the irresponsible or immoral or non-moral life gets nowhere? Orthodoxy says that God will eventually frustrate sinners and punish them forever? Why not have punishment that fits the crime and accomplishes these ends here and now in the hope that wrongdoers will repent and turn freely to God and to the good for its own sake? Hick acknowledges that at first people live self-regarding, pleasure seeking, pain avoiding lives. Only in the long run do they see the futility of their wrong choices. Is there any reason to think that in my proposed world sinners would never come to the same conclusion without the excessive, irrational sufferings that take place in this world? Even if they didn't, they could at least be rendered harmless to others and constantly frustrated in their stubborn attempts to beat the system.

Is there only one set of conditions, the set that includes massive evils, within which persons can discover their true self-hood in fellowship with God? In Hick's scenario and mine scenarios souls are restless until they find their peace in loving communion with God. Why is there not hope in both worlds that they might eventually respond to the persuasive attraction of divine love and find their true destiny? Are undeserved suffering and excessive evil a necessary path to salvation, whereas deserved suffering and controlled evil are not even a possible path? Hick is willing to accept massive horrors, terrors, miseries, and harsh oppression as the necessary price for moving toward spiritual perfection. I am willing to wager that more benign methods may eventually work with far less pain and injustice than Hick's scheme allows or requires.

Good done because it is good is the ideal, of course. A loving God will surely seek human beings for as long as it takes until they are persuaded to respond freely with an answering love. The first concern here and now is for the one harmed. Shall we sacrifice victims for the sake of developing virtue in the victimizer! Are we to prefer the freedom of the evildoer to the life of the one harmed? The Irenaeans on the contemporary scene will say that of course we must, since the soul-making process takes multitudes of lifetimes and deathtimes. Meanwhile, since it is the only way that works, we must let freedom loose and live with the terrible consequences. If it is going to take such a long time to perfect souls anyway, then let us protect would-be victims at the moment and hope that

the development of virtue can be secured in some other
way with less misery. Furthermore, does not violence
unjustly suffered at the hands of others itself create
bitterness and the desire for revenge? Does not injustice tend to corrupt character, to engender hate, and
to set in motion chains of action and reaction by which
evil is reproduced over and over in vicious cycles very
difficult to break into? Is success in our wrongdoing a
means of producing character in either the perpetrator
or the victim?

It might help for the would-be initiator of evil
to experience fully and for as long was redemptively
necessary the feelings and sufferings of the victim had
the intended act been successfully performed. This
sometimes works when rapists are confronted with their
victims and murderers are set before surviving family
members and forced to hear their pain. This might
produce empathy for the other and remorse in the sinner. If we suffered the pain we intended to inflict on
another and felt the good we did for them, we might
come to love our neighbors as we love ourselves. We
would be our neighbors in the sense of experiencing
their joy and sorrow in so far as we contribute to
them. In any case, it is hard to conceive consequences
that would be worse than the present system in which
the relatively innocent are slaughtered daily.

B. The second problem is death. An omnipotent God
could simply grant everlasting time to each new created
person. It has never been clear to me why we must die
in order to go to heaven. It has never been explained
to me why persons can be miraculously sanctified after
death but not here and now. I have never seen a persuasive discourse making it plain why God has so little
problem overcoming death beyond this life but why it is
the unconquered enemy in this vale of tears. Why must

we die before we can become deathless? Hick, of course, speculates that between embodied lives we will live in a disembodied, mind-dependent state in which our desires are reflected objectively in the world, thus forcing us to come to terms with our real selves. Hence, the transition from one life to another itself contributes to the process.[32] Maybe, but must it be that way? If not, other alternatives are permissible. Finally, we must ask how essential immortality is anyway. If everyone could live out the full potential of a healthy, happy but mortal life under conditions of justice and prosperity, death would be less of a threat though still not as desirable as immortality.

C. The third problem is more difficult. Demonic evil would be eliminated by the perfecting of moral character. But will not ambiguity rooted in the nature of things be an inextricable part of every possible world? It seems to be fundamental to ours. In the ideal case, however, two factors decrease its threat to fulfillment. (1) The first is that persons of good will would be willing to adjust to the conflicts between competing values and aims and accept provisional trade-offs, given the assurance that next time the balance will be shifted in favor of whoever sacrifices most this time. (2) The second is a corollary of the first and essential to it. Given everlasting time to work it out, the problems raised, say by the fact that one choice eliminates the others for the time being, would not pose the same difficulties that mortal beings face. Virtues may also be vices. A gentle soul who always seeks harmony and reconciliation may fail to confront evil for fear of causing conflict. Hence, a more balanced set of moral habits might eliminate some of the worst features of ambiguity. This may be naively optimistic. Maybe all we can ever hope for is that the damaging consequences of ambiguity could perhaps be reduced to more tolerable proportions. Yet it gets more complicated. Any increase in capacity for greater ranges and depths of experience -- what Bernard Loomer calls "size"[33] -- means that perils rise with promises, possibilities of evil with possibilities of good, vulnerability with complexity, and so on. This fact appears to be unavoidable. Even for an omnipotent, perfectly loving God, some happiness-reducing ambiguity may be an ineradicable feature of finitude. Would this be true in heaven too? Maybe heaven as a perfect order with nothing to decrease the joy of the saints is not a possibility after all.

D. The final issue is perhaps most difficult of all. Is not physical and psychic pain essential to the spiritual perfecting of rational souls? Are not suffering and joy dialectically related to each other so that we cannot have one without the other? Do not the ills of this life purify our hearts as nothing else can? Are not many made perfect by their sufferings? Given this life and its conditions, as well as the facts and possibilities known through experience, a positive answer to each question can be defended. That moral growth can be facilitated by suffering is undeniable. Must it be that way? Is it not possible for persons to mature by processes of growth that do not require the massive horrors of body and soul that are characteristic of this world? Since we have no experience of any other universe, we cannot be sure. I hope that suffering is not the only road to perfection. Moreover, much suffering crushes the spirit, engenders bitterness, leads to hatred of life, and turns the soul away from God.

166

Why No Agreement is Possible

Oh, how vain are our speculations! Oh, how futile are our imaginings! I, of course, do not know how to instruct God in the design of the best possible world order. My point has been to object to some influential theodicies that have the effect of explaining away the badness in order to protect the virtue of God or to justify misery. I have played with a less tragic alternative that appears to have as good a chance of producing spiritually mature rational souls.

It may be that finite reality necessarily entails ineradicable ambiguities such that even an omnipotent God is caught up in a tragic dilemma: either a world of free rational body-spirits with possibilities of both good and evil or no world at all. If that be so, we can only speculate whether the risk of creation is worth it for God or for us. Is existence necessarily tragic? If so, there cannot be a perfect world of free and rational souls living in a natural and social environment in which neither the possibility or actuality of evil is real. If so, heaven is not possible.

If we had some absolutely certain reason to believe that a God infinite in wisdom, power, and goodness is indeed real, we could not on the basis of our feeble, finite, fallible experience prove that this is not the kind of world such a God might create. There may indeed be reasons unknown to us that could account for all our objections and explain why the evils of this world are compatible with divine existence so conceived. We cannot on the basis of what we experience in this life establish by reason the existence of a God as without flaw. Such was persuasively argued by David Hume in Part XI of Dialogues Concerning Natural Religion. But it is not logically impossible that God permits evil for a good and justifying purpose. That may be reassuring to some, but mere logical possibilities do not go far toward teaching us what is actually the case. Belief in the perfection of God despite suffering requires faith[34] for its foundation and eschatology for its vindication. Finally, one either has such a faith, or one doesn't. I have a different faith.

At this point we hit upon the reason that adherents of competing theodicies so seldom convince or even make points against each other. It is not primarily a matter of right reasoning, logic, skillful display of evidence, and the like. Errors in thought may occur, be recognized, and corrected, of course. The primary consideration, however, is that each theodicy constitutes a peculiar Gestalt with its own organizing center. Each thinker proceeds on the basis of certain assumptions or convictions that are, for that person, compelling. These core beliefs constitute the controlling center of the Gestalt. It determines what will be admitted as counting for or against a particular theodicy. Arguments based on principles and facts that are counter-indicative will be interpreted or explained away in ways that do not threaten the fundamentals that must be preserved. Every system of thought is validated on the basis of criteria internally generated that will not convince anyone who stands outside that particular circle of verification.

To put it differently, many points of view about evil become plausible if enough of the basic assumptions on which they are based are granted. Unfortunately, these fundamental presupposition cannot be shown to be valid. No set of these foundational premises can be known with certainty to be true, regardless of the strength with which they are held. At least, we cannot be sure when or that subjective confidence and objective truth coincide. A particular Gestalt may, of course, be undermined if enough anomalies develop internally or if the controlling center weakens or decays for some adherent. Creative imagination may then proceed to work out the details of a new Gestalt built on the newly dominant assumptions.

Hence, in the last analysis, what I propose is not to wreck the traditional theodicies by the power of argument, logic, and evidence. I simply suggest a competing Gestalt organized around a different set of intuitions that I find operating within myself. A theodicy stands as a whole as some particular reasoner is grasped by its controlling center. This is only another way of saying we all live by faith. We reason in the light of some perspective or another that determines what counts as evidence and how much weight is to be assigned to some fact or argument. I take this to be an Augustinian/Anselmic view of faith and reason.

To conclude, the final question is not what worlds could be if there were a perfect God unlimited in power, wisdom, and goodness. The crucial issues are: Given this world and its possibilities, what interpretation of our experience is most adequate? Which view of God and of human life is most satisfactory for coping with the world we live so as to maximize justice and joy and to increase the love of God and neighbor? The next chapters will offer a perspective on these questions.

ENDNOTES

1. Quoted in Kenneth Cauthen, Systematic Theology, p. 109. See John Calvin, Institutes, I, xvii, 12-13.

2. Millar Burrows, An Outline of Biblical Theology, pp. 206219.

3. Alvin Plantinga, God and Other Minds; God, Freedom and Evil; and The Nature of Necessity.

4. Stephen Davis, Encountering Evil, pp. 69-83.

5. It would be appropriate to ask why so many liberal Christians who reject biblical infallibility still hold to notions of divine perfection. I can only guess that surrender of either the unqualified goodness or the omnipotence of God is far more threatening and generates more sustained efforts to preserve belief in them. Yet the rational difficulties are no less in one case than in the other. To be more precise, either the need to believe in divine perfection or the support for such belief is stronger in them than the apparent contradiction created by the massive and absurd evils in the world, necessitating a frequent appeal to mystery to bridge the gap between experienced facts and a doctrine too precious to be abandoned.

6. Cf. Cauthen, Systematic Theology, pp. 132-155.

7. Emil Brunner, The Christian Doctrine of Creation and Redemption, pp. 175-185.

8. Denial of genuine evil is a major strand in classical theodicies, based on the notion that the presence of sin and suffering lead to an immense, greater, and justifying good that would have otherwise been impossible. A necessary means to a justifying end is at most a relative and not an absolute evil or may be regarded as only apparently but not genuinely evil.

9. Paul Tillich, Systematic Theology, I, pp. 269-270; Langdon Gilkey, Maker of Heaven and Earth, pp. 178-207; and John B. Cobb, Jr. and David R. Griffin, Process Theology, pp. 69-75.

10. By tragic in this connection I mean that the nature of ultimate reality is such that some desired good cannot be had without suffering, evil, or ambiguity. The tragedy is anchored in the fact that not even God can produce some goods without the cost of

unwanted suffering. To say that reality has a tragic
dimension means that the one and only, the only possible, road to heaven goes right through the middle of
hell!

11. I leave aside the question as to whether the
notion of "the best possible world" is a meaningful or
useful one. It seems to be it is, if we mean by it no
more than a world equal in excellence to any possible
world in its basic design and intention, recognizing
the fact that contingent events in any given world will
make it better or worse in fact and in detail than it
might have been or necessarily had to be. See Hick,
Evil and the God of Love, pp. 145-168; Davis,
Encountering Evil, p. 71.

12. Hick, Evil and the God of Love, pp. 327-331;
Davis, Encountering Evil, pp. 49-50.

13. Plantinga, God and Other Minds; The Nature of
Necessity; and God, Freedom and Evil; Davis, Encountering Evil, pp. 69-83.

14. David R. Griffin, Encountering Evil,
pp. 111-112.

15. Hick, Evil and the God of Love, p. 88.

16. Plantinga, God and Other Minds.

17. Hick, Evil and the God of Love, and Encountering Evil, pp. 39-52.

18. See Encountering Evil, pp. 67-68, and Evil
and the God of Love, pp. 304-316.

19. Anthony Flew, "Divine Omnipotence and Human
Freedom."

20. J. L. Mackie, "Evil and Omnipotence."

21. Karl Barth, Church Dogmatics, II, 1,
pp. 257-350.

22. Hick, Evil and the God of Love, pp. 266-277.

23. Granted, an unpredictable element always
attends freedom, if we mean by it, as I do, creative
self-transcendence or "limited creativity"
(Hick). Freedom normally is exercised in the expression of a given set of commitments, convictions, goals,
obligations, unconscious impulses, and so on that

define the operational Gestalt that constitutes "character." Freedom also involves the capacity to create a new Gestalt, to reorient the self around a new ensemble of motives, values, aims, and norms. This occurs when, for some reason, the previous functionally effective system becomes unsatisfactory, unworkable, or too full of anomalies to serve the largest and deepest ends of the self. A creative transcendence of the dissatisfied self may take place by an imaginative reconstitution around a new organizing center of aims and obligations that may be experienced as a spontaneous or intuitive conversion. This is the operation of freedom at its highest and marks the distinguishing feature of human beings in relation to what we know or suspect about other animals, although analogous operations may occur at many levels of nature. See, for example, Arthur Peacocke, God and the New Biology, pp. 133-160. New levels of organization have emerged, for example, in the evolutionary process. In human beings there is a self-conscious, deliberately self-directed dimension about creative self-transcendence that presumably is not present in analogous occurrences in the non-human world. The creation of a new Gestalt, however, is not arbitrary or uncaused even in this case but emerges out of the quest for the apparent good that in its operationally effective form constitutes the master motive of all human choice and action. It takes the form, however, of a new creation.

The situation is more complex than this in that the self cannot by merely taking thought change the actually functioning Gestalt. It is only when the operational system of motives, aims, impulses, and commitments breaks down existentially in the presence of alternatives that a creative reorganization of "character" can occur by an imaginative leap of the will. Every one who has experienced the overcoming of some unwanted or neurotic pattern of behavior knows that change is not easy, and we do not always understand just how it comes about. Sometimes it is experienced as a gift and not an achievement, although deliberate effort and consciously employed techniques can help in selected cases.

The choice of alternative means to achieve given ends occurs more easily, as do minor modifications of behavior that may be directed self-consciously in the light of rational deliberation in the light of some set of governing ends. My choice of "Baby Ruth" rather than "Snickers" at the candy counter feels like a kind of arbitrary choice that I just make by doing so. However, I never choose licorice because I don't like it. A minor Gestalt revolution would have to occur for me to forsake my present tastes in candy!

24. Hick, Evil and the God of Love, pp. 333-336.

25. See the discussion between Griffin and Hick on this point in Encountering Evil, pp. 103-104, 122-123, 129. Both appear to be right in some respects but less than totally correct in all respects. Hick is certainly right that the world would be better off if some particular evils did not occur. Hence, these particulars are genuinely evil. Hick does not have to show that every experience of suffering is necessary. In a contingent world, some evils that occur do not have to occur. Without them the world would be better off in that respect, from whatever standpoint whatever, taking everything into consideration. Griffin is correct, however, in insisting that if the fact of suffering involving some set of particular and real, even if contingent, evils that reach massive and excessive proportions are necessary and that they are justified in the end because they lead to an infinite good, then suffering in this case is, in Hick's own words, not "merely evil." i. e., not totally, only, and absolutely evil. In that sense are they not, in Griffin's terminology, only apparently evil? I think the discussion could be clarified if, instead of contrasting real and apparent evil, we distinguished between absolute and relative evil. The former are evils that are not justified by their being necessary means toward a larger good. The latter are evils that are still evil but only relatively so, since they are justified by their contribution to a larger good that could not have been otherwise enjoyed.

26. Evil and the God of love, p. 364.

27. Evil and the God of Love, pp. 337-386, and Encountering Evil, pp. 39-52, 63-68.

28. This, of course, was the procedure followed by David Hume in his Dialogues Concerning Natural Religion, Parts X, XI. In addition to the inferior quality of the present effort, my attempt differs in that I have tried to include, along with the goal of happiness, the concern of Hick that persons grow into moral and spiritual maturity in which they freely love God and each other. Hick engages in a dialogue with Hume in which he tries to show that to make the world a hedonic paradise is also to render it impotent to be a laboratory of soul-making. See Evil and the God of Love, pp. 322-336.

29. The category of the demonic is too complex to be discussed adequately here. In the background is the myth of superhuman or non-human bad spirits who produce suffering and evil in human affairs but whose own fallenness is a product originally of their own choice. Here it refers to a structural power of evil originating in the past operating effectively and systemically in human life and history in the present beyond the power of simple free choice to overcome in a given situation. Yet since the evil arises from the contingencies of free choice and not from natural necessities, the demonic can be overcome, at least in part, because of the capacity of creative self-transcendence in human beings. Its forms are many and diverse. It may be experienced by individuals as a compulsion or possession, an irresistible urge toward destructive actions known to be so and contrary to conscious intent. It may take the form of neurotic or criminal behavior springing from unknown unconscious forces rooted deeply in early childhood experiences. Parents who were abused as children may, despite their conscious intention, abuse their own. Individuals socialized into unjust social systems may in willing or invincible ignorance perpetuate them without ever being conscious of their demonic nature. Moreover, social systems may themselves be ambiguous, producing both creative and destructive results. Capitalism, for example, exalts individual freedom, distributes economic power, and generates wealth but leads to considerable inequalities and the concentration of wealth in private hands that is used to perpetuate privilege originally acquired by some combination of vigorous enterprise, good luck, fortunate circumstances, merit, and ruthlessness.

Seldom is evil deliberately done for its own sake but most often results from some idolatrous or overzealous or misguided pursuit of what is at least partly good. Circumstances shape but do not determine human decisions, although they may in some extreme cases. For example, slavery flourished in the South because of geographical and climatic conditions aided and abetted by the invention of the cotton gin -- all of which combined to make cotton growing profitable and to generate support of slavery from nature (following Aristotle) and by divine sanction (following Scripture).

Wherever the demonic manifests itself, it creates an enslavement that produces evil in individual and communal life. Yet since it originates in freedom, it can be overcome through freedom, but only through liberating experiences of grace in which the destructive power of the past is recognized in the presence of

alternatives whose promise of new life energizes choice
and generates structural transformation.

This usage is influenced by Walter Rauschenbusch's
notion of the "superpersonal powers of evil" in A
Theology for the Social Gospel, chapters VIII, IX, and
Paul Tillich's concept of the demonic as "a `structure
of evil' beyond the moral power of good will, producing
social and individual tragedy precisely through the
inseparable mixture of good and evil in every human
act." The Protestant Era, pp. xx-xxi.

30. Contingency is a complex notion. A contingent
event is one that happens but that might not have. It
is an event that is not wholly and in every respect
whatsoever determined. There are at least two
types: (1) events that result from the intersection of
two or more lines of activity (two airplanes colliding
in mid-air). Had the prior and contributing circumstances been different, the event would not have happened
However, the intersecting lines of activity might each,
as a relatively autonomous chain, be wholly or partly
determined within itself (two rocks colliding while
rolling down a mountain) and (2) events or entities
that internally exhibit or produce free, spontaneous,
or otherwise non-determined events or entities not
fully reducible to any set of necessary and unavoidable
prior causes. The entities in question may or may not
be persons. A free act of a person who has the metaphysical power of contrary choice would be an example
of the second kind of contingency. If sub-atomic particles exhibit a degree of objective indeterminacy,
contingent events will also occur at some level of
nature.

31. This, of course, sounds like the methods
advocated by the behaviorists. B. F. Skinner, in my
view, is not totally wrong, although there is a fatal
contradiction in the center of his system regarding
human beings. He assumes that people are totally determined and that they are free not only to imagine utopi-
as but to devise the necessary program to achieve them
through the procedures of operative conditioning. If
people are totally determined, they cannot extricate
themselves from the binding chains of necessity to
alter empirical conditions. If people are free to step
outside the chains of conditioned responses that determine their behavior, then his program of reconditioning
will not work as well as he claims, since the trainees
are presumably as free and as creative as the train-
ers. For his programs to work best, there needs to be
some relationship similar to that between a psycholo-
gist and the pigeon, a controller with great powers and

a controllee with limited powers in a controlled environment created or defined by the controller. For Skinner, see Beyond Freedom and Dignity.

However, we learn by positive and negative reinforcement in ordinary situations not contrived by a controller or conditioner. If we come in from the cold and stand by a fire, we can be positively reinforced by standing close enough to be warmed slowly but negatively reinforced if we stick our feet in the fire for a quicker thaw. We achieve healthy and satisfying results by learning in these natural situations in ways that do not turn us into robots. So why could not we learn as persons and not as merely conditioned pigeons if God manipulated our environment in ways that have the same kind of predictability that getting close to a fire has?

32. Hick presumably believes that for all of us living on planet earth at the moment, this is round one.

33. Bernard Loomer, "The Size of God," in The Size of God, ed. by William Dean and Larry Axel, pp. 20-51.

34. Faith is used here since I am not a rationalist who believes that right reasoning based on universal and objective principles can settle these matters. Reason in this sense cannot demonstrate for all competent reasoners by any combination of arguments the reality of God as a perfect being. Since experience does not provide a certain knowledge of the God of traditional theism, the only other recourse is an appeal to divine revelation, and that requires faith for its reception, however much it might be claimed that faith knows for sure. Believers may be convinced that their experience confirms, even it cannot establish, the reality of an Infinite Power and Goodness, but experience tells us very little until it is interpreted. Interpretations are notoriously diverse and contradictory. The same must be said for the intuitions and hunches that inform our reasoning. So faith -- meaning either trust in a divine self-disclosure or an intuition or hunch that unifies our experiences into some Gestalt of belief -- is the ground of our convictions about ultimate matters. Faith in the epistemological sense, then, refers to the organizing perspective that determines what counts and how much for and against a set of truth claims. We all live by faith when it comes to the understanding of meaning of suffering in this life.

Chapter IV
LIFE, EVOLUTION AND GOD:
THEOLOGICAL BIOLOGY

The universe is in the business of creating life. Never mind that we have no compelling evidence that organisms resembling those on earth have emerged anywhere else. Life could not have arisen once were the potential not resident in cosmic reality. Moreover, in a sense it took the whole universe the whole of its past to bring evolution to its present state. Hence, life on earth is a cosmic occurrence that requires an accounting. The potential for life realizes itself with zestful fecundity and tenacity wherever the opportunity arises. This chapter will argue that evolution and the manner of its occurrence suggest a Finite Purpose working opportunistically when and every way it can to create and advance life.

Postulating a Finite Cosmic Purpose moves between two alternatives: (1) the claim that the world process was designed by an Infinite Intelligence and (2) the denial of any cosmic purpose. Not only the reality of massive suffering but also the nature of evolution argues against an Omniscient Omnipotence. The cosmic process is an unpredictable adventure, full of hazards, replete with instances in which by a slight change of circumstances the cosmic trajectory might have gone another way.

Astronomer Bernard Lovell speculates that if the forces
of attraction between protons had been a few percentage
points higher shortly after the "big bang," no galaxies
or stars or life would have arisen.[1] Change the arrangements and interactions that occur at the sub-atomic level
minutely, and no evolution such as we know would have
occurred.[2] Contingency, chance, opportunism, and surprise
abound.

Moreover, life is fragile and encounters many perils
that may bring destruction any minute. Species emerge and
disappear. Uncounted multitudes of living creatures are
produced, large percentages of which are consumed by
predators or die prematurely because of conditions that
yield no food or are otherwise too harsh to sustain
them. All life, says Alfred North Whitehead, is robbery.
Eat and be eaten is the central fact for most species,
although some plants and animal do rot outside of the
digestive system of predators to fertilize the sea or
soil with their substance. It all seems an inefficient,
often cruel, wasteful sight. These points could be argued
at great length with numerous citations of examples and
with quotations from evolutionary theorists. While a
Perfect Omniwisdom might have chosen these procedures as
the means to create, other alternatives are more plausible. Does it, then, all add up to a picture of what David
Hume described two centuries ago as "a blind nature,
impregnated with a great vivifying principle, and pouring
from her lap without discernment or parental care, her
maimed and abortive children?"[3] Maybe, but perhaps a
Finite Purpose is working under constraints of prevailing
conditions doing the best it can under the circumstances
to bring life into being and to develop its potentialities to the maximum.

This latter hypothesis spells out an intuition
elaborated into a speculative hypothesis metaphorically

clothed to describe the facts and evidence provided by observation, correlated with the findings of evolutionary theory. The supposition that at the base of all things is an Adventurous Intentionality functioning opportunistically to produce life and to fulfill its potential is in conflict with no established facts of science and no rules of philosophical reasoning known to me. The alternative explanations of life and its evolutionary history springing from reductionistic, materialistic, mechanistic, deterministic philosophy are implausible.[4] They lack cogency in light of the attempt of reason to elucidate the full range of experience.[5] Much of the rest of the chapter will buttress the evidence.

So far, two points have been made. (1) The universe appears to be in the business of creating, perpetuating, and evolving ever more complex forms of life. This suggests a Finite Cosmic Purpose as its explanation rather than a meaningless nature blind as dirt. (2) Life on earth is a hazardous adventure replete with chance, contingency, inefficiency, and massive suffering. Again, this hints at a Finite Purpose as its source rather than an Infinite Intelligence. Point (3) is that life is a precious gift experienced as intrinsically good and desirable. Put more formally, life is potentially and essentially good, although in fact it may be full of misery, pain, injustice, and cruelty. Indeed, the agony of finite creatures, plus the fact that history is so riddled with natural tragedy and the subjection of the weaker to the powerful, make faith in the goodness of the Creator barely possible for some of us. Yet it must be as emphatically asserted that when the requirements of health and wholeness are being met, life is possessed of a vivid sweetness that is utterly wonderful, awesome, beautiful, and eminently agreeable. No one has been more

eloquent in giving expression to this intuition than
St. Augustine.

> Truly the very fact of existing is by some
> natural spell so pleasant that even the
> wretched are for no other reason unwilling to
> perish, and when they feel that they are
> wretched, wish not to perish but that their
> misery be removed. . . . Do not all irration-
> al animals, . . . from the huge dragons down
> to the least worms, all testify that they wish
> to exist and therefore shun destruction by
> every movement within their power? Nay, the
> very plants and shrubs, . . . do they not all
> seek to conserve their existence by rooting
> themselves deeply in the earth and by casting
> out healthy branches to the sky?[6]

This sense that life matters, that it has inherent
worth, is confirmed in our own experience that it is
good to be. Existence is pleasant, desirable, joyful --
until something goes wrong. When the requirements of
health and enjoyment are present, existence is its own
justification and is experienced as astonishingly pleas-
ing. Food, bodily integrity, and participation in a
nourishing community that provides love from intimates
and justice in the larger setting in a physically pleasant environment in which opportunities are available to
actualize ones capacity in creative work or play suggest
but do not exhaust the requirements of the worthwhile
life. For animals the list is shorter -- food, health,
a sustaining physical habitat, mates, and safety from
predators. Yet when we recognize that not all can be
safe, since the predators would die, a tragic sense of
life is inescapable. When something goes wrong, life can
be dreadful. When things go right, life cannot only be
pleasant but ecstatically sublime indeed.

Three aspects of experience are especially worthy
of note in spelling out how it feels to exist at the
primordial level. The appeal here is to basic human

awareness -- the sense of what it is like to be an existing self in this world. (1) The first fact is the sheer wonder at being alive, the astonishment that we exist, that we are present, conscious and self-aware. I refer to the startling experience that there is something and not nothing, that we are and that we know we are, that we stand out from nothingness as an experiencing subject.

(2) The second fact -- already alluded to and equally amazing -- is that it is good to be, that intrinsically and potentially, life is worthwhile, desirable, excellent, that existence matters. There are pleasures to be enjoyed and joys to be shared if enough goes right to fulfill this potential.

(3) The sheer fact that we are and that it is good to be carries with it the awareness that we did not produce ourselves. If this is not an immediate fact of pure experience, it surely requires only a minimal amount of reflection to lead us to the consciousness that something not ourselves gave us birth. We appeared without being consulted or voluntarily cooperating in our beginning. Our being in a world that is prior to us began without our agency. We were produced, we did not produce ourselves.

Having a mother and a father who begot us only pushes the question back to another level. What is the ultimate source of this coming to be and passing away? Even if we move toward cosmic history, tracing back the evolutionary process to some "big bang" billions of years ago, that does not solve the meta-scientific questions science cannot answer. How is it that the space-time/matter-energy matrix itself was there or came to be? What is the ultimate source of everything else? If the universe itself was always there, then it in effect becomes God (or some part of the God-realm).

Whether the universe was created by (1) Something Else
beyond it or (2) a Creativity within it or (3) emerged
from Nothingness, we are confronted with the impenetrable penetrable mystery of some Ultimate Givenness. How
is it that what Ultimately Is is the way it is, that it
has the character it needed to actualize the possibilities that have come to pass? A trans-scientific level of
inquiry is called for. This line of investigation comes
into play when human imagination searches for final
facts, causes, and purposes. Or perhaps rational speculation must give way to a receptive intuition that is
grasped by or infused with a Sacred Presence too deep
for words. All high religion testifies in myth, ritual,
and formal doctrine to the fundamental congruity between
what is deepest in us and the Ultimate Mysteries and
that if we live in tune with the Final Facts, all is
well. For me, the basis of religious response is a
grateful awareness that we came to be by the operation
of processes that we did not originate. This deepest
sort of knowing involves an intuitive sense of awe,
wonder, and appreciation in the presence of unfathomable
mystery. Science only touches but does not penetrate the
ultimate whence and why, the deepest meaning and purpose
of it all.

Life with its promise of delight is a gift from
beyond our-selves. While some simple sequences of reflection are involved, the experiences are primal. A
capacity for self-transcendence (the ability to make the
world and oneself an object of reflection) and the use
of language are required. Nevertheless, the sense of
being given a gift of a potentially good existence is
pushing toward a level of primal awareness. It is a
first level of witness about what it feels like to be a
self in this world. I do not argue, of course, that my

interpretation of this primal awareness is self-evident or beyond question.

Two lines of converging evidence, then, point to a plausible hypothesis regarding the Primordial Matrix out of which and by whose operations life has appeared on this planet: (1) the facts of evolution as exhibiting a hazardous but persistent urge toward the creation of life and (2) a set of interpreted intuitions about the sheer fact of existing as a self-conscious self experiencing life as a potentially and essentially good gift presented to us as a total surprise. The perceived and interpreted facts of evolution and the internal data of subjective consciousness lead to the postulation of an Opportunitistic Finite Purpose. At the heart of things is a Loving Intention to create and to evolve higher forms of life for the sake of increasing the range and depth of enjoyment. A Cosmic Eros hungers to actualize possibilities in finite organisms who, in their living, experience the joy of being.

Life is an end in itself. Life is for living and for nothing else. What is a cat for? To enjoy being a cat and to produce other cats who can take pleasure in living. Cats enjoy being cats. As long as they are well fed, watered, healthy, and exist in pleasant surroundings, they appear to be "happy." To say that the processes and events that make up being a cat are a set of neutral facts without meaning or purpose is preposterous. A sense of worth, that something matters, accompanies the fact of existing.[7] Every line of evidence external (interpreted observations) and internal (interpreted introspection) testifies to this primal truth.

The two lines of evidence are finally united, or at least connected. We who experience our existence as a good gift are a part of nature. Human beings emerged from the same Womb of Creativity that produced galaxies, dinosaurs, and cats. Our intuition that life is intrinsically desirable and valuable gives rise to the conviction that all life is worthwhile. Our individual experience is a particular clue to a universal fact. Life as felt from the inside coincides with and supplements the observed and interpreted facts of evolutionary history. The result is a hypothesis that is in harmony with everything that science has discovered. Science, as such, however, can neither establish nor contradict any supposition about ultimate meanings, origins, or purposes.

The appearance of life on planet earth, eventuating in the production of human beings who can ask what it all means, requires an accounting. The minimal claim made here so far is that an adequate philosophical explanation necessitates reference to Purposive Agency in some fashion. The nature of the telos at work in creation remains to be specified. That is primarily the task of the next chapter. At this point it will be useful to relate the philosophical and religious claims made already to (1) the current scientific understanding of the process of evolution and (2) the controversies in philosophical biology regarding the nature of life and mind.

LIFE, EVOLUTION AND PURPOSE

References to Purposive Agency are regarded with suspicion among many scientists. Contemporary biologists are generally of the opinion that the evolutionary process can be explained by random mutations in organisms that give them a reproductive advantage as determined by non-random environmental selection. The cumulative selection of reproducing survivors over many generations accounts for the origin of emerging species. Two primary processes are involved: random mutation (change in the transmitted genetic material) and natural selection (environmental determination of which offspring enjoy reproductive success). In the prevailing biological theory the first is a matter of chance, the second is a matter of law.

To refer genetic mutation to chance means that the changes are random with respect to the survival needs of offspring. Mutations occur (or may occur) by strictly determined mechanisms within organisms. Whether the mutation is advantageous given the environment into which the offspring are born is a hit or miss affair, a matter of pure coincidence. Chance only means some fortuitous conjunction of different chains of activity otherwise not directly connected. Each of these chains may be wholly determined by prior causes. Once this chance juxtaposition of mutated organism and environment has occurred, then, according to some, strict necessity takes over. Either the organism can survive and reproduce in its setting, or it cannot. These occurrences are, in the strictest sense, non-purposive. Is this the truth, the whole truth, and nothing but the truth about evolution?

Richard Dawkins thinks he has explained evolution when he elucidates the mechanisms of the process knowable by science. Random mutation and cumulative natural selection over a long period of time produce the organized complexity of organisms without any trace of immanent or transcendent design. This process of non-random survival gradually evolving organic stabilities makes the statistical improbabilities plausible and is the only workable theory ever proposed. Once, he says, our own existence was a mystery, but it is no longer since Darwin. Even so, to respond, this does not account for the fact that matter-energy so arranged into such hierarchical systems as nature produces had within itself the potential for producing life. This is not even to mention that this fund of matter-energy with its potential was there rather than nothing or something else! This is the real mystery, not the externally observable facts. However they got arranged, how is it that atoms and molecules can be so organized as unified wholes and how is it that they have the properties and exhibit the patterns of behavior they do? How is it that the further organization of these components into larger organic wholes produces life and later mind and consciousness? How is it that this potential is there to be realized when the proper forms of organized complexity are produced by evolutionary processes? The mystery is not only that something is present rather than nothing. The further wonder is that this something has the marvelous possibilities to evolve over time into the cosmos we are born into. Life itself with its capacity for enjoyable experience is the fact that begs for interpretation, not the mechanisms biologists can uncover. While the empirical processes known by science provide a necessary part of the total explanation, it is not sufficient.

Random mutation and cumulative selection may (or may not!) solve the empirical problem. It does not even touch the metaphysical mystery. Dawkins seems unaware that there is even a mystery after science gets through. Who is more impoverished in mind or spirit, the author of Psalm 104 who is without benefit of Darwin or the atheistic scientist who thinks that because he has Darwin, no mysteries remain.[8] At least Stephen Hawking, who believes that science will likely soon produce a complete theory about _what_ the universe is, thinks there is a question of _why_ to which we can all turn -- after physics has completed its basic work.[9]

Whether Cosmic Purpose is real is not a question that scientific methods can resolve. The combination of observations and theory that constitutes science can neither detect nor rule out the operation of subjective aims within organisms and within the world as a whole.[10] A scientific world view from which purpose is excluded as an explanatory principle can be sustained only by adopting a philosophical theory that restricts the knowable and the real to what scientific methods disclose. Such a view regarding the nature, scope, and limits of scientific knowledge can itself not be established by those methods of inquiry that constitute science. What observation statements count for or against the proposition that what is not detectable by scientific methods is not real? What necessary assumptions constituting the rational foundations of scientific inquiry dictate such a conclusion? Hence, the assumption that what cannot be known by scientific method is not only not knowable but is non-existent is a philosophical proposition. Moreover, it is a form of methodological absolutism that is vulnerable to careful analysis.

Science gains its precision and potential for testing its claims at the expense of total existential adequacy for interpreting the whole of reality in its full concreteness. The aim of scientific inquiry, I take it, is to provide a complete accounting of human sensory experience by a logically coherent body of theory that systematically correlates at appropriate points with relevant observations. While the distance between theory and observation may be bridged with complicated networks of intervening pathways and logical connections, what makes its laws, formulas, equations, symbols, generalizations, models, concepts, etc. scientific is that theory at some point is connected or connectible to some form of pertinent observations. If no possible or conceivable empirical (sensory) data at any point count for or against a claim, whatever its epistemological status otherwise, it is no part of science as presently practiced. Hence, what can be known and how it can be known is determined and limited by the sort of data that count in the determination of the truth or falsity or probability of scientific statements.

Science necessarily abstract from the whole in order to examine the data relevant for its purposes. This selectivity means that only what is thus admitted serves as a source of knowledge. If there is a more to reality than is thus abstracted, it escapes the methodology employed. This more, if it exists, can be safely ignored for certain purposes, for good reason and with good effect, as the success of science thus conceived powerfully demonstrates. Nevertheless, this success is achieved at the expense of turning what it examines into objects, void of subjectivity.[11] To declare that because science does not capture this more in its net, it is not real is to commit what Whitehead called "the fallacy of misplaced concretion," the identification of an abstraction with the concretely real.[12] If what is methodologically ignored is taken to be non-existent, the resulting picture of reality is faulty. In short, if mind and purpose are present within life at all levels, science cannot not discover it. This limitation is inherent in its method. As Whitehead says, a science that turns all its examines into objects that can be observed from the outside "only deals with half the evidence provided by human experience."[13]

Yet the issues are more subtle and complex than has so far been indicated. It is not that science so conceived cannot speak of anything that is not directly and immediately observable. However, the postulation of non-observable entities requires a chain of logical inferences and necessary (or possible) connections between the theory that requires them and some sensory observation or some set of them. The existence of the non-observable is known by some observable effect. Such theories may be joined with and reinforced by other established (or plausible) theories and their supporting observations. If, however, the data that might require such hypotheses are in principle not available from the observation of objects, then this situation would not arise. Success in explaining the mechanisms of evolution has been so spectacular that the skepticism of scientists regarding purposive factors may be justified <u>from a scientific point of view</u>. A biologist like E. W. Sinnott, who argued that "psychical activity," though non-observable is as real as "biological organization" that can be observed and, if presupposed, can account for what is observed got little hearing among mainstream scientists.[14] Hence, it may be that the view of the cosmos as a set of neutral facts void of intentionality is a conclusion to which science most compellingly points.[15] Only the scientific community can determine by its actual practice what theories are required in terms of its chosen methods. Philosophers will do well neither to ignore nor to make premature alliances with the prevailing outlook of the scientific community. Science gives us a perspective on the world that is defined by prevailing opinions -- involving both consensus and controversy -- within the community of scientific inquirers who accept each other's work as legitimate. Let us note that the dominant neo-Darwinian position on random mutation and natural selection is not beyond dispute on purely scientific grounds.[16] The history of science cautions us against taking any current theories as final.

In any case, the fundamental case for purpose in the universe must rest on grounds that transcend -- in principle -- the capacity of science either to establish or to refute. What science offers is relevant to, but not determinative of, the truth about Final Facts and Cosmic Intentionality. This decision arises ultimately as a primal response of the whole self. Such convictions about ultimates emerge in the context of historically developed frameworks of religious and cultural traditions individually appropriated.

At the root of philosophy and religion is a primordial sense about things felt intuitively and inescapably, a grasping and being grasped that is transrational. Yet this experience when interpreted gives reason its perspectival clue to the nature of the cosmos as a whole. Whether this is called response to divine revelation, a mystical a priori, enlightenment, discovery, inspiration, or what, this primal interprience is basic to all reasoning about ultimates. It means that finally all reasoning about Final Facts is circular. Our interpretations elucidate and finally confirm some deep intuition that is too powerful to be doubted. In this sense, we all live by faith and not by sight or reason alone.

The philosophico-religious faith undergirding this essay is that the cosmos as a whole and in all its parts is infused with Eros driving the evolutionary process toward self-transcendence of any present achievements. Process is infused with purpose, a craving for the good. Eros creates on the frame of Space-Time an evolving universe of ever more complex forms of life capable of enjoying their own existence. It is equally true to say that the cosmos as a whole and it all its parts is drawn by the lure of attractive possibilities that offer forms of actualization. Put otherwise, the possible becomes actual under the lure of the good, where the good refers to the self-enjoyment of experiencing subjects actualizing their potential. This partly conceptual, partly metaphorical, partly mytho-poetic form of expression elucidates an intuition about the nature of things. In the interest of existential adequacy for living the fullest possible life, we venture into trans-scientific territory. Into this region scientists as scientists cannot go but human beings must. Here reason and imagination are stretched to their limits in the effort to articulate depths of feeling pervaded by mystery and awe. At this level we know neither how to pray nor to think but can only hope that the Spirit will instruct us with "sighs too deep for words" (Roms. 8:26 RSV).

Hence, two kinds of questions arise: the theoretical and the practical. The theoretical hangs, in part, on conceptions of the nature, scope, and limits of scientific knowledge. It rests also on the validity of particular trans-scientific, religio-metaphysical judgments. The practical test has to do with the implications of cosmological theory for life in its full concreteness with its threats and terrors and its promise of pleasure in being. The nihilism, even if called humanism, resulting from a scientifically-based outlook that disconnects human aspirations from cosmic purposes is not only theoretically unsatisfying but pragmatically deficient. It requires us to believe that blind, lifeless, aimless matter has produced thinking, feeling, purposive beings. It also results in existential estrangement from the natural matrix that gave us birth.

LIFE AND MIND IN PHILOSOPHICAL BIOLOGY

We turn now to the nature of life and to current controversies about purpose as a factor in the functioning of organisms. What is life? How can the properties and activities of organisms be best explained? In what ways are the various levels of hierarchical organization related to each other? The epistemological, ontological, and methodological questions are baffling.[17]

Much confusion has grown up around the notion of reductionism. Problems are created by the fact of organized complexity. Organisms are hierarchical systems in which various levels of organization must be dealt with. Put otherwise, complicated issues arise around the relationships of wholes to parts. The disputes center around what can and cannot be reduced to or explained in terms of something else: higher levels of organization in terms of the lower, wholes in terms of parts. It will be helpful to distinguish between higher-level processes, on the one hand, and higher-level theories, on the other hand.[18] The first has to do with realities and is an ontological question. The second has to do with knowledge and involves epistemological questions. Can the higher-level theories of biology be reduced logically and epistemologically to the lower-level theories of the basic sciences of chemistry and physics? Can the processes of one level be reduced to and fully explained by mechanisms operating at a lower level? Can organized wholes be fully explained in terms of their parts?

Ernest Nagel has convinced a lot of people that theory or epistemological reduction is impossible. The laws and theories of biology cannot be reduced to the laws and theories of chemistry or physics.[19] The higher-level terms cannot be logically derived from the lower nor logically connected with them through the use of common terms. Concepts such as cell, organ, homeostasis, predator, etc. cannot be defined in physico-chemical language. Nevertheless, methodologically one might insist that reductionist explanation of wholes by parts should be explored as far as possible. Much is learned this way, whether or not it is fully successful.[20] Moreover, ontologically one may believe that the fundamental entities containing the properties and potencies from which all else is derived are those elementary forms of matter-energy dealt with by physics. Whatever they believe epistemologically about the logical relations among the various levels of theory and ontologically about the ultimate realities present in life, methodologically most biologists affirm the validity of reductionism. It is profitable to seek explanations of the higher by the lower, of wholes by the parts. This holds even for those who also insist that the system properties and processes of all higher-levels of organization and of whole organisms require treatment in terms appropriate for that level.

Generally speaking, three views of the nature of life may be distinguished: vitalism, mechanism, and organicism.[21] These positions describe a spectrum of views that crisscross, overlap, and shade off into each other in complex and subtle ways. A multitude of extremely slippery, difficult, and interconnected issues are involved. Problems of logic and of precise definition of terms beguile and trip up even the most seasoned thinkers. A statement may be valid if interpreted in one way or given a carefully restricted and specified meaning but misleading if taken in other ways. Hardly anyone is entirely satisfied with the way anybody else puts the matter.

1. Vitalism

Vitalism maintains that in addition to the physical properties present in non-living things, some life force or non-material vital agent must be presupposed to account for the activities, purposes, and functions exhibited in organisms. It is a dualistic outlook based on the premise that life is a different kind of reality that cannot be explained in the terms that apply to inanimate matter. Henri Bergson's notion of an elan vital[22] and Hans Driesch's postulation of an _entelechy_[23] are the prime examples usually cited.

The striking fact about organisms from worms to humans is that they exhibit apparent purpose. Biologists from Aristotle to Jacques Monod have noted this both in the observed behavior of living things and in the internal workings of their intricately interconnected parts. Why, then, should we not postulate the existence of mind or some purposive agency as the explanation or probable cause? Such assumptions have not proven to be scientifically fruitful or necessary. This is especially the case when some force or principle or entity has been postulated to account for gaps in present theory. When these gaps have been removed by the advance of scientific discovery, it gives rise to the conviction that eventually all phenomena that have been attributed to subjects -- to consciousness, purpose, choice, etc. -- can be fully interpreted in physical terms.

2. _Mechanism_

Mechanistic biologists need not deny that some behavior of organisms and some organic processes within organs and cells are "apparently purposeful." Their claim is that all such phenomena can be fully accounted for by reference to physical mechanisms either already discovered or potentially discoverable by physicists and chemists or at least by molecular biologists. Says Jacques Monod, ". . . anything can be reduced to simple obvious, mechanical interactions. The cell is a machine; the animal is a machine; man is a machine."[24] If all phenomena can be explained in terms suitable to a machine, then the postulation of mind or purpose to describe plants, animals, or people is unnecessary. It would be as foolish as employing those concepts to account for the reality and behavior of an automobile or an electronically controlled robot. Hence, to a mechanist, reference to <u>entelechy</u> (Driesch) to an <u>elan vital</u> (Berg-son) appears to be a violation of "Occams's razor," the principle that entities shall not be multiplied beyond necessity. Frequently quoted is Julian Huxley's remark that to explain evolution by reference to an <u>elan vital</u> is like explaining the motion of a train by an <u>elan locomotif</u>.

This brings us near to the crux of the issue. If there were physical phenomena or observable behavior that could not possibly be accounted for otherwise, then reference to some non-physical reality or principle or force might be acceptable. If investigation revealed missing causal links, gaps, leaps without connecting physical causes, functions without physical structures, etc., vitalists, might get a respectable hearing. How-ever, as long as hope persists that biological and psychological phenomena can be fully explained in physi-co-chemical terms, the mechanist creed will attract believers. At any rate, the implicit if not declared faith of many contemporary biologists was stated by Francis Crick, a Nobel prize-winner as a co-discoverer of DNA. He wrote, "the ultimate aim of the modern move-ment in biology is in fact to explain <u>all</u> of biology in terms of physics and chemistry."[25]

Mechanists, then, are ontological reductionists. They believe that life, in the last analysis, can be fully and exhaustively understood, in principle if not in present or future fact, in terms of the fundamental elements of matter-energy. This is, of course, the province of physics and chemistry. While new proper-ties, behaviors, activities, and capacities appear in organisms that are not present in the inanimate world, they are reducible ontologically without remainder to functions and effects of non-living matter when it is organized in a certain way. The favored analogy for this outlook is the machine. Life is a very complicated machine or is at least machine-like in its structure, functions, and causal connections. The most thorough-going ontological reductionists are "microparticulate derivationists," meaning that everything else is produced by and ultimately is nothing but the smallest particles of matter-energy and their interactions.[26] Any apparently purposive behavior of organisms and all teleonomic functions within the organism are the product of non-purposive mechanisms that have emerged in the evolutionary process. Explanations in terms of final causes are rejected, although the appearance of purpose is not denied. Given the elementary entities that compose the space-time/matter-energy continuum, their properties, and the laws that govern their behavior, all else can be accounted for metaphysically. Ontological reductionists may disagree among themselves on logical or epistemological grounds as to whether, or at least the extent to which, higher-level theories can in fact be reduced to lower-level theories. Nevertheless, the tendency is to urge that physics holds the key to everything with nothing left out, ontologically if not epistemologically, eventually if not now. Living organisms are nothing but complex expressions of certain highly organized forms of non-living matter.

To keep the classifications logically neat, we may distinguish between the extreme mechanists who affirm both ontological and epistemological reductionism and moderate mechanists who assert ontological but not epistemological reductionism. The latter are hard to distinguish from the weak organicists except in emphasis, attitude, and tendency.

It is difficult to understand the fierce hold of mechanism on so many biologists. Certainly it is related to the huge success of the life sciences in penetrating so acutely and minutely into the workings of nature. In particular, the achievements of molecular biology in recent decades are spectacular. A philosophy that allowed that there is more to life than science can ever tell us would still be in possession of that important part of the truth. Surely something else is going on here. Success perhaps has seduced its practitioners into an overweening confidence that scientific methods puts us in touch with bedrock reality. And does this get combined with some deep need for security, for some path to truth that offers closure and finality, for a way of knowing that frees one from the existential terrors of not knowing? Does it reflect some ambition for science to be the messiah of the modern world that can at last reveal the secret of existence? Now that priest, church, Bible, and speculative philosophy have been exposed as fallible, relative, and void of certainty, is the scientist the keeper of the keys to truth? Is the faith in mechanistic science as the only sure foundation of knowledge akin in spirit to the fundamentalist mentality in religion that craves something absolute? What accounts for the claim that the only source of true knowledge is "objectivity" (Monod)? What truly needs explaining is our own "subjectivity." Isn't it possible that "subjects" may be a necessary clue to the full understanding of the "objects" so prized by "objectivity?" Mechanism has to fly in the face of such obvious difficulties that surely more than disinterested devotion to truth is involved. At any rate, it is a philosophical faith not a simple elucidation of scientific knowledge.

Jacques Monod first declares that molecules, cells, organs, organisms, and people are machines, pure objects. Then he confronts with astonishment and shock the surd fact of mind, a free subject that can and must choose values.[27] A human being who can think, write a book about souls, and call upon others to choose between life and death is an anomaly in Monod's world. Thinking soul produced by a blind, purposeless process is a phenomenon totally inexplicable by the philosophy he espouses. Reflecting the themes of the French existentialists Jean-Paul Sartre and Albert Camus, he sees the universe as a cold, silent, aimless, meaningless collocation of atoms that has absurdly thrown us into existence. Monod speaks of living beings as strange. Even stranger is the outlook he shares with multitudes of contemporary scientists. Such reductionism cannot make sense of the central reality of concern, namely, us as inquirers -- hungry, even desperate, to find meaning and purpose in the mysterious gift of our own creation.[28]

As has been frequently noted, behaviorist psychologists and mechanist biologists who sincerely urge us freely to adopt their determinist, ateleological philosophies are exhibiting purposive behavior their conceptual schemes cannot account for.[29] By foregoing any consideration of internal mental events involving thought and intention in favor of external behavior that can be observed, B. F. Skinner is able to explain everything except Skinner purposefully engaged in truth-seeking behavior. His program for social redesign is trapped in an insoluble dilemma. If we are completely programmed by the environment, then no one, not even Skinner, can step outside the chain of causation in order to rechannel the behavior of others into more desirable patterns. If we are able to transcend our programming in pursuit of some freely chosen goal, then environmental determination is not absolute. The faith in mechanistic science is so powerful that not even the sheer contradiction involved in the fact of human self-hood can shake it.

A biological science that eliminates all subjectivity and purpose from non-human organisms is no less adequate as an interpretation of the full reality of life than is behavioristic psychology as a full accounting of human beings. For Skinner and Monod, science deals with observable objects and their behavior. Hence, if subjective purpose is real in nature, science so conceived could in principle never discover it.[30] Whitehead's statement of more than a half-century ago still holds. "Science can find no individual enjoyment in nature; science can find no aim in nature; science can find no creativity in nature; it finds mere rules of succession. These negations are true of natural science; they are inherent in its nature."[31]

3. Organicism

Organicists take a variety of positions in the middle. Some have much in common with the mechanists. Those to the other extreme overlap with vitalism. Minimally, organicists maintain that the appearance of life on earth introduces functions, properties, and activities requiring concepts, models, laws, and patterns of interpretation not reducible to anything else. However important, essential, and necessary reductionist explanations are, they are not sufficient to account for everything. At the same time, the higher levels of organization in hierarchical systems are dependent on and constrained by the lower levels and would not exist or function without them. Moreover, the laws of physics and chemistry are everywhere exemplified. Physical processes are nowhere transcended by the presence of autonomous non-physical entities, and so vitalism is rejected.

Methodologically, organicists typically insist that two kinds of approaches are needed: (1) holistic or compositionist inquiry that studies the properties of wholes and (2) reductionist studies that explain wholes in terms of the mechanisms and relationships of parts. Neither approach is sufficient by itself; each requires the other. The two are complementary and not in conflict. The total understanding of living beings requires an interdependent, multilevel approach.

Organicism includes a variety of approaches. Probably no classification short of describing everyone's views in detail will suffice. Nevertheless, a weak, a moderate, and a strong form of organicism may be distinguished.

a. Weak Organicism

The weak form is concerned primarily to insist on the autonomy of biological theories and laws and hence to deny that reduction can ever be complete or sufficient in all respects. These organicists may be content to insist that holistic as well as reductionist programs of research are necessary. New terms, concepts, and laws have to be introduced at the higher levels that are not present in explanatory schemes operating at the lower levels. Of course, many ontological reductionists (mechanists) agree so far. Epistemological and methodological organicism in this weak form does not seem to amount to much, except as a protest against the "nothing buttery" of the extreme ontological reductionists who think, on "microparticulate derivationist" grounds, that the reductionist explanations are the only ones that ultimately matter. Weak organicists do not agree that when the molecular biologists have finished their work and turned the rest over to the physicists, biology has nothing more to say.

b. Moderate Organicism

The moderate organicists go a step further, although it is a subtle point, as we shall see. They start with the assumption that new properties and processes requiring new theories emerge in higher-level wholes due to the more complex forms of organization. Moreover, the new properties are functions of the complex organization of the ultimately elementary parts but are not possessed by or inherent in them outside of organisms. Hence, they cannot be derived from them as such. Therefore, reduction is not only epistemologically and logically impossible but also ontologically questionable, if not wrong. Since the extreme ontological reductionist thinks that the new properties are derived from the interactions and organization of the elementary realities, the crucial but subtle dividing line seems to be here.

The moderate organicists focus on the newness and uniqueness of the relationships, processes, and functions that occur at higher levels of organized complexity. Hence, they are inclined to see something new in reality, even though they may describe it in terms of processes, relationships, and functions rather than in terms of new entities. Life and mind are atoms and molecules but atoms and molecules organized in special and complex ways in a hierarchy of levels that does indeed bring something new into the world. Yet they are determined to avoid vitalism of any form. They wish to account for the vitalist facts without reference to any vital agents or forces or entities operating on different principles than those found elsewhere in natture. Complex organization of atoms and molecules -- the same atoms and molecules dealt with by physics and chemistry -- is the clue to life. The crucial question is: What is the ontological status of the new processes and relationships produced by the specific kind of complex organization that is or produces the new phenomenon of life?

Do the moderate organicists believe that higher-level processes are in some sense autonomous with respect to lower-level processes? If so, they may be accused of slipping illogically from the highly-defensible notion of theory autonomy (epistemological or logical irreducibility) to a highly vulnerable doctrine of process autonomy (ontological irreducibility) without having sufficient ontological grounds for doing so.[32] Process autonomy, argues Morton Beckner, requires vitalism -- some agent that transcends physical laws operating at the lower levels and indeterminacy at lower levels. Moderate organicists are determined to reject vitalism. Hence, they may be in a dilemma. If they deny process autonomy, they are hard to distinguish from the ontological reductionists. If they affirm it, they may be forced into vitalism.[33]

Put another way, if they insist that life and mind are emergent realities, they may find themselves affirming a sharp discontinuity or dualism in nature. If they reject vitalism, how can they account for the discontinuity? It is not easy to explain how life and mind come from dead matter, from lifeless physical and chemical processes. They seem more prepared to accept frankly these "evolutionary transcendences" (Dobzhansky) and to affirm a dualism of matter and consciousness (Thorpe and Dobzhansky) than to risk even a hint of the dreaded vitalist doctrine.[34]

At this point the analysis has to shift to other grounds. The argument has to do with the metaphysics of organization. If complex hierarchical organization produces novel events, what is the organization of? Is there not something to be gained philosophically and nothing lost scientifically to assume that nature at all levels is life-like in character, everywhere involving both material and mental aspects, objectivity and sub-

jectivity? In this case evolution is the story of the
emergence of new forms and levels of mind-matter. The
higher forms of life are continuous in kind but different in degree in relation to lower forms of organization. Yet each new level produces entities that are
real as wholes, as real as the smaller organisms or
organic events that compose them.

My thesis, learned from Whitehead, is that there
are two kinds of wholes and thus two kinds of relationships in higher level wholes.[35] (1) Some wholes are
hierarchically organized systems of organic events or
organisms. All but the elementary units of matter-energy are composed of these life-like entities or smaller
organisms. Basic reality consists of organisms -- or at
least of organic events or systems -- large and small:
quarks, electrons, atoms, molecules, cells, organs,
organisms, and human beings. They are all subjects in at
least some limited or analogical sense. As subjects or
subject-like entities they exercise some degree of
self-determination in pursuit of internally guided aims.
Like human beings, whose experience of what it is to be
is the model for all basic reality, they have both a
mental and a physical dimension. To put it differently,
they are subjects to themselves and objects to others.

Perhaps a complete analysis would require a complex
classification of organismic wholes, ranging from the
more distinct individuality found in an atom, a molecule, an amoeba, a cat, and a human being, on the one
hand, to less individuated wholes such as cells, tis-
sues, and organs, on the other hand. The term organism
could then be restricted to the highly individuated
wholes. The term organic system could be used of the
less individuated wholes that nevertheless display a
significant degree of dynamic integration and unity.

(2) Some wholes are aggregates of the smaller organisms, or at least of life-like events. They are not themselves organisms -- pencils, planets, stones, automobiles, and machines of all types. These are wholes that are true objects with no element of subjectivity, self-determination, or individual purpose. Extreme ontological reductionists (mechanists) think of biological organisms as wholes after model (2). However, the ultimate composing parts are themselves objects, non-living and void of subjectivity. A living being is nothing more or not much more than an unusually complicated machine. At least it is machine-like in crucial respects.

Some ontological reductionists, however, are Cartesian dualists with respect to human life. They attribute process autonomy and free will to human subjects, for example, J. C. Eccles and Jacques Monod.[36] Leaving human consciousness aside in the weird case of evolutionary Cartesian dualists, problems remain. Even if new system properties and processes emerge as a result of the interactions and relationship of the parts, the causal power proceeds from below. The reality and the potency lie at the lowest levels. There is no reverse influence from the whole to the parts, from the unitary system to its components. The higher level is in no way determinative of the lower level, at least in a presently existing and functioning organism.[37]

Consider a car. It is a hierarchically organized system that functions as a whole. It contains a number of sub-systems which themselves have parts -- the motor, cooling system, electronic system, braking system, lighting system, and so on. The lighting system is made up of bulbs, sockets, wires, switches, electric current, and so on. Even the lighting system parts have parts. The mechanist might well agree that matter organized into an automobile exhibits functions and processes that are something more than the simple sum of its parts taken separately or as unorganized. It can move forward and backward due to the way the parts are systematically integrated in relation to each other. Total system functions becomes possible that are not mere products of the sum of the parts disconnected and thrown on a pile. Nevertheless, a car can be given a reductionistic explanation in materialistic, mechanistic, deterministic terms, level by level right on down to the relationships and interactions among the fundamental particles.[38] It should be noted, however, as Michael Polanyi has argued, that the "boundary conditions" are not so reducible. These are the principles devised by engineers that impose the order, relationships, and interconnections between parts of a machine. The "boundary conditions" are necessary so that it will function in accordance with its humanly intended purpose.[39]

Richard Dawkins specifically uses the analogy of an automobile to explain his biological views as a hierarchical reductionist. He snarls at those who think that to admit to reductionism is like confessing that one eats babies. The mythical reductionist is supposed to believe that complicated things are to be explained directly in terms of the smallest parts or even as the sum of the parts. The real reductionist -- at least the kind he is -- explains complex things immediately only one level down. He insists that, of course, "the kinds of explanations which are suitable at high levels in the hierarchy are different from the kinds of explanations that are suitable at lower levels. This was the point of explaining cars in terms of carburettors rather than quarks."[40] If one proceeds a level at a time, however, one reaches a final explanation in terms of the fundamental particles. In that sense, a car is to be inter-

preted in terms of interactions among the fundamental
elements known to physics. An organism is likewise a
hierarchically organized system of sub-systems and then
of organs, cells, and finally of molecules, atoms,
electrons and quarks. The biologist is done after arriv-
ing at entities simple enough for the physicists to take
over.

Here an interesting question arises. Presumably the
atoms and molecules in a piston behave the same and have
the same properties and functions as part of a functioning automobile as they do when the piston is thrown on
the junk pile later. Suppose we shift from a mechanical
system to an organic system. When the light metal sodium
is combined with the poisonous gas chlorine, salt is produced that is neither metallic nor poisonous. May it be
that the new relationships and properties that arise in
salt signify that organized complexity in an organic
whole is a different thing from organized complexity in
a car? Can it be that a different metaphysical view is
needed to account for that fact? Suppose we make the
organism the basic model of reality and use it analogi-
cally or metaphorically to understand everything else,
or at least all basic reality. That is what I propose to
do.

My argument is that the moderate form of organicism
needs metaphysical clarification. Do moderate organicists accept the analogy of the machine? Do they finally
agree that the really real entities and potencies are
those located in the fundamental particles of matter? If
so, can they build a satisfactory philosophical doctrine
explanatory of the novelty present in living organisms
and human beings? Can they do so merely be referring to
new levels of organization of the elementary particles?
Or is it necessary to refer also to the emergence of new
realities? Perhaps a kind of self-transcending material-

ism that accepts sharp discontinuities in nature but stops short of strong organicism or any form of vitalism will do scientifically. Yet how do the dualists who affirm the reality of the human self account for its emergence if its unique appearance is disconnected metaphysically from prior stages of evolution? Metaphysical clarification is called for.[41]

c. Strong Organicism

In the strong organicism adopted here, the organism not the machine becomes the model not only for understanding life but for understanding molecules, atoms, electrons, and quarks. Moreover, an explicit and intentional shift is made from substance thinking to event thinking. The real does not consist of things with properties but of processes with structures. The elementary processes are life-like pulses of matter-energy, patterns of vibratory happenings. They are finally local distortions or pleatings or enfoldments of space that take time to occur. Space-time/matter-energy forms a field or continuum that has unitary-organic, dynamic-creative qualities. Systems of these activities have the potential to transcend their present states and to reorganize themselves at higher levels in ever more complex hierarchical patterns that finally give rise to animals and human beings. Finally, all organic realities are life-like, having both a psychic and a physical dimensions. What is viewed from the outside by physics as patterns of vibratory energy has on the inside the quality of mental and emotional intensity. What the evolutionary process discloses is not so much the emergence of life and mind but of more complex forms of matter-energy that are at the same time higher forms of psychic life.[42]

Does organicism of this sort inevitably become a new vitalism at least in some weak form? Two points of agreement can be found with the vitalists. (1) Purposive activity is real and not reducible to the mere mechanisms of efficient causation. (2) Reality contains a dimension that is not directly observable or subject to proof or disproof by scientific methods alone. The fundamental difference is that dualism is rejected. Vitalism teaches that matter and life are two different kinds of reality. One is void of purpose and subject to mechanistic laws. The other is full of purpose and subject to laws of its own. Strong organism affirms that nothing is totally lifeless and mindless. Subjectivity and purpose are dimensions of every organic event at every level. A duality is present, however, since every organism or organic system has both mental and physical dimensions. Elements of efficient and final causation are required for a complete interpretation of every organic event. Hence, all organic reality is living or life-like and exhibits a duality between the physical and the psychic. This duality is present at the elemental level of nature and runs up and down the entire hierarchy of organized complexity.

The crucial point, then, has to do with what kind of vitalism we speak of and how it relates to the scope and limits of scientific knowledge. Scientists reject vitalism usually for one or both of the following reasons. (1) Life can be fully explained without reference to a separate and second kind of reality that operates according to laws of its own in sharp discontinuity from the physical realm. (2) It is not a scientifically productive hypothesis. Reason (1) is agreed to, since all nature is life-like and thus the needed continuity of reality and explanation is preserved. If vitalism means that some vitality or reality "exists in living organisms that does not obey the laws of physics and chemistry,"[43] process panpsychic organicism is not vitalism. This is true in the same sense that when a person freely chooses to wiggle a finger, no violations of the laws of physics and chemistry occur. At the same time, we must refer to a free agent who initiates a bodily movement. Moreover, since subjectivity and objectivity are dimensions of every organism or organic event, a theory of knowledge that sees everything as pure objects and explains everything in mechanist terms will, as Whitehead says, miss half the evidence. Panpsychic process organicism agrees with vitalism that there is a reality inaccessible to science, at least directly. Conceivably it might be postulated on the basis of what can be observed. Such a postulation may not be essential to science, since no observable breaks or violations of physical or chemical laws are involved. However, what is accessible fits more an organic than a mechanistic model. At every level of nature, parts serve the system purposes of wholes. To reason (2), then, one only needs to say that nature may not be arranged for the purposes of scientists. Science as normally conceived cannot ferret out all its dimensions. Things may be real that science as science cannot discover. Nevertheless, the kind of weak vitalism presupposed here may be a philosophical option that is irrelevant for science strictly speaking. While an organic model of nature can interpret the evidence available to science, the view defended here cannot be established or refuted by scientific inquiry alone. It is scientifically permissible but not required.

PROCESS PANPSYCHIC ORGANICISM

With this in mind, let me present a brief overview of the position that is to be developed. Consider two sentences. (1) "Jones is writing his will." (2) "Jones is making ink marks on a piece of paper."[44] The second statement may be describing the same event as the first

statement. Nevertheless, writing a will cannot be reduced to making marks on a paper with a pen. Other
conceptual schemes and realms of meaning and types of
events come into play. Writing a will requires a rational agent involved in a community that has created a
realm of legal and social meaning implied by the writing
of a will. Making the marks on the paper with a pen are
mechanisms employed by the agent to accomplish a purpose. When everything involved is taken into account,
making a will is neither identical with nor reducible to
making certain marks on paper with a pen. An ontological autonomy and a downward causation are involved from
the higher-level event (the legal event of making a
will) to the making of the marks on the paper. Yet no
laws of physics and chemistry are violated. Atoms and
molecules are present in and essential to the occurrence
of the event at every level. They are serving the purpose of the human agent.

We get closer to a usable analogy if we concentrate
on the events that lead from an intention in the mind of
Jones through the brain events thus excited to the
movements of arm and hand that guide the movement of the
pen on the paper. Mind has some autonomy with respect to
brain events. Moreover, mind events may not be totally
identical with the correlative brain events. Mind may be
more than simply the same event experienced from the
inside as the brain events studied by neuro-scien-
tists. Mind-brain identism may not be correct. At any
rate, some autonomy of mind events in relation to brain
events is present that is not reducible epistemologically, methodologically, or ontologically to the interactions of electrons and quarks. To exclude a human agent
with purposes using the mechanisms and organs of his
body leaves something out ontologically and epistemologically. The notion that nothing is going on here

but the interactions of elementary particles of matter is true only in a trivial sense. The atoms and molecules of Jones' body do not decide to write a will or determine the content of it. Jones does. This common sense fact must be given an metaphysical basis.

Physicists, chemists, biologists, psychologists, economists, sociologists, lawyers, historians, philosophers, and others could study the event (making a will) and its sub-events from the perspective peculiar to that discipline. Physicists can find molecules, atoms, and sub-atomic particles in Jones' brain and hand, in the ink, in the paper, and everywhere else. Biologists will finds cells and organs at work. Psychologists could seek motives and explanations of Jones' behavior, which might include shutting out some relative from the will.

This high-level event (the mind exerting influence on the brain) provides a model from which analogies can be drawn to apply to the reality and functioning of hierarchically-structured organisms. Organisms, as unitary functioning wholes, have system purposes ("self-programmed programs" -- Thorpe[45]) that are carried out by the organs, cells, molecules, and atoms that compose their bodies. Human beings have purposes that are consciously entertained; not all organisms do. All organisms are and have bodies with system purposes that are carried out by bodily parts that serve the interests and goals of the organism as a whole. At least we can say that organisms or organic systems are self-organizing and self-directing at every level including cells and bodily organs. At the higher animal level this self-directing is located in and carried on by an individual mind at some level. The snapping turtle who waits for a fish and then suddenly grabs it in his jaws is using the organs, cells, molecules, atoms, and electrons of its body to serve a system purpose. Surely we must attribute some emotional tones to the food-getting and mating activities of such animals, as well as elements of memory, perception, anticipation, and purpose. In an analogical way so is the amoeba using its more limited parts in sustaining its life. Purpose does not have to be conscious. Nevertheless, it may involve mind or something analogous to mind, even in cells.

Organisms as inclusive systems of high-level events are dependent on the lower-level processes that go on in their bodies. They are not ontologically reducible to those processes. No causal gaps appear in the patterns of activity that scientists can study from the level of quarks to the level of an egg becoming an organism. Biologists, chemists, and physicists can also discover causal mechanisms at work, patterns in the processes, laws governing events at the level appropriate to their discipline. Each level of organization in an organism from the total system level to the level of atoms and sub-atomic particles can be explained in terms appropriate to each successive level. By reference to the level below it and to all the intervening and cross-level dimensions, explanation can proceed down to the elementary particles. Each perspective abstracts from the whole by a selective process dictated by the discipline and the particular interest at work in a given inquiry. Every discipline may tell the whole truth from its standpoint and offer a perspective on the whole reality. No specialized discipline tells the whole truth about the whole event from the most inclusive perspective.

Metaphysical philosophy is the critic of abstractions and seeks the most comprehensive truth from the largest possible perspective. It can only be partially successful and never convincing to everyone. Philosophy has as its task the discovery of what is concretely real, the whole with nothing left out. This requires that the knowledge we have of ourselves as subjects, as purposive beings, be taken into account and incorporated within a comprehensive view of things. Since we are ourselves an instance of nature, we may generalize from our own reality as mind and body that life in all its forms at all levels is a unitary reality with two dimensions. From the inside we know ourselves to be experiencing subjects with bodily components. All organisms are, from this point of view, subjects composed on subsystems that are also experiencing subjects with bodily components. When observed or prehended from the outside by another subject, they are objects. As known to themselves from the inside they are subjects. These are not two distinct and separate realities but one reality with objective and subjective dimensions.

The brain as observed is a material object resolvable into electro-physico-chemical processes taking place in billions of interrelated cells. Mind is dependent on these physical processes but is not reducible to them. Minds are these physical processes in the brains, or some essential set of them, as experienced by a subject in terms of sensations, memories, thoughts, feelings, intentions, and so on. Minds are centers of activity numerically distinct but not ontologically independent of brain functions. For every psychic event there may or may not be a precise physiological correlate. Interaction certainly occurs between mind and body in which the causal arrows run both ways. Mutual influence takes place in some obvious ways. Anxiety may produce stomach distress. Drugs can alter psychic states. A subjective purpose can move arms= and legs. This view of organisms in no way contradicts any of the findings of science on its own terms. It insists that the whole reality has a private internal reality as a subject as well as an public external appearance as an object.

What is true at the human level may well be true at every organic level, including animals, plants, cells, molecules, atoms, electrons, and quarks. The mentality at each level can be correlated with the physiological structure that supports it. Animals with a central nervous system are different from and have more complex experiences than amoebas. Amoebas are different from molecules and so on. Yet when the categories of mind and body are appropriately extended and modified, the same duality between subject and object, mind and body may hold throughout nature. Even the entities studied by physics may be thought of as having an inner and outer dimension as indicated by Whitehead's claim that "the energetic activity entertained in physics is the emotional intensity entertained in life."[46] In the terms of Charles Hartshorne taken from Charles Peirce, we must speak of both physics and psychics.[47]

In short, then, I want to defend a version of panpsychic organicism that may oppose mechanism and reductionism more on philosophical than on scientific grounds. The fundamental issue has to do with what is concretely real, with what is evolving and emerging. The basic thesis is that all reality is or is composed of life-like events or organisms (quark, electron, atom, molecule, cell, organ, organism, human beings). Stones typewriters, cars, and the like are aggregates of the basic organic actualities. They are, as such, true objects lacking subjectivity, mind, or purpose. The organic realm is made up of a hierarchy of organisms whose functions and activities are partly autonomous and self-governing and partly determined by the causal mechanisms and interactions of its components. Systems of events that make up each level are internally related

or mutually dependent, mutually influential, working
interdependently with each other to create the whole of
which they are parts. Parts influence wholes. Wholes
influence parts.

Even an atom is not a thing but a system of interacting energy-events, a complex of social happenings.
According to the Pauli exclusion principle in a given
atom, no two electrons can have identical states. An
atom behaves like a tiny organism in which the whole has
properties that cannot be derived from its parts. Its
component parts in their togetherness exhibit laws
different from those that govern them in their isola-
tion. The parts and particles of larger systems lose
their individuality and function socially. They surrender in part their own autonomy to the governance of
the larger wholes. The particles appear to be local and
temporary manifestations of an underlying substratum of
vibratory energy. Space-time/matter-energy form a continuum in which smaller and larger organic systems
emerge at various levels of organization. Each new
emergent form has properties and functions not contained
by lower levels of organization. This principle may hold
from the subatomic dimension of matter-energy right up
the scale until human consciousness emerges in the human
brain.[48]

This way of looking at nature may be compared to
the views of three prominent thinkers. I have learned
from each of them. Alfred North Whitehead was an organismic philosopher whose views of more than six decades ago are still ahead of many biologists. Some of
them have not yet transcended the mechanistic outlook
that has long been outdated in physics. His words are
worth quoting at some length:

> The concrete enduring entities are organisms,
> so that the plan of the whole influences the

very characters of the subordinate organisms which enter into it. In the case of an animal, the mental states enter into the plan of the total organism and thus modify the plans of the successive subordinate organisms until the ultimate smallest organisms, such as electrons, are reached. Thus an electron within a living body is different from an electron outside it, by reason of the plan of the body. The electron blindly runs either within or without the body; but it runs within the body in accordance with its character within the body; that is to say, in accordance with the general plan of the body, and this plan includes the mental state. But the principle of modification is perfectly general throughout nature, and represents no property peculiar to living bodies.[49]

Biology is the study of larger organisms; whereas physics is the study of the smaller organisms.[50]

Arthur Koestler, a writer turned biological philosopher, takes this analysis a step further. An organism is a hierarchically organized whole made up of subwholes he calls holons. These are self-regulating open systems that have both the autonomous properties of wholes and the dependent properties of parts. They are thus "Janus-like," looking both upward toward larger holons or wholes and downward toward smaller holons or parts. Each holon is both self-assertive in manifesting its own individuality as a self-governing unit and integrative in subordinating itself to an existing or evolving larger unified system or holon or whole.[51]

Most important of all, in some respects, is the witness of Paul Weiss, an experimental biologist, whose views come from empirical study in the laboratory and in the field. Observation and evidence persuaded him to reject the "elementarian" extreme that individual cells are responsible for everything that happens in an organism. He also disregarded the "totalitarian" extreme that cells are under the unchallenged control of the organism as a whole. Instead, he found that at every point the cell is seen "partly as an active worker and partly as a passive subordinate to powers which lie entirely outside its own competence and control, i. e., supra-cellular powers." Again he concluded that the cell

> . . . is not just an inert playground for a few almighty master-minding molecules, but is a system, a hierarchically ordered system, of mutually interdependent species of molecules, molecular groupings, and supra-molecular entities; and that life, through cell life, depends on the order of their interactions; it may be well to re-state at the outset the case for the cell as a unit.[52]

Weiss concluded that two facts have to be kept clearly in view and reconciled. While (1) "the organism . . . acts as a unitary whole," nevertheless (2) much that happens "can be explained as a fixed linear sequence of component processes, i. e., through mechanisms."[53]

In short, a strong panpsychic process organicism maintains that explanations require reference both to (1) underlying causal mechanisms at lower levels that shape, constrain, and partly determine the organism from below and to (2) the self-governance of emergent realities acting from above as a whole whose parts serve the purposes of the unitary system. Hence, both epistemological reductionism and ontological reductionism are rejected. Neither the theories of higher-level processes nor the higher-level processes themselves are completely reducible to lower-level theories and processes. Autonomy and subordination characterize the functioning of organic systems that are both parts of larger wholes and themselves an intermediate whole. Not only new processes, activities, and relationships emerge at the higher levels of hierarchically organized organic systems but new realities. We must speak of new emergent entities that in varying degrees in different contexts can be thought of both as individuals as members of larger societies. Atoms and molecules that are themselves individual centers of purposive action. They are also societies made up of interdependent wholes. The degree of individuality and sociality may vary from organism to organism up and down the hierarchical scale and in different contexts. This must be determined specifically by careful empirical study and analysis in particular settings.

The degree of autonomy, freedom, and purposive creativity varies with the organism and context. The highest exemplification of subjectivity and mentality are found in the human organism with its powerful brain. Human consciousness is dependent on brain events but is numerically distinct. Mind possesses a capacity of creative self-transcendence as a center of thought, feeling, and choice that is unique on earth. The higher animals, we may speculate, have a lesser capacity. Presumably, as we move down the scale of complexity, consciousness or sentience or subjective awareness gradually fades until it is negligible. Subjectivity merges into organic functioning that nevertheless exhibits degrees of purposiveness centered in more or less individuated wholes that merit the analogical designation of mind. Psychic reality includes elements that are or are at least akin to perception, memory, anticipation, and feeling. We do not know what goes on in the subjectivity of a lion that has spotted food or a potential sexual partner. We may speculate that it involves at least as much emotional intensity as thought! Is there any reason to think that something akin to these dimensions of experience are altogether lacking in an amoeba? Experience in a molecule or an atom certainly is extremely remote from anything that goes on in a human being or a lion or even an amoeba. Nevertheless, the energetic activity present exhibits observed or postulated behaviors that may express an internal subjectivity that is appropriate to the their simpler organization.

Here we encounter the difficult problem of the difference between the interactions of parts in a whole that create new system properties and processes and that whole itself thought of as an emergent individualized agent that partly governs the relationships among its components. The autonomy of individual agents constituted as a society of parts, but distinct from the parts, may be relativity greater in human beings and the higher animals. As Whitehead claims, at this level we may speak of a "dominant occasion" or soul that is a center of consciousness and purposive choice. In highly organized organisms, mind rises above the bodily system, although it is in touch with bodily events. It is a focused center of psychic activity with real though limited powers of freedom and creative self-transcendence. The discreetness of a transcending individual agency is less in simpler animals and least in molecules and atoms. In the latter case, the difference between the autonomous agency of the individualized whole and the product of the interactions among the parts may be negligible.

Maybe there is a more distinct dividing line between organisms in which a dominant center is found (higher animals and human beings, e. g.) and those in which no such central center distinct from the whole, but part of the whole, is present. Charles Hartshorne speculates that in a tree the individual cells are on their own, responding to neighboring cells and to lower level entities -- molecules, atoms, and particles.[54] Nevertheless, is not the tree as a whole an individual with some rule-directed, self-governing, though not self-conscious, autonomy? Do not the cells serve the purposes of the tree as a unitary system of activities, even though there is, as such, no dominant center or "soul"?

The final question is: what is the nature of nature? Is it more like a system of organisms with mental and physical dimensions or more like a machine? The theory held by a given individual tells us something about the whole person. Probably no way exists to settle disputes at this level. A transrational hunch or intuition has the last world. Locating the mystery is the problem. All confront finally a kind of brute givenness about things, some ultimate thatness and whatness impenetrable by thought. This primordial thereness provides framework within which thought and explanation take place. Reason cannot explain the Final Fact but must accept it as the basis for all subsequent explanations. All finally live by faith, a perspective that arises out of a total response to the Totality as experienced.

The perspective briefly developed here cannot be demonstrated, but it violates no evidence known to me. Moreover, it has the pragmatic advantage of providing a humanly satisfying outlook. Persons are viewed in continuity with the whole of nature. Nature is seen to contain dimensions of purpose throughout that make it a more comfortable home for the end-seeking organisms that we ourselves are. Reductionist science posits a surd fact in the universe. Human beings are thrown up by accidents and necessities (chance and law) in a blind process. Hence, they are alienated from the natural matrix that gave them birth. In the cosmos I envision, it is easier to relate to Nature as Mother, although She often seems more terrifying than nurturing.

LIFE AND PURPOSE IN PHYSICS

I see no reason to deviate from the conclusion I reached twenty years ago:

> Scientific knowledge and metaphysical intuition can best be synthesized if the cosmos is regarded as a value-creating system of structured processes capable of self-transcendence. This statement holds as equally important an axiological and an ontological principle. Put together, these two principles indicate that the world is made up of, or at least contains, societies and series of events whose inner meaning is the drive toward the realization of experienced good and whose objective manifestation is analyzable into mutually supporting activities, spatially and temporally interconnected in a way as to constitute a unitary whole. In its parts and in its totality this nature aims at even higher, hence more satisfying, levels of achievement.[55]

Contemporary physics, I argued, seems to require an outlook that stresses two features of the physical world: its organic-unitary and its dynamic-creative character.[56] The first indicates that the universe is one and that its parts have a holistic, organic character in which internal relations as well as external relations are exhibited. Organism is a useful model at every level of reality, including the realm of molecules, atoms, electrons, and quarks. The second specifies the importance of time, process, the emergence of novel forms, and the drive of the universe toward higher levels of complexity and function.

More recent work with thermodynamics and physical systems offers corroboration of these features. Ilya Prigogine's work with "dissipative structures" is pertinent. He shows that certain open systems, ones that receive matter and energy from outside themselves, can maintain themselves in a state far from equilibrium. They can also, under the required conditions, undergo transformations that result in a reorganization at higher levels of complexity. The newly ordered systems can preserve a stable state. Then they reach new points of disequilibrium that are amplified. Finally, a still further reorganization takes place. The supposition is that something like this led to the production of the first living organisms capable of reproduction, muta- tion, and evolution. Out of chaos and chance come order and then disequilibrium and higher orders.[57]

Jacob Bronowski has spoken in a similar way of the principle of "stratified stability," a succession of temporarily stable states. Each stage contains the building blocks of the next level of evolution in a process that is continually open to future transfor- mations into ever more complex systems.[58] This principle seems generalizable extensively to include not only physical or non-living systems but organisms, popula- tions, and paradigms of thought. At any rate, organ- ic-unitary, dynamic-creative tendencies seem to be built into every level of reality from the beginning of this cosmic epoch that presumably began with a "big bang" many billions of years ago to produce at last the world we inhabit today.

I am tantalized by the suggestion of Samuel Alexan- der that "time is the mind of space."[59] Does the reality and duality of life extend even to the primordial level of space-time? If "time is the mind of space," is space the "body" of time? Are space-time energized and per- vaded with a restlessness, an urge toward realization of potentiality? Is the primordial stuff nothing other than primitive life in quest of adventure? Is the whole cosmos pervaded from the beginning with an erotic hunger for actualizing possibility in quest of higher levels of more experience and enjoyment? Is the drive toward self-creation, self-enjoyment, and self-transcendence resident in the original givenness of the universe? Are matter-energy the dynamic flowing, knotting, congealing, evolving adventure of space-time? Are space-time/matter-energy the underlying life/body-mind that is also the history of God as Universal Life/Body-Mind? Such thoughts are obscure at best. They do provide a principle of unity grounded in the notion of life as the mental-bodily reality of the world at all levels of realization.

Finally, this cosmic vision is an intuition about the nature of all things rooted in an experience of what it is to be as a psychic-physical unity. If our own being is the clue to what is, then it is plausible to generalize from our own evolutionary and embryological development to a hypothesis about the universe itself. Hence, my own philosophical reflections about the findings of contemporary science lead to the conclusion that "from the primordial matrix of space-time there has emerged a hierarchy of valuing, experiencing organic beings, whose own duality at the level of biological life may provide a clue to the nature of all reality."[60] Such ambitious musings are metaphorical and even poetic efforts to express the felt mystery of existence that is beyond articulation. At some level even scientists confident in their reductionism and mechanism are giving expression to a deep inner conviction that exceeds their knowledge. It is a pity that some of them have not yet caught onto this human fact. We all "see through a glass darkly" (St. Paul), walking by faith and not by sight.

In short, the universe is indeed, I believe, in the business of producing life and seeking its fulfillment. It is in that sense a value-creating system, since life is intrinsically worthwhile. Its existence is its own justification. Potentially and essentially, life is good. Actually and existentially, suffering may rival

enjoyment. Evil arises because of the tragic destruc-
tiveness and ambiguity implicit in finitude and freedom.
The remaining chapter will develop a doctrine of God
that fits this vision of the cosmos. The central theme
is that God is the All-Inclusive Life of the Cosmos
whose history is the ultimate environment of the adventurous evolution of life on earth.

ENDNOTES

1. Holmes Rolston, III, Science and Religion, p. 69.

2. Ibid., p. 71. Stephen Hawking makes the same point in A Brief History of Time, p. 125.

3. David Hume, Dialogues Concerning Natural Religion, p. 79. For a recent complaint against the processes of nature as cruel, necessitating that moral beings set themselves in opposition, see George C. Williams, "Huxley's Evolution and Ethics in Sociobiological Perspective," Zygon (December, 1988), pp. 383-407.

4. For an example of the mechanistic outlook that is rejected, see Jacques Monod, Chance and Necessity. For views closer to my own, see John Lewis (ed.), Beyond Chance and Necessity. Rolston, Science and Religion, pp. 81-150; Charles Birch and John Cobb, The Liberation of Life, pp. 44-150; John Cobb and David Griffin (eds.), Mind in Nature; Arthur Koestler, Janus; and, of course, the many writings of A. N. Whitehead bearing on the subject, e. g., Science and the Modern World, Process and Reality, and Modes of Thought.

5. For my previous account of the evolutionary process in relation to cosmic purpose, see Science, Secularization and God, pp. 90-130.

6. Augustine, City of God, XI, 27.

7. Cf. Whitehead, Modes of Thought, pp. 149, 184.

8. Dawkins, The Blind Watchmaker, especially pp. ix-xii.

9. Hawking, A Brief History of Time, pp. 174-175.

10. See Rolston, Science and Religion, pp. 81-150; Whitehead, Modes of Thought, part III. For a statement of my views on scientific knowledge in relation to philosophy and theology, see Science, Secularization and God, pp. 49-89.

11. This is explicitly how Jacques Monod describes the essence of science -- the only way to reliable or real knowledge. See Chance and Necessity, pp. 21, 3-33, 160-180.

12. See Alfred North Whitehead, Science and the Modern World.

13. Whitehead, Modes of Thought, p., 211.

14. See E. W. Sinnott, Cell and Psyche, Biology of the Spirit, and Matter, Mind and Man.

15. Cf. Science, Secularization and God, pp. 115-122. See Ian Barbour, Issues in Science and Religion, pp. 337-347, for a discussion of the many meanings purpose may have in scientific and philosophical thought. Some evolutionary theorists speaks of a "quasi-purposive" element or of the appearance of purpose due to the way natural selection works to give advantage to genes favorable to survival (G. G. Simpson, for example), but this has nothing to do with action of any purposive agents, cosmic or local.

16. David J. Depew and Bruce H. Weaver (eds.), Evolution at a Crossroads; and Mae-Wan Ho and Peter T. Saunders (eds.), Beyond Neo-Darwinism. See Michael Ruse, Darwinism Defended, and Taking Darwin Seriously, for an account of current controversies and for a naturalistic interpretation of Darwinian views of evolution.

17. The issues and controversies pertaining to the philosophical understanding of biology can be found in the following volumes: F. J. Ayala and Theodosius Dobzhansky (eds.), Studies in the Philosophy of Biology; John Lewis (ed.), Beyond Chance and Necessity; John B. Cobb, Jr. and David R. Griffin (eds.), Mind in Nature; Stanley Jaki, The Relevance of Physics, pp. 283-329; Arthur Peacocke, God and the New Biology, pp. 1-72; and Charles Birch and John Cobb, The Liberation of Life, pp.44-96. For sharply contrasting individual views, see Jacques Monod, Chance and Necessity; and Arthur Koestler, Janus. See also Ernst Mayr, Toward a New Philosophy of Biology, pp. 1-65.

18. The influence of Morton Beckner on this distinction has been widespread. See "Reduction, Hierarchies and Organicism," in Ayala and Dobzhansky (eds.), Studies in the Philosophy of Biology, pp. 163-177.

19. Nagel, The Structure of Science.

20. Karl Popper has argued that no attempt to reduce subjective experience to biology or biology to chemistry and physics has ever been fully successful. An unresolved residue always remains. However, nothing succeeds more than a successful reduction, and as a method of inquiry reduction should be sought since so much can be learned that way. See "Reduction and the Essential Incomplete-

ness of all Science," in Ayala and Dobzhansky (eds.), Studies in the Philosophy of Biology, pp. 259-284.

21. A brief but splendid history of attitudes on these positions can be found in June Goodfield, "Changing Strategies: A Comparison of Reductionist Attitudes in Biological and Medical Research in the Nineteenth and Twentieth Centuries," in Ayala and Dobzhansky (eds.), pp. 65-86.

22. See his Creative Evolution (1911).

23. See his The Science and Philosophy of Organism, 1907-1908.

24. From a BBC lecture. Quoted by John Lewis (ed.) in Beyond Chance and Necessity, p. ix.

25. In his book Of Molecules and Man, p. 10. Quoted in Arthur Peacocke, God and the New Biology, p. 1.

26. See Donald Campbell, "'Downward Causation' in Hierarchically Organized Biological Systems," in Ayala and Dobzhansky (eds), Studies in the Philosophy of Biology, p. 179.

27. See Chance and Necessity, pp. 20-46, 159-180. When he speaks of organisms as "self-constructing" and "self-reproducing" machines (and is not speaking metaphorically), that itself should warn us! I wish I could teach that trick to my Toyota. Apparently he means that organisms are not like machines but are machines, albeit very complicated ones.

28. Ultimately, we all confront a Final Thatness and Whatness -- the way things just are, the mystery of being -- that must be accepted. But Monod asserts a philosophy that itself confronts a surd reality not accountable for by the philosophy that was supposed to eliminate the unexplained within the empirical world itself. At this level theory ought to contribute to understanding not confound it by having to confront phenomena that should not be at all if the underlying assumptions of the system are correct. Descartes, his hero, at least had God to account for matter and mind. Monod has mind evolve from the machine.

29. For a behaviorist outlook, see B. F., Skinner, Beyond Freedom and Dignity.

30. I am reminded of the old story of the drunk who was looking around under a lamppost at night. When questioned, he announced that he was looking for a key he had lost in the vacant lot across the street and explained that he looked under the lamppost because that's where the light was, confessing that he could never find it in the dark.

31. Whitehead, Modes of Thought, p. 211.

32. Cf. Arthur Peacocke, God and the New Biology, pp. 13-26.

33. Beckner, "Reduction, Hierarchies, and Organicism," pp. 171-177.

34. For Theodosius Dobzhansky, see The Biology of Ultimate Concern, and his articles in the symposia edited by Ayala and Dobzhansky, pp. 1-2, 307-337, and by Lewis, pp. 131-141, and by Cobb and Griffin, pp. 19-24; for W. H. Thorpe, see his articles in the symposia edited by Ayala and Dobzhansky, pp. 109-138, by Lewis, pp. 1-5, and by Cobb and Griffin, pp. 1-11, 35-36. References to the other writings of these distinguished scientists can be found at the end of each article referred to. Thorpe says that he is so impressed with the discontinuities in nature that he is compelled to be a dualist but that if he ever were to become a monist, it would be of the Whiteheadian kind. He further agrees that internal purpose and self-programming are real in organisms. He also suggests that purpose cannot be spoken of in nature until life emerges and resists panpsychism. Hence, Thorpe is close to what I have called moderate organicism with its attempt at fine balance between mechanistic and vitalistic extremes and its knife-edge instability. J. C. Eccles appears to be a Cartesian dualist through and through. At every level below human consciousness he is a mechanist. But he asserts that consciousness is a not reducible to brain states. Moreover, human beings exercise free will that affects brain processes. In the language of Beckner, the higher level of human consciousness has some autonomy with respect to the lower level processes of brain events. He admits that he can give no scientific account of how this can be. See his article in the volume edited by Ayala and Dobzhansky, pp. 87-107.

35. Cf. David R. Griffin, "On Ian Barbour's Issues in Science and Religion," Zygon (March, 1988), pp. 57-81.

36. For Eccles, see his article in Ayala and Dobzhansky (eds.), pp. 87-107; for Monod, see Chance and Necessity.

37. Some insist that "downward causation" may take place over a period of time in the evolutionary sequence as natural selection edits the products of upward, physical causation. The jaws of soldier termites, useful for fighting but making it impossible for them to feed themselves, were selected only because a higher level or sociological division of labor had occurred whereby the workers fed the soldiers. Campbell, "`Downward Causation' in Hierarchically Organized Biological Systems," pp. 179-183.

38. See Richard Dawkins, The Blind Watchmaker, p. 12.

39. Personal Knowledge, and Science 160 (1968), pp. 1308-1312.

40. Dawkins, The Blind Watchmaker, p. 15.

41. Ernest Nagel, Ernst Mayr, Arthur Peacocke, and Morton Beckner are epistemological or weak organicists but ontological reductionists, although not exactly of the same kind in either case. Peacocke and Mayr are closer to the borderline of what I am calling moderate organicism, in that both make much of the fact of emergent relations and processes. Peacocke points out that ontological reductionism is not all of the same type. Sometimes it seems mainly a protest against vitalism. The stronger type urges that organisms are nothing but atoms and molecules and that when physico-chemical explanations are complete, nothing more important need be said. Not even Jacques Monod goes quite that far, since he says he knows of no good molecular biolo-gists who think the organicists could just as well go out of business. All those named in this note so far are ontological reductionists of the milder sort but have various opinions about what more there is to be said. For Monod and Richard Dawkins, not much more. For Mayr and Peacocke still more, so that they at least approach the boundary between weak and moderate organicism. With his stress on discontinuous emergence or transcendences, Theodosius Dobzhansky and W. H. Thorpe qualify as moderate organicists. Thorpe, like C. H. Waddington, was close to a Whiteheadian outlook and a philosophy of organism that applies to atoms and molecules as well. Charles Birch, Sewall Wright, and E. W. Sinnott are panpsychists and close to the strong organicism I advo-cate. Mayr finds touches of vitalism in the latter two,

although not the old-fashioned dualistic kind. Birch distinguishes between himself as a process organicist and panpsychist from Dobzhansky, whom Birch calls an emergent evolutionist, on the one hand, and from E. W. Sinnott, whom he calls a vitalist, but does not see himself as one. It is all very complicated. On the ontological question, perhaps it is better to think of a continuum, or several of them depending on what the issue is, that runs from the strongest kind of materialistic mechanism or monism, one the one extreme, through weaker forms of reductionism into organicism that on its strong side becomes panpsychist and finally ends, on the other extreme, in a dualistic vitalism.

42. Similar, although not necessarily identical, views are found in Birch and Cobb, The Liberation of Life, pp. 44-202; David Griffin and Ian Barbour, Zygon (March, 1988), pp. 57-88; Ian Barbour, Issues in Science and Religion, pp. 273-364; Charles Birch, Nature and God, and in Ayala and Dobzhansky (eds.), pp. 225-240; and John Cobb, David Griffin, Charles Birch, Charles Hartshorne, Sewall Wright, Ann Plamondon, C. H. Waddington, Arthur Koestler, and Richard Overman in Cobb and Griffin (eds.), Mind in Nature. I also find a kinship with the views of Arthur Koestler, Janus; and E. W. Sinnott, Cell and Psyche, and Biology of the Spirit. I find similar themes in their writings and have learned much from them, especially those influenced by the organicism of Alfred North Whitehead. Charles Birch is explicitly a Whiteheadian biologist. W. H. Thorpe is close. See the articles in the volumes edited by John Lewis, Ayala and Dobzhansky, Koestler and Smythies, and by Birch and Cobb. C. H. Waddington is not far from the Whiteheadian kingdom. Sewall Wright is a panpsychist. I am remarkably in agreement with myself as expressed in Science, Secularization and God, pp. 90-130. But I am not as close to Paul Tillich and Teilhard de Chardin as I was two decades ago.

43. Mayr, Towards as New Philosophy of Biology, p. 2. Mayr sees a remnant of vitalist notions in Alistair Hardy, Charles Birch, and Sewall Wright because they appear to "believe in some sort of non-material principle in organisms." p. 13.

44. This section has been influenced by the analysis of Morton Beckner in Ayala and Dobzhansky (eds.), pp. 163-177, although my final position differs from his.

45. W. H. Thorpe in Cobb and Griffin (eds.), Mind in Nature, p. 5.

46. Ibid., pp. 231-232.

47. "Physics and Psychics: the Place of Mind in Nature," in Cobb and Griffin (eds.), Mind in Nature, pp. 89-96.

48. See Ian Barbour, Issues in Science and Religion, pp. 294- 298.

49. Whitehead, Science and the Modern World, pp. 115-116.

50. Ibid., p. 150.

51. See Koestler, Janus, especially pp. 23-56, 289-311, and "Beyond Atomism and Holism," in John Lewis (ed.), Beyond Chance and Necessity, pp. 61-72.

52. Quoted by June Goodfield, "19th and 20th Century Reductionist Attitudes," in Ayala and Dobzhansky (eds.), Studies in the Philosophy of Biology, p. 78.

53. Ibid., p. 75.

54. I was gratified after becoming aware of this problem to find Charles Hartshorne, who usually has an answer for most everything, pondering the distinction between (1) members of a set of interacting individuals being influenced by each other and (2) any member being influenced by the whole formed by the whole set. He then asks what is added to the interactions among the parts (1) by speaking of the totality of these individual agents as itself an agent (2). See Cobb and Griffin (eds.), Mind in Nature, p. 66.

55. Cauthen, Science, Secularization and God, pp. 94-95.

56. Ibid., pp. 109-115.

57. See Peacocke, God and the New Biology, pp. 62-65, 133-160.

58. Ibid., pp. 156-157.

59. Alexander, Space, Time and Deity, II, p. 44.

60. Cauthen, Science, Secularization and God, p. 105.

Chapter V
THE GOD OF LIFE AND
THE LIFE OF GOD

Once only Possibility and Eros were. Nothing
else was, no-thing, no light, no darkness, no
time, no space, no water, no land, no fire, no
air. Eros united with Possibility, hoping to
give birth to Good. Possibility produced not
a living child but an egg. When they saw it,
they said, "This is not the Good we wanted;
let us destroy it." When they attempted to
crush it in their hands, it burst open in
blazing light. Thus was their daughter-son
born. When Possibility and Eros looked upon
the tiny, helpless infant, they were moved
with compassion. They loved the child and
called it Space-Time, whose other name was
Mixed Blessing. When they were in a philosophical mood, they called the child Ambiguous
Potential. The infant grew, spread out, and
moved ahead in all directions. Possibility and
Eros nourished the child and cared for her/him
as best they could. The child was wayward,
stubborn, slow to learn, capricious, frequently disobedient, and sometimes violent. Nevertheless, Space-Time was tender, loving, imaginative, ambitious, and resourceful. Possibility and Eros were now filled with hope and
again with despair as they watched their child
increase in size and ability. "All we ever
hoped for was Good," said they, "and what we
got was this unpredictable child who one day
promises to be the Heavenly One we sought and
another looks like the Bad One that above all
else we did not want." On their worse days,
they felt like killing Space-Time, but they

never did. It was not only love that stayed
their hand but hope that Mixed Blessing would
someday, somehow, become the Good child they
wanted. Still they hope. Still they weep and
wait.

A Modern Myth[1]

Where did the world come from -- ultimately? Nobody
knows. The reigning scientific theory informs us that
the universe has evolved over billions of years.[2] From
whence came the energy of the "big bang?" Whether ours
is the first or only the latest example of an everlasting (or indefinite?) series, we cannot presently tell.[3]
Are there worlds beyond our knowledge? We cannot determine how many layers of reality lie between our world
and what is ultimate. Maybe there was "nothing" before
the present universe, and something just began to be.[4]
Perhaps some primordial chaos or energized potential
generated from possibilities within itself initiated the
present trajectory of becoming. Unless one believes that
some relevant actuality is prior to every potentiality,
everything can be easily thought away except possibility and perhaps "nothing."[5] Possibility presumably just
is.[6] If so, what else is required to produce the world we
live in? As Immanuel Kant said, at this level pure
reason is like a bird with no air to fly in. Speculative thought at this level provides no certainty.
Agnosticism is the only defensible posture for human
beings with regard to Ultimate Mystery.

A DI-POLAR GOD

Many proposals have been made concerning Ultimate
Mystery and its relation to the world available to
experience. A brief list will illustrate the point.

PRIMORDIAL FACTORS	MODE	THE PRESENT WORLD
Gen. 1 God and Primeval Chaos	Fiat	Heavens and the Earth
Aristotle Actus Purus, Plato Forms, The Good, The Receptacle	Desire Construction by Demiurge	Formed Matter Formed Matter
Plotinus The One	Emanation	Chain of Being
Deists Deity	Design and Construction	World-Machine
Hegel The Idea	Dialectical Development	Processive World
Buddhism Emptiness	Manifestation	Phenomenal World
Naturalism Nature	Evolution	Evolving Cosmos
Alexander Space-Time	Evolution	World-Deity
Whitehead Creativity, God, Eternal Objects	Persuasion,	Processive World

---

Allowing for many variations and combinations, an oversimplified scheme of logical options would include the following: (1) The presently actual world began from "nothing" (creatio ex nihilo) by some absolute contingency or necessity (atheism or naturalism).[7]

(2) The presently actual world came from previous states of itself (atheism, naturalism, or scientific pantheism).[8] The world itself is everlasting, self-existing, self-sufficient finitude.

(3) The world exists in a necessary unity or identity with God to constitute an all-inclusive Whole (classical pantheism). The God-dimension is eternal, absolute, necessary, perfect, and immutable. The world-dimension may go through various stages and transformations.

(4) The world is everlasting in so far as its matter is concerned but is given form and concrete actuality by the operation of a Divine Reality (Greek theism).

(5) The form and matter of the world were created _ex nihilo_ by a Perfect Omnipotent Being who has total control over all finite things (classical Christian theism). A variant would be an Eternal Spirit of unfailing good will but with limited power to prevent or overcome evil.[9]

I propose a theory compatible with elements from all these types but not clearly identical with any one of them.[10] Uncertainty about final facts requires that several options be considered as possibilities. We cannot know, for example, whether the world is temporal, as (1) and (5) allow, or everlasting, as in (2), (3), and (4). Is pure possibility primordial, necessary, and eternal, or is it the first emergent from "nothing?" But even the emergence of possibility must have been a possibility. Types (1), (2), and (4) are most promising when properly construed. Types (3), (4), and (5) assume a Perfect Fullness of Being that does not fit well with a naturalistic outlook in which time, process, contingency, emergent evolution, and the ambiguities of life are taken with full seriousness. They become candidates only when rendered in some form of di-polar panentheism or neo-classical theism along lines proposed by Hartshorne and Whitehead. These two thinkers, however, also attribute unsurpassable perfection to one pole of the divine reality. I affirm a model of Imperfect Primordial Becoming.[11] An alternate version of (5) postulating an Eternal Finite Spirit motivated by love to create a world, whose growing life is the divine body, is a possibility that must be entertained. That alteration would move it toward a variant of (4). To types (1) and (2) I add Eros aiming at Ideal Possibility to provide meaning and purpose within am ambiguous cosmic process. What do these revisions add up to when incorporated into a vision of the God-world relationship? Answering that question is the next step.

Despite our invincible ignorance about ultimates, I will specify a set of factors that could be the ultimate explanation of the way the world has come to be.[12] The proposed theory is an attempt to give a credible and useful interpretation of experience in its widest ranges. I begin with the assumption that if something is real that once was only possible, some way is needed to account for the transition between that possibility and the present actuality. In the evolution of the cosmos over billions of years, something new has been produced. This suggests a distinction between the Created (our actual world) and the Uncreated (the primordial conditions explanatory of its emergence). If type (1) above in its most radical form is correct and something can come from pure, blank Nothingness by some absolute contingency (or necessity?), the Uncreated is "nothing" or Pure Possibility. Mere possibility seems insufficient to account for the emergence of something real. Cosmic becoming requires in addition to possibility a hunger for realization of the good -- Eros. I reason this way because "our own experience of creative becoming seems to involve the actualization of some possibility under the attraction of some ideal (the good)."[13] I generalize that experience into a primordial cosmic principle.

In any case, the Uncreated accounts for the fact that the Created -- the evolved and evolving cosmos that once was only a possibility -- now is real. God is the name given to the di-polar reality that includes the Uncreated and the Created. The Uncreated is the Primor-

238

dial Ground of the created.[14] The Created is the novelty
that emerges in time and in the processive cosmos. It is
the universe produced and being produced by the Uncreated Factors to which we have no epistemic access,
except through what is experienceable. The Created is
both God and is in God. I propose, then, to add to the
conversation a form of naturalistic panentheism. The
world is in God, but is not, as such, the whole of God.
To identify God with the World as a Whole, as Bernard
Loomer does, is to unify the Uncreated and the Created
into one concrete reality.[15]

The following scheme spells out additional formal
features of the di-polar God.[16] The term God when used
without specific reference to one pole encompasses
both. These polar distinctions are abstractions from the
concrete whole that is the one undivided God. The further task will be to clothe these descriptive structures
with content.

THE DI-POLAR GOD

THE UNCREATED	THE CREATED
Transcendent	Immanent
Utter Mystery	Limited Meaning
Ultimate Referent	Immediate Reference
Absolute	Relative
Eternal	Temporal
Necessary[17]	Contingent
EROS-POSSIBILITY	EVOLVING WORLD

In this form of empirical theism, God created the
world and us. This means that factors ontologically and
temporally prior to the presently actual world account
for our existence and for the possibility of meaningful
life. God is our Cosmic Parent, our Heavenly Mother-
Father. Following the earlier empirical theists, an

organism-environment scheme will be employed as a useful way of organizing our experience and giving us a comprehensive frame of reference. We are organisms living in an immediate environment of time and space and nature that sustains our bodies. God is the name for the Cosmic Environment in which "we live and move and have our being" (Acts 17:28 RSV). As far as he went, Shailer Mathews was on a useful track with his definition of God as the concept we have of "the personality-producing, personality-sustaining factors in the cosmos."[18] A more detailed and precise conceptual scheme than he provided is helpful for theoretical purposes.

GOD AS COSMIC ORGANISM

Let us, then, assume a distinction between the Uncreated and the Created. Uniting these aspects, but keeping them in mind, let us proceed. God is a Cosmic Organism in whom Divine Eros has woven on the frame of Space-Time/Matter-Energy a world, actualizing its potential in quest of Possible Good or Ideal Possibility. The Evolving World is the Created. The Uncreated factors are Eros and Ideal Possibility (Possible Good), with Space-Time/Matter-Energy as either a co-equal original partner or perhaps the primordial product of their union. Mythically, I imagine that Space-Time is the first child of Eros-impregnated Possibility.

THE DIVINE LIFE

SPACE-TIME

EROS   Evolving World   POSSIBLE GOOD

MATTER-ENERGY

THE GOD—WORLD

THE WORLD AS A SOCIETY OF ORGANISMS

It is (intrinsically) good to be, since potentially and essentially, being is experienced as good. Good occurs when the potential for enjoyment in experiencing subjects is being actualized in a healthy or just way. By experiencing subjects I mean primarily animals and human beings in whom there is subjective awareness or feeling that varies with the complexity of the organism. At the lowest level, this includes at least the capacity for feeling pleasure and pain. In the higher animals and in people, experience is much more complex and rich. At every level of awareness the distinction holds in some form between the positive and the negative dimensions of experience, i. e., enjoyment and suffering, happiness and misery, pleasure and pain, health and sickness, and so on.

Probably plants are not sentient. By analogy, plants, molecules, atoms, electrons and quarks (or perhaps strings[19]) may also be called experiencing subjects in the sense that they are individuals or organic systems with life-like characteristics. They are able to act selectively and responsively with their environment to actualize their potential. Plants certainly do live out a life in which their potential is more or less actualized. We recognize readily the difference between healthy and sickly ones. Below the level of sentience, enjoyment is identical with healthy functioning. Health refers to a state of activity characterized by dynamic organic wholeness in which the structures, processes, and components of an organism function to facilitate the maximum fulfillment of potential. Put otherwise, a healthy organism is one in which all its parts work in a mutually supporting fashion to achieve and sustain the normative goals and functions of the system as a whole and of the larger systems of which it is a part.[20]

In these extended senses it seems plausible to suggest that reality is made up finally of nothing but experiencing subjects or organisms large and small.[21] The primary ingredients of the universe, then, may be thought of as life-like events or as systems of such events. They are organized activities or energies with a career or history intent on actualizing their potential.[22] This philosophical view conflicts with nothing in contemporary physics regarding the elementary particles or of the universe as a whole. Its aim is to provide a cosmic and human meaning to physical theories and equations.

Life, I believe, is the best candidate for a universal category that applies at all levels.[23] Human beings are somewhere in the middle between the largest and the smallest entities in the universe. We get our clue to what life is from our own experience of what it means to be and to aim at some internally guided end. As far as we know, only human beings and other complex animals are conscious. Nevertheless, by analogy we may extend the abstract concept of life -- the process by which ends internal to individual entities or societies are sought -- down to the smallest elementary particles and up to include God. Symbolically, God may be considered as a Cosmic Life whose aim at self-realization is also an aim at self-realization for all sub-societies and individuals within the Divine Body. God is both the All-Embracing Society and the Universal Individual.[24]

At some point in the evolutionary drama, organisms emerged with the capacity of subjective awareness or feeling or sentience in the ordinary sense of the terms. Below the animal level, if the term experience is to be used, it refers to organic functioning in which life-like units of energy at various levels and combinations in larger systems interact with their environment in accordance with their natures and potentials. Subjectivity may exist at every sub-human level, if that means only minimal capacity for some degree of contingent initiative or response or selective activity guided by internal ends, which by analogy can be called creativity or freedom. In all organisms, then, good, experience, and enjoyment refer to healthy systemic functioning or dynamic organic wholeness. In some middle range organisms -- human beings and other animals -- experience, enjoyment, and good are connected with some form of inner or subjective awareness, sentience, or consciousness.

GOD AS PERSON

We have no way to determine whether God is everlastingly conscious, an emergent consciousness, conscious only in finite consciousness, or not conscious at all. God can be imagined metaphorically as a Cosmic Person whose body is the world. In other contexts, God can be thought of as the Mind of the cosmos. While we have no compelling basis for saying that such a Mind or Person exists as a self-conscious subject of experience, we do have experiential reasons to affirm that God is present to and operative in experience as if God were a self-conscious experiencing Person. Life is experienced as a good gift from God. Possibilities of meaning and enjoyment are generated in life processes that are cosmically produced. Pragmatically, it would be the same in terms of the events of real life in all its public and private dimensions if God were an intelligent, purposive, conscious, feeling Person.

The world process can be described, then, as the possible becoming actual under the lure of the good. Eros is the hunger for actualizing potential that yields satisfaction or enjoyment. It is the driving energy that pushes the process into creative advance. The Cosmic Organism is driven by Eros in quest of the Good. Or God may be described as the Life of the World, where life means the process by which potential is actualized in

accordance with internally guided ends. This Adventurous
Life is in the process of actualizing the potential of
the cosmos. Internally driven by eros in quest of the
good, the body of God lives and grows. Organisms, whether God or goldfish, are driven by eros "to live, to live
well, and to live better."[25] God may be metaphorically
described as the World as a Whole struggling to actualize to the fullest in variety and qualitative richness
the potential of the Primeval Atom as it exploded and
evolved into the expanding galaxies and into earth's
biological evolutionary spectacle. God is the Cosmic
Life in whom we live our lives.

In such a metaphorical scheme, sin and evil may be
compared to a cancer that destroys life by disrupting
the processes that sustain the life of the host
organism. Human suffering is a wound in the body of God
felt alike by the finite organism and the Cosmic Organism. Analogously, we can say either, "When my foot
hurts, I hurt," or "I hurt in my foot." In fact, in this
scheme, God has no pain that is not, in that sense,
related to the pain of one of the members of the divine
body. In this framework, the imagination is set loose
with a rich potential for developing images that relate
us to God in ways grounded in immediate human experiences that are identifiable and specifiable.

SPEAKING OF GOD

Symbol, image, and metaphor are being used with no
particular discrimination among them. Analogy might have
been used as well. The precise definition of each in
relation to the other is a matter of considerable controversy. Is symbol different from metaphor and analogy
or identical with the one in contrast to the other or a
general term encompassing both plus perhaps other non-
literal attributions? Disputes about the matter cannot
be resolved. We do not know, cannot know, the exact way

in which our language does or not correspond to or correctly describe in some fashion the objective referent. Metaphors, symbols, and images specify an element in our interpreted experience of God. They point to God as experienced and believed in. They relate something felt as God to the whole of our experienced and interpreted world. They are valid for us if they function effectively in that way. Precise definitions and discriminations among the variety of non-literal references to God may be useful for some purpose.[26] It will be sufficient for the present purpose to say that these terms indicate similarity between some known finite reality and the experienced reality of God. More precisely, they suggest a likeness or identity in one or more respects between the symbol and that which is symbolized but unlikeness in other respects.

A myth presents a set of religious and philosophical convictions in the form of a story about the gods. To talk of God as a Person who thinks, feels, and acts like a human being and who does things in the world is to use language mythically. Ordinary language, including anthropological terms, referring to finite realities are employed to interpret experienced aspects about God or ultimate facts. Myths are not literally true, of course, but they articulate felt meanings that function pragmatically as if they were. They intend to point to something really present in the objective sphere that cannot be precisely expressed in the vocabulary used. Mythological statements do not misrepresent the ultimate situation in so far as the significance of reality for our experience is concerned. They are existentially adequate and religiously useful though not conceptually exact. My myths assume the world-picture of present-day science as incorporated into a philosophical scheme that intends to explicate the religious meaning of reality as experienced.

We cannot be sure how accurately our myths, concepts, and metaphors describe objective reality. We can live by the faith that reality as experienced is not misrepresented by our functionally operative theories. Our language is not misleading and, therefore, not untrue in the pragmatic sense. If it functions to provide understanding and a way of coping with life that leads to the actualization of the potential for meaning and enjoyment, it is validated. The most adequate religious vision would be that one that led to the maximal actualization of the possibilities for justice and happiness in this world. It may be that a plurality of visions may function equally well in this regard. In so, they are equally true if they meet all the standards of theoretical and practical reason within the perspectives that sponsor them and for the persons who believe them and live by them. This does not mean that anything goes. We must stand by and even fight for, at whatever level of defense or offense is appropriate, those values produced by religious visions that are essential in our minds to justice and human happiness.[27]

A GOD WHO ACTS

In the Bible God has a direct and immediate relationship to every event. It is as though God says to the sun every morning, "Get up, and do it again."[28] God acts ordinarily and faithfully in the regularities of seedtime and harvest and of night and day to maintain the natural order. God acts in extraordinary ways on certain occasions to achieve a particular purpose. Whether in normal or exceptional events, God is directly and immediately the source of all things. God sends the rain, hardens the heart of tyrants, rolls back the water of the Red Sea, and raises Jesus Christ from the dead. All this occurs in a straightforward way so that God is presented as an Agent who acts among other agents (Ex. 3:2-4; Ex. 14:21; Jonah 1:4, 17). As the supreme and sovereign ruler of all things, God's will is law and God's word is irresistibly and instantly effective. No autonomous realm of natural law or of secondary causes stands between God and the world (Is.19:24). At the same time, God may govern through intermediaries such as the kings of Israel (I, II Samuel). Moreover, God may employ the intentions and actions of human beings as instruments of divine purpose (Is. 10:5-11; 45:1). To this extent, the general history of the world in which the free choices of individuals and nations have some independence are caught up in a specific salvation history by which ultimately God's aims are accomplished.[29] This is a mythological view of the world. When taken literally, it becomes a naive outlook on things.[30]

What shall we make of this today when nature is seen as embodying laws, patterns, and parameters to which there are no exceptions? The network of events is uniform throughout so that each local phenomenon stands in direct continuity with a history that defines the boundary conditions it will obey in form and effect. The whole of nature is a continuum that displays no breaks with the universal features that govern the occurrence and interrelationships of events. Even if there are non-determined contingencies, unpredictable happenings, emergent novelties, and elements of chaos, they exhibit an overall structure that governs all events. They happen only when requisite conditions are present and take place within limits defined by the total context in which they occur. Hence, all events fall within a range that does not violate the general patterns that pervade all things. Whatever elements of surprise, creative chaos, and objective indeterminacy may be present, this

in no way lends support to the possibility of miracles
that supernaturally disrupt the natural order with
whatever elements of determinism and indeterminism it
ordinarily contains.

In this setting, God is not seen as a Sovereign
Agent who alters the course of events at will.[31] Nevertheless, for an empirical outlook the question becomes
one of evidence. Does experience require a place for
exceptions to the general order of things (where order
is an inclusive term that includes whatever elements of
chaos, objective indeterminacy, creativity, novelty, or
unpredictable contingency that an adequate scientific
view of the world requires these days)?[32] It is a subtle
and complex question.[33] While miracles in the traditional
sense cannot be absolutely ruled out, they play no role
in this account of God's activity.

What, then, shall we conclude? Three propositions
must suffice for the moment. 1. We can develop no theory
of how God acts in the world that can be known to correspond exactly to the facts. Physicists may now be on
the verge on discovering ways of understanding everyday
things like pendulums and turbulence.[34] The story is that
on his deathbed Werner Heisenberg, the great quantum
theorist, revealed that he would have two problems for
God: relativity and turbulence. He was convinced that
God could answer his questions only about the first![35]
Should we not be modest, then, about proposing theories
about God's activity in events?

The most compelling attempt to provide such a grand
theory in recent times has been made by Alfred North
Whitehead in Process and Reality. His cosmology meets
tests of internal coherence, adequacy to evidence, and
applicability to specific areas of experience as well as
any attempt is likely to do. It is also relevant as a
guiding vision when its moral and religious implica-

tions are spelled out in ordinary language for persons
unequipped to handle (and uninterested in!) the formidable metaphysics involved. As a pragmatically useful
theory, the philosophical vision of Whitehead has much
to commend it. In what sense can it be held to be
true? If it does not provide a description that corresponds exactly with the facts, shall we regard it as
a philosophical "myth,"[36] a likely story? Yes, but in
that case is it not unnecessarily complex, detailed, and
ambitious for its purpose? A more modest proposal is
offered here.

2. While God's ways with the world cannot be described literally, our theories attempt to elucidate
something experienced (or at least thought to have been)
and thus in that sense objectively real in the nature of
things. Framed in concept, myth, metaphor, and symbol,
our theologies relate what we otherwise experience and
believe to the ultimate questions of life. Our beliefs
about God must connect with and satisfactorily elucidate
our ordinary experience. Theology attempts to relate
worldly experience of self, others, and nature to final
matters of fact. How shall we speak of God acting purposefully in ways that make sense of life in the context
defined by our existence in the world we inhabit?[37]

Suppose we say that "acting purposefully" involves
one agent (or more) among other agents performing public
(in principle) deeds at particular times and places in
an external environment that lead toward a consciously
intended goal. A baseball team or a man cutting firewood
would exemplify this standard paradigm. God does not fit
this pattern exactly. God as the Unified Whole is, in
one sense, an agent among other agents, one causal
source among many. In an equally important sense, God as
the All-Inclusive Society is at work everywhere all the
time in and through the whole system of finite beings,

causes, and purposes. Again, God acts not on things external but on things internal to the agency in question. Moreover, finite actors operate within the framework of laws and processes that are given, not of their own making. God is either the source of such structures, or they define the structure of the divine being. Finally, God does not alter some events among others, as does a man cutting firewood. Rather God works in and through the whole set of operations that constitute nature and history to accomplish the divine purpose. Hence, since the world is the body of God, it may be useful to hold that God acts in the world analogous to the way we act through our bodies.[38]

We must proceed with caution, however, since at least three distinguishable meanings can be assigned to this analogy. (a) Finite agents act on entities that are outside and other than themselves, as, for example, when we use our limbs and muscles to pull a saw back and forth to cut wood to burn in a fireplace.[39] Nothing is external to God in the sense that saws and wood are external to us. (b) We also act within our bodies, as, for example, when our internal organs digest the food we eat.[40] "I digest my food," and "My stomach digests my food" are alternative ways of expressing the same thing in ordinary language. We also grow new cells within our bodies and create thoughts in our minds. (c) Midway between are the processes by which we consciously move parts of our body.[41] A mental purpose affects cells of the brain that in turn initiate muscles and so on. Like (a) this results in or in part involves a particular, public, external act (or a series of them) consciously intended, but like (b) it has to do with operations internal to our own being, in this case, the translation of a mental aim into a physical event. Since the rele-

vant points can be made under (a) and (b), (c) will be
ignored here.

(a) We can speak mythically of God as an Agent
working in the world, striving and suffering with it,
creating, judging, and redeeming its creatures, and
directing all things toward fulfillment. Translated into
concepts, this means that in and through the structures
and processes of nature and history as a whole and its
parts, a creative purpose is present. When we assert
that God acts purposefully in the world, we point to a
telos that is present in things. Eros is active by which
the possible becomes actual under the lure of the good.
When we speak of God acting, we refer to the goal-seek-
ing activities in nature, the inner-directedness in
things that drives them toward an end.[42] Nature discloses
a capacity for creating new organic wholes capable of
more complex forms of functioning. Emergent evolution is
the story of the creativity and purposiveness that
unfolds in cosmic and earthly history. Component parts
serve as means by which the aims of an organism to live
and to strive for fulfillment are achieved. The molecules, cells, organs, and systems of organs within
living beings function cooperatively and interdependently to achieve the goals of the organism as a whole while
mutually sustaining each other.

Purposes pervade the workings of nature. When we
say that God acts, we refer to this telic dimension in
the world. God works in and through the whole system of
nature with the aim of actualizing the potential for
enjoyment in organisms large and small. God's aim for
all finite creatures is to increase the quality, intensity, and richness of experience. God's will seeks
pleasure, enjoyment, justice, happiness for all human
beings. God wants to increase loving relationships
within the community of persons and between all people

and Her/Himself. All processes that increase richness of experience and enjoyment are the work of God. This includes what went on in the first few seconds after the "big bang" by which the course of cosmic evolution was set. It embraces what occurred when hydrogen was turned into helium. Later God was at work in the hot, deep interior of stars producing the heavier elements essential to life on earth.[43]

Put simply, to say that God acts means that we detect purposiveness in the world that is accounted for by reference to a Final Fact. God has <u>a general purpose</u> to actualize possibility in quest of the good and <u>particular purposes</u> for particular occasions to increase enjoyment in living beings. God is involved as Ultimate Ground wherever an occurrence takes place that contributes to the achieving of those purposes. In short, the story of life and its evolution can be told mythically in terms of the outworking of Cosmic Personal Purpose. To speak mythically means to tell a story about God that functions pragmatically to enable us to understand and to respond to something real in the cosmos. We speak knowing that the story, while not literally true, is adequate for its existential or practical purpose. Since it is not taken literally, questions about double causation of the same event do not arise. The mythical claim that God acts has to do with the perceived meaning of existence and of the purposes detected immanently within the processes of nature and human life.

(b) As the self, a bio-spiritual whole, works through its members to actualize its potential, so God as the Universal Society may be seen as acting through the systems and subsystems of the world to actualize the potential of the divine life. The organs, cells, and molecules of the body work together to sustain the functions of the system as a whole. Each part carries

out specific goals that are marvelously coordinated so
that the overall goal of healthy functioning is a-
chieved. Even more instructive for the purpose at hand
is the fact that from the moment of conception the
developing organism organizes itself so that orderly
growth toward maturity is set in motion. The fertilized
egg becomes an adult human being by a set of internally
guided processes aimed at the actualization of the
potential within it.

When the mythical interpretation suggested in (a)
that imagines God as an Agent working purposefully in an
external environment is translated into conceptual
content, it merges and becomes identical with the metaphorical interpretation of (b). Both ways add up to the
same vision of the world in relation to God. In summary,
to speak of God acting intentionally in the world to
achieve ends means that the cosmos may be thought of as
a Divine Life in process of actualizing its potential. The Divine Life has a di-polar nature whereby we
can distinguish between the world process (God as Created) and its ultimate foundation (God as Uncreated).
God as the Cosmic Whole including both the uncreated and
created dimensions is both a Particular Individual (the
unity of the All) and a Universal Society (the system
that contains all other systems).

3. While God is present in all events, not everything that happens in all respects is the direct causal
result of divine action, except in a sense to be specified. This qualification is necessary in order to make
a place for freedom in the creatures and to account for
evil without making God fully responsible. Human freedom
is the capacity to originate genuine novelty. It is
creative self-transcendence that involves the power of
contrary choice (at least in some complex, limited, and
varying sense). In one respect, of course, God is the

source of all that happens. All that is non-ultimate ultimately proceeds from what was or is ultimate. This holds for the free acts of created beings and for evil that results immediately from proximate sources, even if these free acts or evil occurrences could have been otherwise.[44] God creates creators of free acts and contingent events. God, as the Source of the sources, is indirectly the source of all things,[45] although evil occurrences are not the intention of God.

As noted before, many options are available for conceptualizing the Final Facts in approximate plausible correspondence with the facts of experience. Speaking mythologically, if God has loving intentions but lacks the power to fulfill them perfectly, many of the evils of life can be accounted for. God is limited by the free choices of the creatures and by the structures of finite reality. Moreover, the possibilities for good and for evil are inextricably intertwined so tightly that ambiguity is inescapable. Speaking empirically, if human beings experience a creative love in those nearest to them and a loving creativity at the base of things, they may be moved to respond with gratitude toward God and love toward neighbor despite the threat of destructive evils and frustrating ambiguities.

Speaking mythically, God's special work is generating the cooperative response in creatures that is necessary to actualize the potential for enjoyment given with the gift of life. God's general work is creating the foundational structures and processes that make life and its fulfillment possible. Both the special and the general work are mediated through the eros in all life that drives it toward the good. At the human level, conscious discernment of divine purpose can facilitate a cooperative response that enables people to attune themselves to the divine intention. They can strive opportunistically with the facts of life to maximize creative possibilities despite the threat of destructive evils and frustrating ambiguities. Christians respond to God by preaching the Gospel and demonstrating love that seeks justice.

GOD AND EVIL

With this background in mind, the doctrine of God can be further developed by a consideration of the problem of evil. A number of definitions and distinctions are helpful. By evil in the broadest sense is meant the occurrence of less than the best possible within some relevant set of circumstances. It is the coming to pass of the worse rather than the better possibility that could have happened in its place, all things considered. This definition includes a strong aspect whereby some structured potential for good is disrupted or destroyed. The result is pain, misery, or other torments of body or spirit. Evil also refers to the shadow side, which is the good that is missed. All evil casts a shadow, of course, since the destruction of a potential for enjoyment necessarily prevents some good from being realized. A shadowy dimension is also present, however, wherever the better and the best are missed, even though some positive but lesser good was attained. Strong evil is the actual experience of misery, suffering, and injustice. Shadow evil is the negative side -- the dark badness of what might have been within some appropriate frame of reference.[46] The strong element is usually the primary reference. The evils that break our hearts are those instances of agony and affliction that threaten or shatter the pleasure of living -- raging famine, ravaging illness, tragic accidents, uncaring cruelty to people and animals, natural disasters that destroy life and property, senseless murder of the innocent, vicious subjugation of the helpless, and the like.

Evil refers more specifically to suffering and injustice. By suffering is meant the experience accompanying the blockage or frustration of a potential for enjoyment. This potential refers to what is either present or that would have been present had the given organism been gifted with a complete set of fully functioning capacities or if circumstances had been ideally different. A child born blind suffers in the sense of lacking the ability to see. A child who contracts a painful and debilitating disease of the eye suffers a blockage of a potential for enjoyment that was originally given. The varieties of enjoyment are many and thus are the forms of suffering. Physical pain, disease, anguish at being unloved or unwanted, loneliness, not belonging, having no home, hunger, abject poverty and want, failure in the pursuit of desirable goals, meaninglessness, despair, premature death -- these indicate but do not exhaust the forms of torment to which we are heir in this sometimes terrible world.

Injustice refers to the deprivation of rights, privileges, and opportunities to which persons have a legitimate claim as free and equal members of society. It is the denial of the personal and social goods to which we are entitled. Injustice is itself one form of suffering. It denies the enjoyment that comes from full participation in a community to which ideally we contribute according to our abilities and receive according to our just claims.[47]

Suffering and injustice can in turn be related to the categories of the sinful (moral evil) and the tragic (natural evil). The sinful (moral evil) refers to the suffering and injustice caused by irresponsible human action. Under sin is included deliberate action that is intended to harm or done despite the fact that it does. Also embraced is accidental or non-intentional harm done to others resulting from carelessness. Persons are responsible for misery caused by avoidable ignorance and for harmful acts that could have been prevented had they done their personal best. The driver who, while intoxicated or because of failure to exercise due caution in backing out of a driveway, non-intentionally kills a child is guilty of sin.

Under tragic (natural evil) is included the suffering and injustice arising in the nature of things that involve no irresponsible human choices and actions.[48] Injustice may be done and suffering caused where none was intended and where unavoidable ignorance was present. Tragic injustice is closely related to the moral ambiguity involved in human choices. Fully honoring the rights or needs of some may infringe on the just claims of others. Parents who give extra time to a handicapped child may deprive their other children of needed attention. Justified preferential hiring to benefit women who have been unfairly excluded previously may do an injustice to individual males who bear no responsibility for past discriminations. Raising minimum wages will help workers in low paying jobs but may increase unemployment. Accidents involving no human irresponsibility may produce suffering but involve no sin. In addition, the usual list of natural evils includes such things as disease, intractable pain, bodies badly deformed and disabled, and natural catastrophes -- the legal "acts of God," such as flood, storm, earthquake, lightning, and the like. Obviously, some suffering arises from a mixture of human irresponsibility (freedom) and non-human factors (nature). People who knowingly build houses over a geological fault that eventually produces a devastating earthquake participate in their calamity in ways that those who build there in innocent ignorance do not. The lines between what involves human irresponsibility and what does not may be hard to draw in many instances.

The relationship between suffering and evil is complex. In this connection, some make a distinction between genuine and apparent evil.[49] Genuine evil is suffering that is pointless, destructive, unnecessary, and leads to no compensating good. The world would have been better off without it, all things considered. Apparent evil is suffering that eventuates in or is the means to a larger good or is compensated for in some larger context. Before the invention of anesthesia, the amputation of a gangrenous leg to save a life would by this definition be an apparent evil. Here I object. While there is a compensating good, the pain is excruciating. The screams are real. Hence, the designation of this event as an "apparent" evil trivializes the badness involved.

I prefer to distinguish between absolute evil and relative evil. Absolute evil is suffering that is pointless, unnecessary, purely destructive with no redeeming elements or outcomes for anyone ever. Relative evil is suffering that is partially, wholly, or more than compensated for in some larger context or in the long run. The connections of suffering and evil to some compensating good are multifarious. Consider the following list that, by and large, runs from unqualified evil to suffering that is so trivial as to be insignificant.

1. Events that are totally pointless, destructive, unredeemed, and unnecessary: the torture and eventual murder of a child by a parent that has only negative effects on all touched by it over a long period of time.

2. The involuntary suffering of some that leads to an immense good for others: a minor earthquake that

kills hundreds leading to precautions that later save thousands of lives in a major tremor.

3. <u>Evil acts that have unintended consequences for good in the long run</u>: Joseph's being sold into slavery by his brothers becoming the means by which he later saved his family from famine (Gen. 45).

4. <u>Deliberate harm or violence done to a person or group in order to prevent or overcome a larger moral evil</u>: a policeman who finds a brief but opportune moment to kill a crazed gunman systematically murdering a group of hostages in a bank. Consider also participants in a justified war who kill the enemy as a last resort to overcome cruel tyranny and oppression and to achieve greater justice when all non-violent attempts have failed.

5. <u>Voluntary suffering that benefits others</u>: A person who volunteers to undergo medical experimentation that kills him but leads to the discovery of a drug that saves thousands of lives. Christians will also think of Jesus and his path to the cross.

6. <u>Suffering that leads to moral and spiritual maturity hardly imaginable otherwise</u>: a man who loses an arm to cancer testifying that he would not have it back if he could because the experience taught him so much about life and love that he never knew before.

7. <u>Pain that is avoidable, voluntary, and temporary, endured for the sake of some personal goal</u>: the agony of a marathon runner after twenty-five miles who could stop anytime she/he chooses.

This list could be indefinitely extended. It serves to illustrate the complexity of the situation. Three factors can be noted that enter into the relativising of evil.

a. Is the suffering a necessary and unavoidable means to the eventual larger good, or is some other path to the same goal available with less suffering?

b. Is the suffering experienced by the same individual, group, or generation that is compensated, or do some suffer while others reap the benefits?

c. Is the suffering voluntary or involuntary?

The more the first alternative in each pair prevails, the more relative is the evil involved.[50] Obviously, in specific cases it is not possible or easy to measure the exact relativity of evils or to designate some as purely and simply absolute without qualification.

Evils, whether absolute or relative, vary in kind (physical or psychic) and severity (massiveness, intensity, duration, numbers of people involved, etc.). Some relative evils may be comparatively worse than some absolute evils. For example, the agonizing amputation of a leg without anesthesia is greater in intensity although it saves a life (relative evil) than a mild cold that does no one any good whatsoever now or later (absolute evil). All suffering is relatively evil, however, even when it is a necessary means to some desired and worthy gain that justifies it. This is another dimension of the fact that the world contains a tragic element. It would be better if the highest ends of life could be achieved by sufficiently stern challenges that did not require excruciating pain and heart-breaking misery.

It only needs to be added that individuals are in part responsible for their own suffering, as well as for the injustice they do to others. By their foolish, inept, or irresponsible choices, they bring misery upon themselves and their neighbors. Sin occurs when individuals are <u>unwilling</u> to choose the better instead of the worse alternative. A tragic dimension enters when

they are <u>unable</u> because of ignorance or personal defi-
ciency to do the best that could be done in a given
situation. It may be, of course, that free choices in
the past have resulted in inability to choose in the
present. Sometimes people hurt themselves and others
when they most deeply want to do what is right and good
but don't know how or lack the requisite ability. Hence,
suffering and injustice may result from sin or exhibit
elements of tragedy -- or both. Unhappiness in marriage
and loneliness are examples that come to mind that may
involve both sin and tragedy.

Injustice is, however, not the mere sum total of
the actions of individuals acting wrongfully against
their neighbors. It is also manifested in the institutions and patterns of social life. Racial, ethnic, and
cultural minorities, along with women and the poor, are
especially subject to deep-rooted, long-standing prejudices that pollute the social atmosphere and rob them as
individuals and as groups of opportunities and benefits.
Society is nearly always organized in ways that systemically help some and unfairly harm others, even when individuals act lawfully. Even in democracies, the rich
and powerful repeatedly manage to arrange things through
money and influence so that the outcome of transactions
within the social system preserve and promote their
interests. They are often aided and abetted by the
moderately well off who believe (perhaps rightly) they
have more to gain in prestige, psychic identity, or
economic advantages by becoming the allies of the elite
than by identifying with the plight of the poor. As long
as they are doing well, those in the broad center cannot
be easily enlisted massively on the side of the worse
off. The changes necessary to eradicate poverty and
primary need would be costly to the middle class as well
as to the wealthy.

The varieties and sources of injustice are too numerous to outline here. Oppression takes a multitude of forms peculiar to given societies. No one has analyzed the social evils of modern industrial societies more profoundly than Reinhold Niebuhr. However, in his preoccupation with the complexities and ambiguities of collective evil, he neglected the positive moral force exerted on individuals by group standards (or gave the impression he did). Societies are generally more moral in the norms and ideals they seek to inculcate in their citizens than are some members of the group. Individuals may be better or worse than the prevailing social ethos. It is in their relationship to other collectives that races, classes, and nations are often more immoral than many of the individuals who compose them.[51]

Individuals are both relatively autonomous and deeply interdependent as they play out their social roles. Their actions are configured by the prevailing institutions in ways that feed into a systemic whole that have consequences they neither intend nor can prevent or escape. My lawfully buying grapes may contribute to the support of a system oppressive to migrant workers thousands of miles away. On the other hand, individuals can in limited ways make choices that to some degree decrease the destructive effects of institutional patterns and contribute to reform. I may along with others boycott grapes to put pressure on producers and lobby for legislation to benefit the workers. Beyond that individuals can refuse to cooperate with social institutions and practices and join reform or revolutionary groups to bring about systemic change. Nevertheless, some of our actions will always have unwanted and unintended evil consequences when channelled through social structures as we live out our lives as citizens and workers in our everyday roles. It is impossible to live a completely pure life that does no evil to no one. As Reinhold Niebuhr pointed out, even Jesus could incarnate perfect love only by becoming powerless on the cross, symbolically and literally lifted above the ambiguities and complexities of interconnected life in society.[52]

The presence of suffering and injustice springing from the sinful and the tragic constitute the reality of evil. The consequence is an ambiguous world. Good and evil, right and wrong, beauty and ugliness, justice and injustice, suffering and enjoyment are entwined together in the fabric of life. Ambiguity, however, does not mean merely that good and evil are both present in the world. The deeper reality is that good and evil in some measure are dependent on the other. Or perhaps they, to some degree, spring from a still deeper source that is the origin of both. Often we cannot have one without the other. Well-intentioned actions that have predominantly good consequence may unavoidably have others that are destructive, there being no choice that is wholly positive with no negative outcomes. In some cases, neither divorce nor continuing the marriage can relieve deep suffering for the couple and their children. The only choice is the lesser of two evils or the better of two ambiguous goods. Our vices often seem the other side of our virtues. Good and evil are to this extent inseparable twins, like the wheat and the tares in the story Jesus told.[53]

Then there are those situations in which ordinary good people are doing the best they can with the finest of intentions toward all. Nevertheless, because of a lack of personal skills, accidents, disease, the perfidy of others -- and a host of unavoidable vicissitudes -- end up leading disappointing, miserable lives. Children starve in Africa for a combination of reasons involving

both natural forces and historical factors that inter-
mingle the sinful and the tragic in baffling ways. Pal-
estinian children and young Israeli soldiers violently
confront each other (1988-1990), caught up in forces
that they did not create and cannot overcome. Yet in
limited ways, they can still choose how they will respond to particular situations as they arise. Behind it
all are legitimate needs for a home, security, economic
opportunity, and national integrity, on the one hand,
and a multitude of prejudices, long-standing hatreds,
and exaggerated self-interests, on the other hand. Parents do unintentional psychological damage to their
children due to a tortured past that encompasses many
generations of interwoven freedom and destiny. The
factors contributing to the world's massive ills are the
product of decades, even centuries, of sinful and tragic
history. Against these demonic powers, the forces of
reason and good will often seem impotent. Across the
years human life attains a complexity and a mystery of
iniquity that defies rationality nearly to the point of
producing despair in the tender-hearted.

The evil we know in this life consists of real
suffering and injustice along with the evil constituted
by the good that might have been but is not. Evils
abundant are interwoven with good in a fabric of complex
ambiguity and rooted in a combination of the sinful and
the tragic. What hope is there? What hypothesis about
God is theoretically required, or at least pragmatically
permitted, by an interpretation based on our experience
of the world we live in here and now? Theory can be
satisfied with a number of alternatives. One can account
for much evil by qualifying the divine power, goodness,
or wisdom. To put it in simple, ordinary language, God
might be:

1. perfectly good and unlimited in power but dumb, **or**

2. perfectly good and supremely intelligent but weak, **or**

3. infinitely wise and almighty but with a mean streak, **or**

4. lacking in two or all of these perfections.

Speculative reason is suspended among these alternatives with no compelling reason to prefer one to the others.[54] There are, however, experiential and pragmatic reasons for believing that God is perfect in intention but lacking in the ability to actualize either (a) the most excellent world possible in principle or (b) a perfect world free of all evil in fact. This hypothesis cannot, of course, be proven. One cannot even demonstrate its theoretical superiority over the options listed. It is finally a matter of intuition, of a hunch about what is going on. We live by faith. We "see through a glass darkly." My intuition about ultimate things rests on the experience that it is good to be, that life is a gift that is potentially and essentially excellent, worthwhile, desirable, and marvelously wonderful. I conclude that the Cosmic Giver of Life is unbounded love whose intention is to create a world and to actualize as much of its potential for meaningful enjoyment as possible. This goal is worked out within a context of ultimate and immediate conditions that constrain what can be done. Hence, I believe God is perfectly loving but limited in power.

None of the traditional theodicies is satisfying. It is not that they lack merit. Nevertheless, after all the insight they contain is added up, they leave too much unexplained on the basis of their initial assumptions. They end up one way or the other rationalizing

the bad away in deference to divine perfection or ac-
knowledging defeat by resort to mystery and divine
transcendence when experience contradicts their attempted resolution. Sometimes they put the blame back on
us. We lack faith or virtue. We have the wrong attitudes
toward life and so on. The realities of life and the
testimony of experience justify attempts to formulate
alternatives to the traditional theodicies. This world
is not equal in excellence in principle and in structure
to some possible world. A completely perfect finite
world (one with abundant good and no evil) does not seem
to be possible. Nor does this world seem to be a path
toward some eventual perfection. The hope that God will
in the end miraculously rid the world of natural and
moral ills, seems improbable. These are intuitions and
hunches, not assured knowledge or demonstrable theses.
This world, of course, could be factually better than it
is, had a different set of contingent events occurred
and a different set of free decisions been made. Nevertheless, a world better in basic design seems possible,
one that would be more likely to produce a greater net
gain of good over evil, even if it would not be free of
all afflictions whatsoever.

Only a suffering God will do. More precisely, only
a finite, struggling, suffering, loving God will suffice
pragmatically to account for the experienced good of
this life in the midst of ambiguity and evil. The affirmation that at the base of things lies a perfect
intention of love to create life and to direct it toward
fulfillment provides a framework for human commitment,
for religious devotion, and for moral action. Our worship and work consist in responding in gratitude and
praise to the divine intention by aligning our own
efforts with the striving of God to create a community

of loving persons who live happily in a just, harmonious, and prosperous society.[55]

The idea of God as Creative Suffering, Struggling Love affords a basis for faith and ethics, i. e., a life of worship and a life of active good works. Moreover, the idea of a finite God perfect in intention but not in power fits well with the known facts about cosmic and biological evolution. The spectacle that before our wondering eyes does appear gives evidence of purpose. The universe appears to be in the business of creating life in as many varieties as the environment will permit. Moreover, time displays a one-way trajectory that has an upward thrusting push toward organisms of greater complexity. These more highly developed life-forms are capable or wider ranges and depths of experience and of potential enjoyment than their simpler ancestors and contemporaries.

The cosmic process has produced human beings with the strange habit and ability to ask from whence all this comes and what it all means. These beings have a capacity for a qualitative richness and density of complex experience unique to the creatures of earth. They can love each other, create and enjoy great music, invent religious visions of the origin and destiny of all things, set forth high standards of conduct for themselves and others, and do all sorts of other wonderful things. Yet the height of their creativity in increasing the joy of life is matched by their destructive tendencies by which violence and hate cover the earth to their shame. The cosmos must have in it "personality--producing capacities" (Mathews), since it has in fact produced persons.[56]

Yet the evolutionary process seems more opportunistic in producing what it can under the circumstances, rather than having the ability to produce some definite outcome. People were invented by the process. We have no assurance that this was the predetermined consequence of some omnipotent aim. Purpose is immanent in the cosmos. The evidence does not sustain belief in a purpose for the process, i. e., some foreordained end that will in good time come to pass no matter what. More specifically, the cosmos seems to be the story of the emergence of life in abundance, life with varying capacities for experiencing the goodness inherent in being. A persistent and deep Eros in the very matrix of becoming hungers to lure the possible into reality with the intent of maximizing richness of experience felt as enjoyment. The forms that life takes, or whether it develops at all, depends on circumstances. The Creative Purpose at work in the cosmos is real but limited in its capacities to bring to infallible perfection the creatures it thrusts from its fecund womb. Hence, the process is ambiguous, a mixture of good and evil, of pain and pleasure, of success and failure, and -- in Christian imagery -- of crucifixion and resurrection.

GOD AND HOPE

Finally, the concept of a loving but limited and opportunistic God provides a realistic basis for hope that can be tested by experience. An empirical theology of history will be based on three assumptions:

(1) The structures and processes operative in nature and history now are the same as those that have been present throughout the human past.

(2) The principles to be employed in understanding the past are to be derived from an interpretation of experience in the present.[57]

(3) Human experience here and now when critically interpreted reveals no exceptions to the general structures, processes, and possibilities present in everyday events in the world.[58]

A contemporary empirical theology of history will include the following points.

1. The cosmic process has created human beings with a moral consciousness and a hunger for a better life. Thus endowed, humanity over the centuries has produced visions of justice and of the good and of the better set forth as norms and goals of human behavior. For Christians the imperative of counting the neighbor's need and good equal to one's own can hardly be improved on. Also unsurpassable is the definition of the goal of life as a community united by praise of God and love of neighbor -- the Commonwealth of God. This norm and this goal reflect aims ingredient in the creativity at the base of things. The fact of human moral and teleological consciousness in its highest reaches provides evidence of a purposive God whose character is love.

2. A plausible interpretation of thousands of years of human experience yields the conclusion that moral progress is potential in the historical process while not certain or inevitable. The past and the present are ambiguous, a mixture of good and evil. The future is unpredictable and likely to be remain ambiguous for reasons offered by Reinhold Niebuhr and Bernard Loomer.[59] History exhibits patterns of moral advance and of moral regression, as well as of stagnation and inertia. Yet in the midst of this some patterns of genuine progress are undeniable.[60] Contrary to some current liberation and eschatological theologies, it is unrealistic to suppose that social perfection will be reached on earth somehow, sometime by a mighty deed of God or by a combination of divine and human action.[61] Likewise, the liberal hope for a gradual movement of society toward peace, justice, harmony, and well-being is too simplistic. The dialectic of Reinhold Niebuhr is more convincing. On the one hand, history exhibits indeterminate possibilities for good;

no prior limits can be put on the extent to which justice may be achieved in society and to which love may become the ruling norm of individual lives. On the other hand, any achieved good can be corrupted and lost; fresh outbreaks of evil are possible. Moreover, the perils rise with the promises so that greater possibilities of good bring greater possibilities of evil. Since sin springs from freedom at the depths of the human spirit, it is an ever present possibility. Hence, no accumulation of social gains can ever guarantee the full and final triumph of righteousness. Yet every situation contains some potential for greater justice, harmony, and human fulfillment that we are obliged to achieve.

3. In particular, kairotic moments appear in history produced by a convergence of factors that create a potential "Gestalt of grace" whose actualization can at least partially overcome the reign of the demonic (Tillich).[62] In language more congenial to process-relational thought, now and then right and ripe moments appear full of new possibilities of justice, peace, prosperity, and joyful self-realization. These are occasions of hopeful opportunity calling for midwives of the divine Commonwealth to facilitate the birth of the new and better reality with which history is pregnant.

While prior human activity is the proximate creator of these novel potentials of fulfillment, the ultimate source lies in the objective nature of things. The ground of hope is the creativity of God by which goodness itself is real and new possibilities of its actualization emerge when certain conditions are present. Human beings did not originally create themselves. Neither did they create the capacity for enjoyment resident in all living beings. In the greater cosmic scheme, then, human action, strictly speaking, can only actualize possibilities of good latent in the givenness of things. That justice as possibility exists is a God-given fact and not a human creation, although its embodiment in particular situations is.

A pregnant moment of history occurred in the 18th century that gave birth to democratic government and ideals of human rights to life, liberty, equality, and the pursuit of happiness. Another transpired in the mid-twentieth century that gave rise to the Civil Rights Movement led by Martin Luther King, Jr. Doubtless other potential leaders as ably equipped and as committed as King had come along earlier, but the time was not ripe. In previous eras they would have been crushed immediately by the reigning demonic powers.

4. Hope is expectation that some appropriate good will be actualized in a situation in which the chances lie somewhere between impossibility and certainty. As a subjective attitude, it may be strong or weak, either because of or in spite of the objective probabilities. A distinction can be made between two overlapping and interdependent forms of hope. Realistic hope is contextual, particular, and more concrete. It relates to a real potential in a given situation in the near term. Utopian hope is non-contextual, general, and more abstract. It pertains to what is logically possible without regard to whether the means for actualizing it are presently understood or available. It is a wish that no one yet knows how to make come true but which could come true if the right steps were taken. The hope that the human race can live in perpetual peace in circumstances of ideal justice under sustainable conditions of prosperity in which no one lacks the material goods and social opportunities to live a long, healthy, and happy life is utopian at the present. The hope that a national health insurance plan can be achieved in the United

States in the next few years that will provide basic and catastrophic medical care to all is realistic.

Realistic hope is for the short run. Goals and strategies can be specified in some detail with reasonable expectation of success. It defines the immediate tasks. Utopian hope is for the long run -- the stuff of dreams. It defines the ultimately desirable that is eventually possible but for which no set of steps can be laid out that would achieve the goal. In its widest and highest reaches utopian hope yearns for the absolute ideal. It imagines at its acme the nearest thing to perfection that is possible, even wishing for the perfect itself, even if it is not fully possible in terms we can understand. Realistic hope needs to be nourished, sustained, and guided by utopian hope lest it become too timid, weak, and complacent. Utopian hope needs to be held in check and balanced by realistic hope lest it degenerate into mere daydreaming that neglects the real potentials at hand. Utopian hope too long unrealized can begin to look like an illusion and may turn into despair. These two forms of hope form an unbroken continuum and flow into each other, so that a clear demarcation is impossible. The form and content of each vary with time, place, and circumstance. Isaiah 11:1-9 and Revelation 21:1-4, as well as I Corinthians 15: 24-28, 51-55, are instances of utopian hope from earlier eras. Each arises out of a particular situation but reach out to embrace an absolute future void of evil.

5. In empirical theism hope cannot rest on the proposition that history will be perfected on earth at some indefinite future by a mighty coercive act of God. In fact, the hope of eventual perfection here or hereafter cannot be a matter of basic doctrine, although such a belief may be entertained as an uncertain pos-

sibility. In the present theology the notion of <u>utopian</u>
<u>hope</u> occupies the place that the expectation of a per-
fect social order inaugurated by an act of divine will.
This form of hope held in more orthodox views, including many contemporary eschatological and liberation
theologies, has been invalidated by historical fact.
None of the expected promises of a perfected social
order whether in the Old Testament or the New have been
fulfilled. The actual history recorded by the Bible
itself is evidence enough, not to mention the nearly two
thousand years that have ensued since. The scoffers who
challenged the author of II Peter in the second century
were right then, and they are still right: "all things
have continued as they were from the beginning of creation" (3:4 RSV).

To hold that the events referred to in biblical
eschatologies are yet to come is to stretch exegesis
beyond reasonable bounds. To suggest that an alternate
version is literally true except for the time frame is
a desperate expedient that misses the point of the
mythology in which they are contained. The biblical
myths must be taken as a whole and reinterpreted as a
whole, not broken into pieces so that what has not been
refuted can be preserved intact while discarding the
rest.

The Bible assumes that a perfect or at least a very
good world existed in the beginning (Gen. 1-3) and that
a new, transformed, and unambiguously good world will be
established at the end (Roms. 8:18-28; I Cor. 15; Rev.
21: 1-4). Modern eschatologies readily give up the
notion of a paradise in the past. Science and historical
evidence have refuted the notion. Yet liberal, neo-orthodoxy, and liberation theologies alike hold in various
ways to the hope that the world and a righteous remnant
of persons will be perfected at a divinely-wrought

consummation. In contrast, a modern <u>Gestalt</u> is offered here that reinterprets the biblical <u>Gestalt</u>. Perfection at the beginning is replaced by ambiguous potential, while hope is held out for a better but not a perfected future. Disaster for the human race on earth cannot be ruled out. Neither can a future here or in a heaven beyond that embodies a good so wondrous that human imagination cannot now discern its form and details. The ultimate possibilities for the future disappear into mysteries beyond human comprehension. Hope outruns the facts presently available to us and carries no guarantees for anything beyond the moment.

More concretely and specifically, in any given situation in which we find ourselves, history is pregnant with possibilities for good. Our task is to discern and actualize them and, when we cannot, to play our hunches and commit our lives to the most promising and probable prospects. In faith and hope beyond the facts, we live our lives, yet respecting the facts when they are known. In some immediate circumstances, there is no hope for what we want most or even for what would be best, all things considered. People get sick, and sick people die. Oppression and violence crush lives right and left. Yet when the context is sufficiently widened or narrowed,[63] hopeful possibilities emerge even from the worst of presents, allowing us to make the most of them when and if we can. Reality is relentless, inexorable, and ruthless. Often the best possible in a given situation is not very good. The lives of the tender-hearted must always be tinged with sadness and a sense of the tragic. Yet life can be very good and can nearly always be made better. No more and no less is the meaning of hope.

FICTIONAL NON-FICTIONAL NON-CONCLUSION

Let us end as we began. I offer another modern myth, a story that presupposes a whole nest of theoretical assumption.[64] Such stories are naive but, properly interpreted, are perhaps more sophisticated than our rational speculations.[65]

> In the beginning God was lonely and hungry to create something to love. So God said, "Let there be a world, fully equipped with everything." Nothing happened. So God said, "Well, all right then, let there be light, and we will take it from there." Nothing happened. God was frustrated and walked around wondering what to do. Finally, a deep exhaustion set in. God fell asleep. When God woke up, lo and behold, a big seed, a very big seed, was lying right there. Nobody knows where the seed came from. The Nothingists say that God's Word produced it. The Tiamatists say it came from God's body. The Classicists say it had always been there. Anyway, God looked at it and said, "I am still lonely." So in disappointment God buried the seed, expecting never to see it again. Sometime later, God was by that way again. A little plant, no two little plants, had appeared side by side. One was beautiful and shiny green. God loved it. The other was ugly and full of thorns. God hated it. So God tried to dig up the ugly one. Its roots were all tangled up with those of the pretty one. God nourished the flower and cut back the weed. Both grew alongside each other. Sometimes the weed would look sick. God hoped it would die. It always came back. The flower grew too. Sometimes it bloomed with beautiful petals. The weed was always near by. Its tendrils threatened to choke the flower. Nobody knows how it all turned out.

ENDNOTES

1. The modern myth is my own attempt to present a set of religious and philosophical speculations in the form of a story about the gods within the framework of the world-picture of present-day science. I assume that the classical creation myths of Babylon and of Israel did a similar thing for their own time. See Bernard Anderson, Creation versus Chaos.

2. See Stephen W. Hawking, A Brief History of Time.

3. Ibid, pp. 115-141. Hawking's interpretation of present scientific evidence is that the universe is self-existent and has no beginning nor end. Shifting into a philosophical mode, he then wonders what need we have of a Creator. However, a theologian may be forgiven for noting that the great physicist seems to be innocent of all views of God except a deistic one.

4. The distinction between relative non-being (me on) as no particular thing or mere potentiality and absolute non-being (ouk on) as pure nothingness or total negation is well known. Cf. Paul Tillich, Systematic Theology, I, pp. 186-192. Here I intend the absolute nothingness presupposed in the Christian doctrine of creatio ex nihilo, the guarantee in orthodoxy of the complete sovereignty of God, since there was "nothing" over against God, no power or being in addition to God that could resist the divine will.

5. Why, then, do I not accept the logic of the ontological argument for the existence of non-surpassable perfection? If perfection is possible, must it not exist necessarily, since even the conceivability of its non-existence is a flaw? Hence, it would appear that perfection is either impossible or that it exists necessarily. One good reason for skepticism is that the great minds over the centuries have divided on the question. In our generation the appeal to the neglected argument in Anselm by Charles Hartshorne has proven no more successful than previous attempts to convert the doubters. Besides, do we know for sure that perfection is conceivable? Even if we did, could we be sure that the necessary connection between thought and being holds in moving from conceivability to necessary existence? See Hartshorne, Anselm's Discovery, and The Logic of Perfection.

6. The distinction between abstract logical possibility, i. e., anything conceivable, meaning anything not self-contradictory, on the one hand, and real

potentiality, i. e., something for which the essential
conditions for actualizing some possibility are present
here and now, on the other hand, may be relevant here.
Perhaps we need only be concerned practically about real
potentials. Yet must not even possibility as abstract
logical possibility have some ontological status?
Possibility is more than pure nothingness and less than
real being. Or is nothing identical with pure possibility? Is not its status eternal and necessary? It is
difficult to imagine possibility having to become
possible. Wasn't the possible always possible (eternally
in a non-temporal sense) and necessary? Who knows, but
it seems so to me.

7. For recent scientific speculation positing
"nothing" as the primordial situation, see Sten F.
Odenwald, "A Modern Look at the Origin of the Universe,"
Zygon (March, 1990), pp. 35-37.

8. See ibid., pp. 38-39, for recent scientific
speculation of this type. This is also the supposition
of the eminent theoretical physicist Stephen Hawking, A
Brief History of Time, pp. 136-141. Samuel Alexander
starts with space-time. See his Space, Time, Deity.

9. Edgar S. Brightman fits this pattern. See A
Philosophy of Religion, pp. 281-314. See also his The
Problem of God.

10. For a long time I have wandered around and away
from the cosmologies of Alfred North Whitehead and Samuel
Alexander. See Alfred North Whitehead, Process and
Reality; and Samuel Alexander, Space, Time, Deity. Cf.
my Science, Secularization and God, p. 165.

11. I worked out this model in conversation with
Hartshorne, Tillich, and others in Science, Secularization and God, pp. 131-194.

12. Some theological revisionists specify the
necessary conditions that underlie the possibility of any
experience whatsoever. See David Tracy, Blessed Rage for
Order, pp. 53-56, 146-171. Certainly all forms of
thought, including science, presuppose order, pattern,
rationality, and intelligibility of some sort. But what
are the theological implications? Here the results are
less than conclusive. Contrary interpretations arise
among the competent. I find plausible the investigations
of common human experience that yield signals of transcendence. I do not take them as beyond dispute. No system
of thought regarding these matters convinces anyone
outside the circle of those who share the fundamental

assumptions on which the conclusions to be verified rest. It is a circular process. Conversion is, of course, possible if a paradigm breaks down. This is more rare than a defense against opposing views. For an attempt to demonstrate the reality of a religious dimension to experience, see ibid., pp. 91-118. That such investigations can produce certainty with regard to the ultimate facts is unconvincing.

13. Cauthen, Science, Secularization and God, p. 154.

14. This language sounds Tillichian. A similarity is found in the fact that it seems plausible that the Source or Ground of finite being is not a realm of existence separate from finite being. The notion of God as the "depth dimension" of finitude suggested by his notion of a "self-transcending naturalism" is appealing. Yet the primordial factors may be more "within nature" than at "the bottom or base of things." The spatial metaphors indicated by the choice of prepositions in both cases can be contrasted with those that suggest that God is beyond or above and separate from the world. My model seems closer to the (3) "ecstatic naturalism" of Tillich than it is to what he designates as (1) supranaturalism or (2) naturalism, or maybe it is somewhere between (2) and (3). See his Systematic Theology, II, pp. 5-10. I, of course, reject his view of Being-itself, since he is only half cured of the "monopolar prejudice" (Hartshorne) that denies relativity and potentiality to God in a proper sense, and thus he remains close to actus purus.

15. In this respect, I agree with Bernard Loomer, "The Size of God." If there are structural factors within the world that in some sense underlie or at least account for its particular processive, evolving character, then Loomer's position and mine may not much different.

16. I give credit to Whitehead and Hartshorne, from whom I learned the di-polar model. I offer a revised non-standard version.

17. Maybe nothing or nothing but nothing is absolute, necessary, and eternal. Formal analysis leads to some final point of reference beyond which there is no going further. Hence, something is actually ultimate and thus absolute in the sense of being independent of all else, or so it seems. But do we know that it must be that way and no other? And maybe the ultimate in this sense is not some-thing but no-thing. And what does eternal mean as contrasted to temporal at this level? Could not

something have just begun to be in an absolutely contingent fashion? But from what? Nothing? Was this an eternal possibility? When could this have happened, and what could "when" mean in this context? Thought is lost at this level. I include absolute, necessary, and eternal at this point in the text, guessing that they refer to Eros and Possibility.

18. Shailer Mathews, The Growth of the Idea of God, pp. 210-234.

19. Hawking, A Brief History of Time, pp. 158-169.

20. If there are elementary particles, as presumably there are, they would not, of course, have parts but would be individuals. They might have dimensions and/or phases, as do actual entities in the cosmology of Whitehead.

21. I have learned most in this regard from Alfred North Whitehead, although I make no pretense of simply repeating his views. See Science and the Modern World, Modes of Thought, and especially Process and Reality. I have also been influenced by the provocative cosmology of Samuel Alexander set forth in Space, Time, Deity. Fragments of the thought of both these philosophers, especially Whitehead, wander around in my head.

22. For a brief but fascinating account of the effort in modern science to discover the elementary particles, see Hawking, A Brief History of Time, pp. 63-79. Cf. Rolston Holmes, III, Science and Religion, pp. 33-80.

23. A remnant of the influence of Paul Tillich is evident at this point. See his Systematic Theology, III, pp. 11-110. However, I came to this world-metaphor out of my own developing convictions as I was influenced by process philosophy. I first used the metaphor in Science, Secularization and God more than two decades ago.

24. Cf. Charles Hartshorne, A Natural Theology for Our Time, pp. 5-12, 34-41, 136.

25. Alfred North Whitehead, The Function of Reason, p. 8.

26. For an illuminating discussion of complexities, similarities, and differences between metaphor and symbol, see Paul Ricouer, Interpretation Theory, pp. 45-69. For a more detailed study of the history and meaning of metaphor, see his The Rule of Metaphor. For a techni-

cal analysis of the different kinds of language about God, see Schubert Ogden, The Point of Christology, pp. 131-147.

27. Does this view lead to an indefensible relativism? Does it make any practical difference whether we believe our way of looking at things corresponds with objective reality and that contrary views are wrong or whether we are just sufficiently subjectively convinced of our views when it comes to working wholeheartedly for their realization and appropriately resisting what is believed to be evil and destructive of justice and well-being? It appears to me that it is the strength of conviction itself that is finally determinative, not whether objectivist or relativist views of truth are held. Moreover, I have insisted that theologians and philosophers aim at objective truth and intend their views to correspond with reality. The problem is that we cannot be sure when belief and knowledge coincide. But when issues of justice and injustice arise, we have to fight for the good and the right as we see it as if we were in possession of the truth. I know of no way to escape relativism with respect to the ultimate questions of God and the good, but I wish there were. Granted many would willingly instruct me in the way beyond the dilemma of objectivism and relativism, but I have yet to be convinced that any proposed resolution is more than a tepid compromise. Besides the great thinkers propose different ways, so I still have to make a subjective choice among them, since I do not know how to determine which one is objectively true. The deeper question, perhaps, is whether relativism when embraced does not inevitably lead to a loss of passionate commitment. How can one give oneself without reserve to something unless one is pretty sure that the supporting belief is really true? I believe that it is enough for people to be convinced of the meaningfulness of life and that the ideas and values they hold are important enough to live by, to promote, and to defend. Maybe it differs from person to person. Anyway, since any kind of final certainty is not possible for me, only some kind of relativism is an option, regardless.

28. Somewhere in my memory this way of putting it is associated with G. K. Chesterton. Willis Glover relates a similar remark to Chesterton. See his Biblical Origins of Modern Secular Culture.

29. No short summary can do justice to the complexities of the biblical witness to the providence of God and to the manner of God's acting within the world. For a less brief summary with numerous scriptural

references, see Gilkey, Reaping the Whirlwind, pp. 241-242, 409-413.

30. I mean here a way of thinking that expresses a religious and metaphysical vision of the relationship between the ordinary world and its transcendent ground in which the ultimate powers are described by stories about the gods represented anthropomorphically. It is in this sense that the God of the Bible is an Agent among other agents. Thus, in its literal form the myth constitutes a naive way of looking at things. When the myth is deliteralized and translated into a philosophical conception of the relationship between the world and its ultimate source, it contains a sophisticated option that can be compared with other metaphysical visions ancient and modern. To say that it is naive is not a value judgment but a description. My own remythologizing is naive too in the same way but naive in terms of contemporary experience and culture.

31. As Gordon Kaufman points out, it is not merely the improbability of miracle that is the problem but the very intelligibility of a notion such as the virgin birth when we try to relate it to scientific views of nature. See "On the Meaning of `Act of God,'" in Owen C. Thomas (ed.), God's Activity in the World, pp. 145-147, 158-159, n. 11. Yes, but if one believes in the "miracle of Christmas" (Barth), one can simply say that Mary was once not pregnant and now she is. How it happened, we do not know, except that it was God's special work without the participation of Joseph. Once one assumes an omnipotent God who can and does intervene empirically, everything but the logically impossible becomes possible. So what, if it is not humanly intelligible?

32. See James Gleick, Chaos: Making a New Science.

33. The outcome depends on how actuality and possibility are related to each other in our minds. Each defines and limits the other. Excluding for the moment questions of logical possibility, we develop notions about what is empirically possible on the basis of what we have, for whatever reasons, concluded to be actual, i. e., the way the world really works not how it might possibly work. We cannot admit as being actual what we cannot believe is possible. Something might be possible and not be actual. Yet what we are convinced is actual must obviously be possible. At any given moment each one of us has convictions about what is possible and therefore could be actual. Likewise, we have assumptions about what cannot be actual because it is not possible. An

event alleged to be an exception to the general order of things will be disallowed if we have concluded, on whatever basis, that it could not have happened, since it is not possible. We will insist that non-miraculous explanations exist, whether we ever find them or not. We might, however, be persuaded on either rational or empirical grounds that our present convictions about what could possibly happen and what has actually happened are wrong. What it will take to bring about a conversion of perspective for any given person cannot be specified in advance. It depends on the depth of conviction or faith or stubbornness present at the time, as well as the potency of the evidence.

Three categories are involved:

Logically Possible	Factually Possible	Factually Actual
Not self-contradictory concrete	Not violating general cosmological principles	Real in fact

I might be convinced that it is logically and factually possible for Jones to have murdered Smith but be convinced by the evidence that Jones did not actually murder Smith. I would need evidence about concrete facts not about cosmological possibilities to settle the question. If, however, the charge were that Jones murdered Smith by sticking pins in a voodoo doll when Smith was 10,000 miles away, I would have to be convinced that it was cosmologically possible (the world actually works this way in its laws, principles, and structures) for this to happen before I could even entertain the question of whether it really did happen in this case. If enough empirical evidence were put before me that such things as murdering a real person by sticking pins in a doll do occur, I might change my mind about what is possible and thus be open to the empirical question as to whether Smith was factually murdered in this instance by Jones. It would, however, take a lot of convincing.

Arguments about the resurrection of Jesus, it seems to me, exhibit this pattern. The alleged evidence in the case is interpreted within such a complex set of assumptions held by the disputing parties that hardly ever is anyone convinced by the argument. Yet conversions do take place with respect both to what people believe is possible because actual and not actual because not possible. Such transformations of perspective probably don't happen often, since such convictions have to do with fundamental matters about how the world works in its basic structures and processes.

34. Gleick, _Chaos_, pp. 39-53, 121-153.

35. Ibid., p. 121.

36. If myth is an appropriate term here, it means a conceptual system that forms a world picture elucidating the origin and nature of things that serves the same function as the stories of the gods in the ancient cultures. Whitehead's metaphysics provides a way to organize the whole of our experience in a systematic fashion useful for understanding the ultimate meaning of things and for coping with the religious questions about matters of "ultimate concern" (Tillich). The ancient myths of Israel, Babylon, Africa, and India did the same.

37. For a selection of essays representing various ways in which the notion of God's activity has been treated in recent theology, see Thomas (ed.), God's Activity in the World.

38. This is an analogy used by process theologians. See Schubert Ogden, "What Sense Does it Make to Say, `God Acts in History'?" in ibid., pp. 77-100.

39. Frank G. Kirkpatrick makes a case for this analogy. He maintains that events like the rolling back of the waters of the Red Sea can be admitted as divine action without violating natural law. He points out that human beings can act without interfering with the finite order of causes. I move my arm, and yet the same act can be given a full physiological and neurological accounting by the various sciences in terms of muscles, bones, electrical impulses to and from and within the brain, etc. Neither perspective interferes with the other. See Frank G. Kirkpatrick, "Understanding an Act of God," in Thomas (ed.), God's Activity in the World, pp. 163-1-80. Commenting on Ex. 14:21, Kirkpatrick says, "Just as a human agent does not violate natural law by deciding to raise his arm, so God does not violate natural law by deciding to move the wind in order to dry up the sea." p. 178. Kirkpatrick, however, does not go on to say how a sudden strong wind caused by God is related to the whole set of meteorological conditions that preceded it and caused it. How could a storm that was not already in the making and ready to happen by natural causes be caused on the spot by divine action without violating the orderly processes that meteorologists deal with? In part he does this by a neat trick of defining (following John Macmurray) natural law as a description of what transpires when no agent interferes. I am more inclined to believe that either one must give up the notion of an autonomous realm of natural law or give up the notion of miracle, unless miracle is seen as a violation of natural law.

40. See Hartshorne, A Natural Theology for Our Time, pp. 9-12.

41. This is obviously related to (a). However, that point had to do with actions of the body that affect something external to the body. Here the emphasis is on processes by which organs of the body are themselves in action, without reference to any effects on anything outside the body.

42. Here my position is closely related to that of Paul Tillich. See Systematic Theology, I, pp. 263-267.

43. Here my position is close to that of Gordon Kaufman, who distinguishes between the "master act of God" that is accomplished in the whole of the cosmos and human history and "subacts" that as stages along the way contribute to the fulfillment of the "master act." See "On the Meaning of 'Act of God,'" in Thomas (ed.), God's Activity in the World, pp. 137-161.

44. In this sense, in contrast to Whiteheadian process theology, I make God more explicitly responsible for the being as well as the goals (initial aims) of creatures. The God of Whitehead is primarily persuasive, offering a set of relevant possibilities for each new moment of becoming. God is the Intelligent Visionary Eros that lures the world process into creative advance. Hence, Whitehead must posit Creativity to account for other factors in the primordial situation. But since Creativity and Eternal Objects as well are uncreated, they too belong to the God-realm, as do the structural necessities that limit and channel the creative efforts of God to maximize value. By combining God and Creativity, my myth is more Hebraic than Whitehead's more Platonic outlook.

45. In this sense merit can be found in the traditional distinction between God as primary cause in contrast to secondary causes. For a recent restatement of this point of view, see Etienne Gilson, "The Corporeal World and the Efficacy of Secondary Causes," in Thomas (ed.), God's Activity in the World, pp. 213-230. Yet the traditional view ran the risk of eliminating finite freedom and thus making God the determiner of all events in their entirety, including those that involved evil and suffering. That must be avoided. I do so by affirming a doctrine of human freedom as the power of contrary choice or creative self-transcendence or the capacity to originate genuine novelty in the world.

46. Obviously, some limits have to be drawn and some appropriate framework assumed. A child starving to death might be better off today (or never have been born) if some more favorable set of possible events in the indefinite past had occurred instead of what did happen. Eventually we are pushed back to the origin of the world and to the ultimate causative factors that generated just this kind of world and established the determining conditions that set in motion some set of contingent events leading to the present and to the child's birth. Any number of things could have been different along the way that would have made the present situation more promising. The evils that disturb us most are the events that represent a worse rather than a better outcome within some circumscribed set of real potentials more or less nearby in time and space.

47. See my Process Ethics and The Passion for Equality.

48. The distinction between natural and moral evil is variously made. For John Hick the difference is in the agency involved. Natural evil is produced by non-human agents and moral evil by human agents. See Evil and the God of Love, p. 12. For David Griffin, the difference is between suffering intended (moral evil) and suffering undergone, regardless of the agent (natural evil). See God, Power and Evil, pp. 27-28. I prefer my distinction since it deals better with the in-between category of accidents, that may or may not be caused by human carelessness. Suppose a person who was exercising due caution hit and killed a child who suddenly darted out in the street right in front of him. Unlike Hick, I would not call accidental harm done by a person who was not irresponsible in the situation moral evil. Suppose the driver was not paying attention and hit the child unintentionally when due caution would have prevented the accident. Unlike Griffin, I would call unintended harm done to another by a person who was acting carelessly moral evil.

49. See David Griffin, God, Power and Evil, p. 22.

50. The distinction between absolute and relative evil makes it possible to accommodate those who want to say that some events are both genuinely evil and that they will or can be compensated or more than compensated for by their contribution or association with some larger eventual good. David Griffin and John Hick argue inconclusively over what is genuinely evil and what is merely apparently so. The distinction between absolute and relative evil may allow both to have their point but in

a less confusing or paradoxical way. See their exchange in Encountering Evil, pp. 103-104, 122-123, 129. See also footnote 25 in Chapter III of the present volume.

51. This is to say that the relationship between the morality of individuals and of groups is more complex than appears in Niebuhr's early work Moral Man and Immoral Society. See also, The Nature and Destiny of Man and Faith and History, as well as most of his other numerous works on economic, social, and political forms of injustice.

52. Reinhold Niebuhr, The Nature and Destiny of Man, II, pp. 35-97.

53. I have given examples and provided extensive discussion of these issues in my Process Ethics, pp. 195-310.

54. One can locate errors of reasoning in the defense of various positions. Some might be so fundamental as to negate the proposition itself, but no theory can be established positively as most assuredly and certainly true.

55. I have defined the good life, the good person, the good society, justice, happiness, and enjoyment in a series of works over two decades. See Science, Secularization and God, pp. 227-228; Christian Biopolitics, pp. 103-153; The Ethics of Enjoyment, pp. 64-100; Process Ethics, pp. 37-82, 125-315; and The Passion for Equality, pp. 1-30, 63-177.

56. See Shailer Mathews, The Growth of the Idea of God.

57. In other words, I accept as "canons of historical inquiry" the principles of homogeneity and analogy. All events of the past and future exhibit the same patterns and possibilities, and events in the past must be interpreted as analogous to events that occur in the present. In this respect I am in complete agreement with Whitehead that an interpretation of history rests on experience in the here and now. See Religion in the Making, p. 82. Cf. my Science, Secularization and God, pp. 198-200. Hence, I disagree with Barth, whose confidence in revelation allows him to ignore or by-pass scientific understandings of nature based on ordinary secular experience that would preclude virgin births and bodily resurrections. See Church Dogmatics, I, 2, pp. 172-202; III, 2, pp. 439-455; IV, I, p. 341. I also disagree with Wolfhart Pannenberg, who thinks that one

can rationally prove the resurrection of Jesus. Proof is
a function of perspective. It is based on a network of
assumptions internal to the total outlook within which
particular claims are made. Pannenberg can prove that the
resurrection was an objective historical event only to
those who share his more general assumptions about how
we know and what we know. It would be foolish for him to
claim that those who disagree with him are irrational or
incompetent. All interpretations of such complicated
matters are relative, and no absolute universality can
be claimed for them. Specifically, Pannenberg could not
give credence to the evidence that the resurrection is
a unique event unless he were already prepared on other
grounds to conceive the possibility of such an event. One
might argue that the evidence for some events is so
powerful and irresistible that it may destroy previous
belief in their non-possibility and force acceptance of
their possibility on the basis of their actuality. However, it is difficult to see how the evidence
for the resurrection can be of this paradigm-shaking
sort. The evidence is limited, second hand, difficult to
assess, and other explanations are readily available that
adequately account for the data. See Basic Questions, I,
chapter 2. For a similar view, see Jürgen Moltmann,
Theology of Hope, pp. 172-190. In this respect I agree
with Langdon Gilkey. See his brief but succinct analysis
of the philosophical issues in Naming the Whirlwind,
p. 361, note 35. The neo-orthodox are right in claiming
that belief in the possibility of the resurrection is a
"faith judgment." It only needs to be added that dis-
belief in the possibility and actuality of the resurrection of Christ as a supernatural cosmic event is also a
"faith judgment," where faith means not the response to
a supernatural revelation but a particular intellectual
perspective not susceptible of rational demonstration to
all competent and unbiased persons. Skeptics and believers all live by faith in this sense.

58. This gets to be quite a subtle point. One might
argue that one of the general principles operating in the
world is that exceptional events are possible. One could
further assert that if one believes in an omnipotent God
whose will determines all things, the possibility of
exceptional events is a necessary principle. Hence, if
Jesus were born of a virgin or was raised from the dead,
this would be an exceptional event in that virgins do not
generally give birth and the dead generally are not
raised. Yet these events would violate no general
principle, since one general principle is that exceptions
can occur. Whether they have occurred is a matter for
inquiry and debate. One might then argue that the virgin
birth and/or the resurrection of Jesus actually did occur

based on the evidence presented by the Scriptures as a reliable witness. Obviously I am denying both the possibility of radical contingency as a general principle operating in nature and history and the fact of radical contingency with respect to particular occurrences. If one has sufficient grounds for assuming the existence of a free, transcendent, almighty Lord or for establishing the Scriptures as a witness whose claims cannot be contravened in a system of thought in which all these assumptions and beliefs cohere and are mutually supportive, then one has a sufficient basis for entertaining both the possibility and the actuality of the virgin birth and the resurrection of Jesus, along with any other miracles that are supported by Scripture or experience.

Since my theology rests on principles that are derived from present experience, I have no grounds for assuming either the incontrovertible veracity of Scripture or the reality of an omnipotent divine will. Moreover, the human experience available to me first hand provides no grounds for the assertion of radical contingency either as a possibility or as a necessity. No exceptional events in the required sense in question here have occurred in my experience or in the experience of many others whose witness I trust most. Yet I must be cautious here, since the evolutionary process does give rise to the new and to the unexpected. Yet the mutations that produce new species spring from potentialities that emerge gradually over the course of time and do not exemplify the kind of radical contingency that miracles in the old-fashioned sense call for.

I need not repeat the argument that debates about such matters as complicated as this admit of no universal or certain resolution. We are all finally grasped by a Gestalt that we cannot deny and to which we must give witness.

59. Niebuhr, Faith and History; Loomer, "The Size of God."

60. This includes not only medical discoveries that control pain and disease but other technologies that improve the human lot and make life easier. In the social and moral sphere as well, the rise of democratic ideals and doctrines of human rights based on the liberty and equality of all persons represent an advance over notions of the divine rights of kings and other doctrines that justified non-consensual government. Certainly the lot of blacks, women, and native Americans in this country shows improvement over the last century and a half, although much remains in current practice that is scandalous to justice. In some respect both moral ideals and moral practice move upward. In the 19th century

learned persons defended slavery and opposed suffrage for women. They used both Scripture and natural law to justify prevailing customs. No one who did so today would be taken seriously. Yet the murder of six million Jews by a highly educated, supposedly advanced nation is a twentieth century phenomena. Cruelty, violence, terrorism, and oppression are still widespread sponsored by states as well as by individuals. The fact that hunger, disease, and poverty that could be prevented are still the lot of millions of people at this very hour gives us reason to be cautious about making claims regarding the advance of moral practice. Moreover, the possibility of ecological disaster during the next century casts doubt on the ability of human beings to act wisely and sufficiently in time to counteract the increasing hazards produced by the very technology that was supposed to emancipate us.

61. See my Systematic Theology, pp. 392-398; and Gilkey, Naming the Whirlwind, pp. 226-238.

62. See The Protestant Era, pp. xvii-xxi. See also his The Interpretation of History.

63. When a loved one dies, the context must be widened so that the living who remain can seek meaning and enjoyment in their own lives from that day forward. For those about to die and for loving family surrounding them, the context must be narrowed so that what is hoped for is not deliverance from death but that whatever possibilities of physical comfort and human companionship arise from day to day can be realized before death opens up the wider context.

64. "One can imagine a hermeneutic style where interpretation would conform both to the notion of concept and to that of the constitutive intention of the experience seeking to be expressed in the metaphorical mode. Interpretation is then a mode of discourse that functions at the intersection of two domains, metaphorical and speculative." Ricoeur, The Rule of Metaphor, p. 303.

65. "Does that mean that we could go back to a primitive naivete? Not at all. . . . But if we can no longer live the great symbolisms of the sacred in accordance with the original belief in them, we can, . . . aim at a second naivete in and through criticism. In short, it is by interpreting that we can hear again." Ricoeur, The Symbolism of Evil, p. 351. And when we have critically interpreted, we can then reinterpret the primitive symbolisms for our age, rewrite them, and

include our revised non-standard version along with our
conceptual efforts.

REFERENCES

Alexander, Samuel. Space, Time, Deity. 2 vols. New York: The Macmillan Co., 1920.

Allen, Diogenes. Christian Belief in a Post-Modern World: The Full Wealth of Conviction. Louisville: Westminster/John Knox, 1989.

Anderson, Bernhard W. Creation Versus Chaos. New York: Association Press, 1967.

Arbib, Michael A., and Mary B. Hesse. The Construction of Reality. Cambridge: Cambridge University Press, 1986.

Arnold, Harvey. Near the Edge of the Battle, 1866-1960. Chicago: Divinity School Association, University of Chicago, 1966.

Augustine. The City of God. New York: Random House, 1950.

Axel, Larry E., W. Creighton Peden, and Lori Krafte-Jacobs (eds.). "Bernard Meland and the Future of Theology," American Journal of Theology and Philosophy. May and September, 1984.

Ayala, F. J., and Theodosius Dobzhansky (eds.). Studies in the Philosophy of Biology: Reduction and Related Problems. London: The Macmillan Press, 1974.

Barbour, Ian G. Issues in Science and Religion. Englewood Cliffs: Prentice-Hall, 1966.

_____. Myths, Models and Paradigms. New York: Harper & Row, 1974.

_____. Religion in an Age of Science. San Francisco: Harper & Row, 1990.

Barclay, William. The Gospel of Matthew. Philadelphia: The Westminster Press, 1975.

Barth, Karl. Church Dogmatics. 4 vols. Edinburgh: T & T Clark, 1936-1969.

Bernstein, Richard. Beyond Objectivism and Relativism: Science, Hermeneutics and Praxis. Philadelphia: University of Pennsylvania Press, 1985.

_____. Philosophical Profiles: Essays in a Pragmatic Mode. Philadelphia: University of Pennsylvania Press, 1986.

Birch, L. C. Nature and God. London: SCM Press, 1965.

Birch, L. Charles, and John B. Cobb, Jr. The Liberation of Life: From the Cell to the Community. Cambridge University Press, 1981.

Brightman, E. S. The Problem of God. New York: Abingdon Press, 1930.

_____. A Philosophy of Religion. Englewood Cliffs, NJ: Prentice-Hall, 1940.

Brown, Delwin. To Set at Liberty: Christian Faith and Human Freedom. Maryknoll, NY: Orbis Books, 1981.

Brunner, Emil. The Christian Understanding of Creation and Redemption. Philadelphia: Westminster Press, 1952.

292

Bultmann, Rudolf. "New Testament and Mythology," <u>Kerygma</u> <u>and Myth</u>. Ed. by Hans Werner Bartsch. London: SPCK, 1954. Pp. 1-44.

_____. <u>Jesus Christ and Mythology</u>. New York: Charles Scribner's Sons, 1958.

Burrows, Millar. <u>An Outline of Biblical Theology</u>. Philadelphia: Westminster Press, 1946.

Calvin, John. <u>Institutes of the Christian Religion</u>. 2 vols. The Library of Christian Classics, Vol. 20. Philadelphia: Westminster Press, 1960.

Cauthen, Kenneth. <u>The Impact of American Religious Liberalism</u>. New York: Harper & Row, 1962. Reprinted Washington: University Press of America, 1983.

_____. <u>The Triumph of Suffering Love</u>. Valley Forge: Judson Press, 1966.

_____. <u>Science, Secularization and God</u>. Nashville: Abingdon Press, 1969.

_____. (ed.) <u>Jesus on Social Institutions</u>. By Shailer Mathews. Originally printed, 1897. Philadelphia: Fortress Press, 1971.

_____. <u>Christian Biopolitics</u>. Nashville: Abingdon Press, 1971.

_____. <u>The Ethics of Enjoyment</u>. Atlanta: John Knox Press, 1975.

_____. <u>Process Ethics: A Constructive System</u>. New York: The Edwin Mellen Press, 1984.

_____. <u>Systematic Theology: A Modern Protestant Approach</u>. New York: The Edwin Mellen Press, 1986.

_____. <u>The Passion for Equality</u>. Totowa, NJ: Rowman & Littlefield, 1987.

Cobb, John B., Jr. and David Griffin. <u>Mind in Nature: Essays on the Interface of Science and Philosophy</u>. Washington: University Press of America, 1977.

_____. <u>Process Theology: An Introductory Exposition</u>. Philadeladelphia: Westminster Press, 1976.

Cobb, John B., Jr. <u>A Christian Natural Theology</u>. Philadelphia: Westminster Press, 1965.

_____. <u>Process Theology as Political Theology</u>. Philadelphia: Westminster Press, 1982.

Cone, James H. <u>God of the Oppressed</u>. San Francisco: Harper & Row, 1975.

_____. <u>A Black Theology of Liberation</u>. Revised ed. Maryknoll, NY: Orbis Books, 1986.

Crenshaw, James L. (ed.). <u>Theodicy in the Old Testament</u>. Philadelphia: Fortress Press, 1983.

Daly, Mary. <u>Beyond God the Father</u>. Boston: Beacon Press, 1973.

_____. <u>Gyn/Ecology: The Metaethics of Radical Feminism</u>. Boston: Beacon Press, 1978.

Davaney, Sheila Greeve. "Journey From the Heartland," A Time to Weep, a Time to Sing. Ed. by Mary Jo Meadow and Carole A. Rayburn. Minneapolis: Winston Press, 1985. Pp. 119-131.

_____. "Problems with Feminist Theory," Embodied Love: Sensuality and Relationships as Feminist Values. Ed. by Paula M. Cooey, Sharon A. Farmer, and Mary Ellen Ross. San Francisco: Harper & Row, 1987. Pp. 79-95.

Davis, Stephen T. (ed.), John B. Cobb, Jr., David R. Griffin, John H. Hick, John K. Roth, and Frederick Sontag. Encountering Evil. Atlanta: John Knox Press, 1981.

Dawkins, Richard. The Blind Watchmaker: Why the Evidence of Evolution Reveals a Universe Without Design. New York: W. W. Norton, 1986.

Dean, William. American Religious Empiricism. Albany: State University of New York Press, 1986.

_____. History Making History: The New Historicism in American Religious Thought. Albany: State University of New York Press, 1988.

_____, and Larry E. Axel (eds.). The Size of God: The Theology of Bernard Loomer in Context. Macon, GA.: Mercer University Press, 1987.

Depew, David J., and Bruce H. Weber (eds.). Evolution at a CrossRoads: The New Biology and the New Philosophy of Science. Cambridge: MIT Press, 1985.

Dobzhansky, Theodosius. The Biology of Ultimate Concern. New York: The New American Library, 1967.

Eichrodt, Walter. Theology of the Old Testament. 2 vols. Philadelphia: Westminster Press, 1961, 1967.

Eldredge, Niles, and Ian Tattersall. The Myths of Human Evolution. New York: Columbia University Press, 1982.

Fine, Arthur. The Shaky Game. Chicago: University of Chicago Press, 1986.

Flew, Anthony. "Divine Omnipotence and Human Freedom," New Essays in Philosophical Theology. Ed. by Anthony Flew and Alasdair MacIntyre. New York: The Macmillan Co., 1955. Pp. 144-169.

Frankenberry, Nancy. Religion and Radical Empiricism. Albany: State University of New York Press, 1987.

Geuss, Raymond. The Idea of a Critical Theory: Harbermas and the Frankfort School. Cambridge: Cambridge University Press, 1981.

Gilkey, Langdon. Maker of Heaven and Earth. New York: Doubleday, 1959.

_____. Naming the Whirlwind. Indianapolis: Bobbs-Merrill, 1970.

_____. Reaping The Whirlwind. New York: The Seabury Press, 1981.

_____. "Cosmology, Ontology, and the Travail of Biblical Language," God's Activity in the World. Ed. by Owen Thomas. Chico, CA: Scholars Press, 1983.

Gleick, James. Chaos: Making a New Science. New York: Viking, 1987.

Glover, Willis B. Biblical Origins of Modern Secular Culture. Macon: Mercer University Press, 1984.

Goodman, Nelson. Ways of Worldmaking. Indianapolis: Hackett Publishing Co., 1978.

Griffin, David. God, Power and Evil. Philadelphia: Westminster Press, 1976.

_____. (ed.). Spirituality and Society: Postmodern Visions. Albany: State University of New York Press, 1988.

_____. God and Religion in the Post-Modern World. Albany: State University of New York Press, 1989.

Hacking, Ian. Representing and Intervening: Introductory Topics in the Philosophy of Natural Science. Cambridge: Cambridge University Press, 1983.

Hanson, Paul. Dynamic Transcendence. Philadelphia: Fortress Press, 1978.

Hartshorne, Charles. The Logic of Perfection. LaSalle: Open Court Publishing Co., 1962.

_____. Anselm's Discovery. LaSalle: Open Court Publishing Co., 1965.

_____. A Natural Theology for Our Time. LaSalle: Open Court Publishing Co., 1967.

Harvey, Van. "The Pathos of Liberal Theology," Journal of Religion. October, 1976. Pp. 382-391.

Hawking, Stephen W. A Brief History of Time: From the Big Bang to Black Holes. New York: Bantam Books, 1988.

Hesse, Mary. Revolutions and Reconstructions in the Philosophy of Science. Bloomington: Indiana University Press, 1980.

Heyward, Carter. The Redemption of God. Washington: University Press of America, 1982.

Hick, John. Evil and the God of Love. Revised ed. San Francisco: Harper & Row, 1978.

_____. Death and Eternal Life. San Francisco: Harper & Row, 1976.

_____, and Paul F. Knitter (eds.). The Myth of Christian Uniqueness: Toward a Pluralistic Theology of Religions. Maryknoll, NY: Orbis Books, 1987.

Ho, Mae-Won, and Peter T. Saunders (eds). Beyond Neo-Darwinism: An Introduction to the New Evolutionary Paradigm. New York: Academic Press, 1984.

Hofstadter, Douglas R. Metamagical Themas: Questing for the Essence of Mind and Pattern. New York: Basic Books, 1985.

Hume, David. Dialogues Concerning Natural Religion. New York: Hafner Publishing Co, 1948.

Hynes, William J. Shirley Jackson Case and the Chicago School: The Socio-Historical Method. Chico, CA: Scholars Press, 1981.

Jaki, Stanley L. The Relevance of Physics. Chicago: University of Chicago Press, 1966.

James, William. Pragmatism (and Four Essays from The Meaning of Truth). New York: Meridian Books, 1955.

Jennings, Theodore W. (ed.). The Vocation of the Theologian. Philadelphia: Fortress Press, 1985.

Jones, W. R. Is God a White Racist? Garden City, NY: Doubleday, 1973.

Kaufman, Gordon. Theology and Imagination. Philadelphia: Westminster Press, 1981.

_____. Theology for a Nuclear Age. Philadelphia: Westminister Press, 1985.

Koestler, Arthur, and J. R. Smythies (eds.). Beyond Reductionism: New Perspectives in the Life Sciences. London: Hutchinson, 1969.

Koestler, Arthur. Janus: A Summing Up. New York: Random House, 1978.

Kuhn, Thomas S. The Structure of Scientific Revolutions. 2nd ed. Chicago: University of Chicago Press, 1970.

_____. Essential Tension. Chicago: University of Chicago Press, 1977.

Lakatos, Imre. The Methodology of Scientific Research Programmes: Philosophical Papers. Vol. 1. Cambridge: Cambridge University Press, 1978.

Lakatos, Imre, and Alan Musgrave (eds.). Criticism and the Growth of Knowledge. Cambridge: Cambridge University Press, 1970.

Lewis, John (ed.). Beyond Chance and Necessity. London: The Garnstone Press, 1974.

Lindbeck, George A. The Nature of Doctrine. Philadelphia: Westminster Press, 1984.

Loomer, Bernard. "The Size of God," The Size of God: The Theology of Bernard Loomer in Context. Ed. by William Dean and Larry Axel. Macon, GA: Mercer University Press, 1987. Pp. 20-51.

Madden, Edward H., and Peter H. Hare. Evil and the Concept of God. Springfield: Charles C. Thomas, 1968.

McCarthy, Thomas. The Critical Theory of Jürgen Habermas. Cambridge: Massachusetts Institute of Technology, 1978.

McFague, Sallie. Models of God: Theology for an Ecological, Nuclear Age. Philadelphia: Fortress Press, 1987.

Mackie, J. L. "Evil and Omnipotence," God and Evil. Ed.
by Nelson Pike. Englewood Cliffs, NJ: Prenti-
ce-Hall, 1964.
McNeil, John. The Church and the Homosexual. Kansas
City: Sheed Andrews and Mcmeel, 1976.
Mathews, Shailer. The Faith of Modernism. New York: The
Macmillan Co., 1924.
_____. The Atonement and Social Process. New
York: The Macmillan Co., 1930.
_____. The Growth of the Idea of God. New
York: The Macmillan Co, 1931.
Mayr, Ernst. Towards a New Philosophy of Biology.
Observations of an Evolutionist. Cambridge: Harvard
University Press, 1988.
Meland, Bernard: Fallible Forms and Symbols: Discourses
on Method for a Theology of Culture. Philadelphia:
Fortress Press, 1976.
Moltmann, Jürgen. Theology of Hope. New York: Harper &
Row, 1967.
Monod, Jacques. Chance and Necessity. New York: Alfred
A. Knopf, 1971.
Moore, A. D. Pragmatism and its Critics. Chicago:
University of Chicago Press, 1910.
Nagel, Ernest. The Structure of Science. New York:
Harcourt Brace and World, 1961.
Niebuhr, H. Richard. Christ and Culture. Harper &
Brothers, 1951.
Niebuhr, Reinhold. Moral Man and Immoral Society. New
York: Charles Scribner's Sons, 1932.
_____. The Nature and Destiny of Man. One
vol. ed. New York: Charles Scribner's Sons, 1949.
_____. Faith and History. New York: Charles
Scribner's Sons, 1949.
Niebuhr, Richard R. Resurrection and Historical Reason.
New York: Charles Scribner's Sons, 1957.
Nygren, Anders. Agape and Eros. London: S.P.C.K., 1957.
Ogden, Schubert. The Reality of God. New York: Harper &
Row, 1966.
_____. The Point of Christology. New York: Har-
per & Row, 1982.
Pannenberg, Wolfhart. Basic Questions in Theology. 2
vols. Philadelphia: Westminster Press, 1970-1971.
Peacocke, Arthur R. Creation and the World of Science.
Oxford: Clarendon Press, 1979.
_____. God and the New Biology. San Francis-
co: Harper & Row, 1986.
_____. Intimations of Reality. Notre
Dame: University of Notre Dame Press, 1984.
Peden, Creighton. The Chicago School: Voices in Liberal
Religious Thought. Bristol, IN: Wyndam Hall Press,
1987.

Pittenger, Normal. Gay Lifestyles. Los Angeles: Universal Fellowship Press, 1977.

Placher, William C. Unapologetic Theology: A Christian Voice in aPluralistic Conversation. Louisville: Westminster/John Knox Press, 1989.

Plantinga, Alvin. God and Other Minds. Ithaca: Cornell University Press, 1967.

_____. The Nature of Necessity. Oxford: Clarendon Press, 1974.

_____. God, Freedom and Evil. San Francisco: Harper & Row, 1974.

Polanyi, Michael. Personal Knowledge. Chicago: University of Chicago Press, 1958.

Proudfoot, Wayne. Religious Experience. Berkeley: University of California Press, 1985.

Putnam, Hilary. Reason, Truth, and History. Cambridge: Cambridge University Press, 1981.

Rajchman, John, and Cornell West (eds.). Post-Analytic Philosophy. New York: Columbia University Press, 1985.

Rauschenbusch, Walter. A Theology for the Social Gospel. New York: The Macmillan Co., 1917.

Rescher, Nicholas (ed.). Scientific Inquiry in Philosophical Perspective. New York: Lanham, 1986.

Religion and Intellectual Life. Summer, 1985. Pp. 7-67.

Ricoeur, Paul. The Symbolism of Evil. New York: Harper & Row., 1967.

_____. Interpretation Theory. Fort Worth: Texas Christian University Press, 1976.

_____. The Rule of Metaphor. Toronto: University of Toronto Press, 1977.

Roberts, Deotis. Liberation and Reconciliation. Philadelphia: Westminster Press, 1971.

Roderick, Rick. Habermas and the Foundations of Critical Theory. New York: St. Martins Press, 1986.

Rolston, Holmes, III. Science and Religion: A Critical Survey. New York: Random House, 1987.

Rorty, Richard. Consequences of Pragmatism (Essays 1972-1980). Minneapolis: University of Minnesota Press, 1982.

_____. Philosophy and the Mirror of Nature. Princeton: Princeton University Press, 1982.

Ruether, Rosemary Radford. Sexism and God-Talk. Boston: Beacon Press, 1983.

Ruse, Michael. Darwinism Defended: A Guide to the Evolution Controversies. Reading: Addison-Wesley, 1982.

_____. Taking Darwin Seriously: A Naturalistic Approach to Philosophy. Oxford: Basil Blackwell, 1986.

Russell, Letty. Human Liberation in a Feminist Perspective -- A Theology. Philadelphia: Westminster Press, 1974.
_____. The Future of Partnership. Philadelphia: Westminster Press, 1979.
_____. Growth in Partnership. Philadelphia: Westminster Press, 1981.
Scanzoni, Letha, and Virginia R. Mollenkott. Is the Homosexual My Neighbor? San Francisco: Harper & Row, 1978.
_____, and Nancy Hardesty. All We're Meant to Be. Waco: Word Books, 1974.
Schüssler Fiorenza, Elizabeth. In Memory of Her: A Feminist Theological Reconstruction of Christian Origins. New York: Crossroad, 1984.
Sheldrake, Rupert. A New Science of Life: The Hypothesis of Formative Causation. London: Blond & Briggs, 1981.
Sinnott, E. W. Cell and Psyche. Chapel Hill: University of North Carolina Press, 1950.
_____. Biology of the Spirit. New York: Viking Press, 1957.
_____. Matter, Mind and Man. New York: Harper & Brothers, 1957.
Skinner, B. F. Beyond Freedom and Dignity. New York: Bantam Books, 1971.
Smith, Huston. Forgotten Truth: The Primordial Tradition. New York: Harper & Row, 1976.
_____. Beyond the Post-Modern Mind. New York: Crossroad, 1982.
Smith, John E. The Spirit of American Philosophy. New York: Oxford University Press, 1963.
_____. Experience and God. Oxford: Oxford University Press, 1968.
_____. Purpose and Thought: The Meaning of Pragmatism. New Haven: Yale University Press, 1978.
Smith, Kenneth L. Shailer Mathews: Theologian of Social Process. Ph. D. Dissertation, Duke University, 1959.
Stout, Jeffrey. The Flight From Authority. Notre Dame: University of Notre Dame Press, 1981.
_____. Ethics after Babel: The Languages of Morals and Their Discontents. Boston: Beacon Press, 1988.
Suchocki, Marjorie. God, Christ, Church. New York: Crossroad Publishing Co., 1982.
Surin, Kenneth. Theology and the Problem of Evil. New York: Basil Blackwell, 1986.
Taylor, Mark. Erring: A Post-Modern A/theology. Chicago: University of Chicago Press, 1984.
Thomas, Owen (ed.). God's Activity in the World. Chico, CA: Scholars Press, 1983.

Tillich, Paul. The Interpretation of History. New York: Charles Scribner's Sons, 1936.
_____. The Protestant Era. Chicago: University of Chicago Press, 1948.
_____. Systematic Theology. 3 vols. Chicago: University of Chicago Press, 1951, 1957, 1963.
Toulmin, Stephen. The Uses of Argument. Cambridge: Cambridge University Press, 1964.
_____. Human Understanding. Vol. I. Princeton: Princeton University Press, 1972.
_____. The Return to Cosmology: Post-Modern Science and the Theology of Nature. Berkeley: University of California Press, 1982.
Tracy, David. Blessed Rage for Order: The New Pluralism in Theology. New York: The Seabury Press, 1975.
_____. The Analogical Imagination: Christian Theology and the Culture of Pluralism. New York: Crossroad Publishing Co., 1981.
_____. Plurality and Ambiguity: Hermeneutics, Religion and Hope. San Francisco: Harper & Row, 1987.
_____, and Nicholas Lash. Cosmology and Theology. New York: The Seabury Press, 1983.

von Rad, Gerhard. Old Testament Theology. 2 vols. New York: Harper & Row, 1962, 1965.
Whitehead, Alfred North. Science and the Modern World. New York: The Macmillan Co., 1925.
_____. Religion in the Making. New York: The Macmillan Co., 1926.
_____. Process and Reality. New York: The Macmillan Co., 1929.
_____. The Function of Reason. Princeton: Princeton University Press, 1929.
_____. Modes of Thought. New York: The Macmillan Co., 1938.
West, Cornell. Prophesy Deliverance! An Afro-American Revolutionary Christianity. Philadelphia: West-Westminster Press, 1982.
_____. The American Evasion of Philosophy: A Genealogy of Pragmatism. Madison: University of Wisconsin Press, 1989.
Wieman, Henry Nelson. The Source of Human Good. Chicago: University of Chicago Press, 1946.
Wilmore, Gayraud, and James Cone (eds.). Black Theology: A Documentary History, 1966-1979. Maryknoll, NY: Orbis Books, 1979.
Zygon: Journal of Religion and Science.

INDEX OF PERSONS

INDEX OF SUBJECTS

TORONTO STUDIES IN THEOLOGY

1. Robert R. N. Ross, **The Non-Existence of God: Linguistic Paradox in Tillich's Thought**

2. Gustaf Wingren, **Creation and Gospel: The New Situation in European Theology**

3. John C. Meagher, **Clumsy Construction in Mark's Gospel: A Critique of Form-and Redaktionsgeschichte**

4. Patrick Primeaux, **Richard R. Niebuhr on Christ and Religion: The Four Stage Development of His Theology**

5. Bernard Lonergan, **Understanding and Being: An Introduction and Companion to** *Insight*, Elizabeth A. Morelli and Mark D. Morelli (eds.)

6. John D. Godsey and Geffrey B. Kelly (eds.), **Ethical Responsibility: Bonhoeffer's Legacy to the Churches**

7. Darrell J. Fasching, **The Thought of Jacques Ellul: A Systematic Exposition**

8. Joseph T. Culliton (ed.), **Non-Violence - Central to Christian Spirituality: Perspectives from Scripture to the Present**

9. Aaron Milavec, **To Empower as Jesus Did: Acquiring Spiritual Power Through Apprenticeship**

10. John Kirby and William M. Thompson (eds.), **Voegelin and the Theologian: Ten Studies in Interpretation**

11. Thomas I. Day, **Dietrich Bonhoeffer on Christian Community and Common Sense**

12. James Deotis Roberts, **Black Theology Today: Liberation and Contextualization**

13. Walter G. Muelder *et al.*, **The Ethical Edge of Christian Theology: Forty Years of Communitarian Personalism**

14. David Novak, **The Image of the Non-Jew in Judaism: An Historical and Constructive Study of the Noahide Laws**

15. Daniel Liderbach, **The Theology of Grace and the American Mind: A Re-presentation of Catholic Doctrine**

16. Hubert G. Locke (ed.), **The Church Confronts the Nazis: Barmen Then and Now**

17. M. Darrol Bryant (ed.), **The Future of Anglican Theology**

18. Kenneth Cauthen, **Process Ethics: A Constructive System**

19. Barry L. Whitney, **Evil and The Process God**

20. Donald Grayston, **Thomas Merton: The Development of a Spiritual Theologian**

21. John J. McDonnell, **The World Council of Churches and The Catholic Church**

22. Manfred Hoffmann (ed.), **Martin Luther and the Modern Mind: Freedom, Conscience, Toleration , Rights**

46. Franklin H. Littell (ed.), **A Half Century of Religious Dialogue, 1939-1989: Making the Circles Larger**

47. Douglas J. Davies, **Frank Byron Jevons, 1858-1936: An Evolutionary Realist**ä

48. John P. Tiemstra (ed.), **Reforming Economics: Calvinist Studies on Methods and Institutions**

49. Max A. Myers and Michael R. LaChat (eds.), **Studies in the Theological Ethics of Ernst Troeltsch**

50. Franz G. M. Feige, **The Varieties of Protestantism in Nazi Germany: Five Theopolitical Positions**

51. John W. Welch, **A Biblical Law Bibliography: Arranged by Subject and by Author**

52. Albert W. J. Harper, **The Theodicy of Suffering**

53. Bryce A. Gayhart, **The Ethics of Ernst Troeltsch: A Commitment to Relevancy**

54. David L. Mueller, **Foundation of Karl Barth's Doctrine of Reconciliation: Jesus Christ Crucified and Risen**

55. Henry O. Thompson (ed.), **The Contribution of Carl Michalson to Modern Theology: Studies in Interpretation and Application**

56. David G. Schultenover (ed.), **Theology Toward the Third Millennium: Theological Issues for the Twenty-first Century**

57. Louis J. Shein, **The Philosophy of Lev Shestov (1866-1938)**

58. Hans Schwartz, **Method and Context as Problems for Contemporary Theology**

59. William C. Marceau, **The Notion of the Eucharist in Theodore de Beze and François de Sales**

60. Ronald D. Srigley, **Eric Voegelin's Platonic Theology: Philosophy of Consciousness and Symbolization in a New Perspective**

61. John Musson, **Evil --Is it Real?: A Theological Analysis**

62. Kenneth Cauthen, **Theological Biology: The Case for a New Modernism**